Eastern European Adoption

Eastern European Adoption

Policies, Practice, and Strategies for Change

Josephine A. Ruggiero

Routledge
Taylor & Francis Group

LONDON AND NEW YORK

First published 2007 by Transaction Publishers

2 Park Square, Milton Park, Abingdon, Oxfordshire OX14 4RN
711 Third Avenue, New York, NY 10017

Routledge is an imprint of the Taylor & Francis Group, an informa business

First issued in paperback 2017

Copyright © 2007 Taylor & Francis

Library of Congress Catalog Number: 2007019702

Library of Congress Cataloging-in-Publication Data

Ruggiero, Josephine A.
    Eastern European adoption : policies, practice, and strategies for change / Josephine A. Ruggiero.
        p. cm.
    Includes bibliographical references and index.
    ISBN 978-0-202-30976-7
    1. Adoption—Europe, Eastern. 2. Adoption—Former Soviet republics.
I. Title.

HV875.58.E852R84 2007b   2007019702
362.7340947—dc22

ISBN 13: 978-0-202-30976-7 (hbk)
ISBN 13: 978-1-138-50934-4 (pbk)

Dedication

This book is dedicated to the people who have changed my life most: first, to my parents, Vera and John Ruggiero, in memoriam—you gave me a good start in life and supported my choices and dreams along the way as loving parents do; next, to my husband, Helmut Reinhardt—without your help, support, and willingness to take on extraordinary child-care and household responsibilities, this project would have taken even longer to complete; and, finally, to the children "of my heart" both near and far, especially Crista Tatiana, Marissa Leanne, and Jonathan Valery—survivors all, and much more. Being your mother has taught me a lot!

Contents

Preface   xi

Acknowledgements   xvii

Part I.
An Introduction to International Adoption from Eastern Europe

Chapter 1.   Adoptions from Eastern Europe   3
                to the United States

Chapter 2.   Understanding What Motivates Americans   19
                to Adopt a Child or Children Internationally

Chapter 3.   Similarities and Differences in Issues Relevant   27
                to International and Domestic Adoption

Part II.
Studying Older-Child and Sibling Group Adoptions from
Eastern Europe

Chapter 4.   Parents Speak About the Process   47
                of International Adoption and
                Their Satisfaction-Dissatisfaction with
                Their Decision to Adopt Internationally

Chapter 5.   Embarking on the Journey of a Lifetime: 65
                Breathing Life into the Data through
                Case Narratives

Chapter 6.   Case Narratives of Satisfied Adopters   73

Chapter 7.   Case Narratives of Families Who Typically Feel   85
                "Caught in the Middle"

Chapter 8.   Case Narratives of Adopters Whose Children   99
              Have Many, Serious Problems

Chapter 9.   Parents Speak About State   117
              and Federal Government Involvement in
              Regulating Agencies Engaged in Placing
              International Adoptees with Americans

Part III.
Interventions and Policy Shifts

Chapter 10.   Impacts of Existing Adoption Policies   125
              and Practices: When Private Troubles Become
              Public Issues

Chapter 11.   Mapping Changes Needed in Adoption Policy   141
              and Practice

Chapter 12.   Solutions and Strategies That Are Linked   149
              to Clients' Rights and Agencies' Responsibilities

Part IV.
Producing Positive Changes for the Long Run

Chapter 13.   Bringing about Changes That Are in   171
              the Best Interest of Adoptees and
              Their Adoptive Families

Epilogue: Out of the Past and into the Future   179

Postscript: A Survey Approach: How? Why? Who?   183

Appendix: Enhancing the Success of Older-Child   193
          Adoptions from Eastern Europe

Bibliography   209

Name Index   217

Subject Index   219

List of Tables

Table 1.1   Russian Adoptees to the United States   5
by Sex and Age, 1993-2005

Table 1.2   Ukrainian Adoptees to the United States   6
States by Sex and Age, 1993-2005

Table 1.3   Romanian Adoptees to the United States   7
by Sex and Age, 1990-2005

Table 1.4   Kazak Adoptees to the United States   8
by Sex and Age, 1998-2005

Table 1.5   Bulgarian Adoptees to the United States   8
by Sex and Age, 1992-2005

Table 1.6   Other Eastern European Adoptees   9
by the United States by Sex and Age, 1990-2005

Table 4.1   Differences in Respondents' Satisfaction   54
by Characteristics and Issues of Adoptees

Table 4.2   Differences in Respondents' Satisfaction   55
by Post-Adoption Issues and Needs

Table 4.3   Differences in Respondents' Satisfaction   57
by Seven Agency-Performance Variables
(Pre-Adoption Stage)

Table 4.4   Differences in Respondents' Satisfaction   58
by Three Agency-Related Variables (Pre-Adoption)

Table 4.5   Differences in Respondents' Satisfaction   60
by Three Children's Post-Placement Needs and Issues

Table 4.6   Differences in Respondents' Satisfaction   61
by Four Other Variables

Table 9.1   Variations in Respondents' Support   118
for a Hard Line Stance for State and Federal
Governments to Take on Selected Policy Issues,
Reported in Percentages and Ranks

Table 9.2   Respondents' Support for a Hard Line   121
                   Stance on Specific Policy Issues at the
                   State Level by Satisfaction-Dissatisfaction
                   with the Decision to Adopt Their First
                   and/or Second Child Internationally

Table 9.3   Respondents' Support for a Hard Line Stance   122
                   on Specific Policy Issues at the Federal Level
                   by Satisfaction-Dissatisfaction with the
                   Decision to Adopt Their First and/or
                   Second Child Internationally

List of Figures

Figure 1.1a   Distribution of Russian Adoptees   10
                   to the United States by Sex, 1993-2005

Figure 1.1b   Distribution of Russian Adoptees   11
                   to the United States by Age, 1993-2005

Figure 1.2a   Distribution of Ukrainian Adoptees   11
                   to the United States by Sex, 1993-2005

Figure 1.2b   Distribution of Ukrainian Adoptees   12
                   to the United States by Age, 1993-2005

Figure 1.3a   Distribution of Romanian Adoptees   12
                   to the United States by Sex 1990-2005

Figure 1.3b   Distribution of Romanian Adoptees   13
                   to the United States by Age 1990-2005

Figure 1.4a   Distribution of Kazak Adoptees   13
                   to the United States by Sex 1998-2005

Figure 1.4b   Distribution of Kazak Adoptees   14
                   to the United States by Age 1998-2005
Figure 1.5a   Distribution of Bulgarian Adoptees   15
                   to the United States by Sex 1992-2005

Figure 1.5b   Distribution of Bulgarian Adoptees   15
                   to the United States by Age 1992-2005

Figure 1.6a   Distribution of Other Eastern European   16
                   Adoptees to the United States by Sex 1990-2005

Figure 1.6b   Distribution of Other Eastern European   16
                   Adoptees to the United States by Age 1990-2005

Author's Preface

As an application-oriented sociologist, I have often been motivated to research and write about topics and issues because of their potential value to others and because of the implications for change embedded in the work. So, perhaps I should further subtitle this book "Feeling Good about Trying to Do Some Good." I say this in the context of my work on international adoption because I hope its contents provoke discussion that stimulates multilevel changes in the ways international adoptions are viewed and handled.

Usually, people who write about adoption have been touched by adoption in some way. Similarly, most authors of books about international adoption are either adoptive parents or people connected with placing children. Many people who write about adoption do so with great passion. These authors believe that the issues and experiences about which they speak just have to be shared. I can understand the passion of authors who write from the heart.

Many books on international adoption fall into one of two broad categories: autobiographical or how-to books. Although some books have aspects of both, most usually emphasize one aspect over the other. My book is neither autobiographical nor a book about how to adopt internationally. Neither is this book about the adoption of newborns or young infants.

Rather, my book is about how risk factors and adoption policies impact on the opportunities for successful functioning of real families who adopt children with known or suspected pre-adoption histories of adversity and about strategies for improving the success of this type of adoption.

Like many others who have written books on international adoption, I am an adoptive parent. Like some adoptive parents, my husband and I decided to adopt siblings rather than a single child. Like even fewer adoptive parents, we adopted three children, simultaneously. None of the three were infants at the time we adopted them. So, like many children adopted beyond infancy, our children came to us with a pre-adoption history of neglect and abuse. Unfortunately, no one told us anything about their past experiences or issues—not the private adoption agency we used, or their Russian facilitator, or the orphanage directors in charge of the child homes (detsky dom) where our children lived. We believe that very important background information was known to these sources and should have been shared with us in the pre-adoption phase, before we accepted the referral.

Our children came to us after living for fourteen months in two different Russian orphanages. Because of their ages, both of the younger children went to an orphanage for children under three years old. The oldest child, who was just over three, was placed in an orphanage for children aged three through seven.

Although *Eastern European Adoption: Policies, Practices, and Strategies for Change* contains insights gleaned from many adoptive parents' stories, it focuses mainly on the issues involved in the international adoption of non-infants and siblings from Eastern Europe. Through survey data, this book looks in depth at both pre- and post-adoption issues: how well prepared to adopt their child/children did these parents think they were? What kinds of post-adoption support and services did these families and their children need after the adoption(s) was (were) completed. *Eastern European Adoption: Policies, Practices, and Strategies for Change* looks at what goes right and what can go wrong in the adoption process and with what effects. Therefore, this book includes coverage of important areas that dovetails with issues involved in the adoption of older children and sibling groups domestically through the child welfare system.

* * * *

The reader might wonder what motivated me to write this book. I knew that the time for a book like this to be written was past due. I also knew that it takes more than courage to write about controversial topics, especially a topic like adoption. Writing this book takes perspective, experience with how adoption works, and the determination to bring the discussion of the downside of adoption to a wider audience than professionals in one's own discipline. Besides being an adoptive parent, I have also been a foster parent to two sibling groups born in the United States and a resource to a child living in a group home. I know the important issues involved in the adoption of older children, both domestic and international. Equally important, I am an experienced researcher and a "seasoned" application-oriented sociologist who has researched issues in both domestic and international adoption for many years.

I am not sure whether this book chose me or I chose it. It has been that kind of journey—a journey of the heart and of the gut. This book, not hastily written, evolved over time as I struggled to find the best and fairest way to present and discuss the issues. I decided to combine my ideas as much as possible with the voices and comments of other adoptive parents. By incorporating both qualitative and quantitative data from my research, I allow adoptive parents to speak about their experiences and to identify the important issues in the adoption of their child or children internationally. Because my personal and professional expertise is in the area of adopting children beyond the age of infancy from Russia and Eastern European countries, I chose to especially target families who had adopted a child age two plus, a sibling group, or "simultaneous multiples" (two biologically unrelated children adopted at the same time).

Writing about adoption is both challenging and controversial. The writer must take a position. Some readers will agree with the position the writer takes. Others will disagree with that position. Some readers will pick up this book and may conclude, after a cursory look, that I am against adoption because I raise issues about current adoption policies and practices. I want to make clear that I am FOR creating or adding to families through adoption, both domestic and international. I have been FOR adoption since I was a child, born to two parents who struggled, unsuccessfully, to produce more than one biological child.

Before I met and married my husband of more than twenty years, I had seriously considered adopting as a single person. After we married and faced issues of infertility, we came to the decision to adopt as a positive choice. We did NOT view that decision as second best to having a biological child. We still do not. However, what we experienced about the politics and the process of adoption, both domestic and international, in conjunction with the challenges we have faced since we adopted our three children, are what motivated me to write this book. Like many people who adopt, we had expected to adopt a child or children domestically. That is where we started. We were interested in adopting two siblings. However, after five years of getting nowhere, despite being very proactive, we explored the possibility of adopting a child or children internationally. Ultimately, we decided to adopt from Russia because this country allowed non-Russians to adopt siblings and sometimes two unrelated children at the same time and because a contact referred us to a licensed, private adoption agency in the U. S. that had begun to arrange adoptions of Russian children "successfully."

Our experiences, as we worked on the adoption process and, especially, as we "lived" the many post-placement challenges that our children experienced, motivated me to reach out to other families who had adopted internationally, especially those who had adopted older children and sibling groups from Russia and other Eastern European countries. What kinds of experiences did other families who adopted from Eastern Europe have? What guidance, perspective, and support could we, together, offer to the various constituencies of the adoption "community?"

I knew that our aggregated experiences could offer important insights to the staff of adoption agencies, both those doing home studies for people planning to adopt an older child/ children internationally and those placing children with waiting families. I also knew that those who make adoption policies could also benefit from an "insider perspective" on the issues.

So, in May of 1998, I embarked on a lengthy odyssey that brought me into contact with more than 120 other parents who had also adopted internationally. Most had adopted a child or children from Russia. Some adopted from other Eastern European countries. Many of these respondents had adopted an older child or children.

I wanted to speak to as diverse a cross section of these adoptive families as possible and I believe that I accomplished that objective successfully. The adoptive parents who participated in my study come from across the United States and a few from outside the United States. These willing and wonderful people shared their experiences and insights, their joys and sorrows, with me honestly.

Many of these parents reported successful adoption stories. Some parents had the courage to admit that their child/children had serious problems for which they were unprepared and which rocked the foundations of their lives. Without my longer-than-anticipated detour to survey these parents and to allow them to "speak" to the issues, this book would have been less powerful and not as complete as it is. Their wisdom and collective experiences help to shape the core of this book.

Through *Eastern European Adoption: Policies, Practices, and Strategies for Change* I hope that the many constituencies interested in and/or involved with the adoption of older children—international or domestic will gain valuable insights about what it takes to build happy, successfully functioning adoptive families. I also hope that policy makers, social service professionals, health providers, and others who are in positions to create positive change in the field of adoption in general will take parents' experiences to heart and will become "change makers" who make decisions which are in the best interests of children and their adoptive families. Being "part of the solution" involves finding ways to turn stumbling blocks into stepping stones so that families who need services for their children and/or support for themselves will be able to obtain what they need, when they need them.

Acknowledgments

To come to fruition, a project like this one needs the support of many people at various stages. I wish to acknowledge the support of Providence College and the Committee to Aid Faculty Research through which funding was provided to help finance the data preparation and analysis phases of this research. I specifically want to thank Dr. Thomas Canavan, (retired) Vice President for Academic Administration at Providence College, who granted me sabbatical leaves in the spring, 1997, and again in spring, 2004. During that first sabbatical, I got the initial phases of my review of the then published literature on adoption and international adoption started and then mapped out the central issues in older child and sibling adoption. During the second sabbatical, I completed major portions of this manuscript and conducted a follow-up survey of many of the parents that I first "met" through my Phase I survey. I also wish to thank Connie Cameron and Janice Schuster, Research Librarians at Providence College, for their assistance with literature searches and statistical research at various points over the years during which this project took shape. Thanks to my colleague, Richard Elkington, of the Art and Art History Department, for his help in setting up and updating the Faculty Research webpage that described the details of my research plan and my search for families to participate in my study. My appreciation goes to another colleague, Jane Lunin Perel, of the English Department and Women's Studies Program, for her suggestions on matters of style in communicating my ideas. I am also grateful to the following groups and/or people for their help in publicizing my research (1) on their websites: the Board of Families for Russian and Ukranian Adoption (FRUA) and Ernie Jones; Dr. Teena McGuiness (ARIA), (2) in the newsletters of their organizations: Joan Clark, Executive Director of ACONE (formerly known as The Open Door Society of Massachusetts) and Thais Tepper and Lois Hannon, co-founders of the Parents Network for Post-Institutionalized Children (PNPIC), and (3) in support groups. Special thanks to Jean R. Scott of the U. S. Department of Homeland Security for her assistance in forwarding information on immigrant orphans admitted to the U. S. and to Patricia Irwin Johnston of Perspectives Press for her thoughtful comments on an earlier draft of this manuscript. Projects like this one also require the help of many research and technical assistants along the way. I have had the good fortune to have six former, and one current, student work with me on this project. I thank them for their help and support in both the early phases of my work and in the later phases which involved coding the information from the Phase I Questionnaire and assisting in data coding and analysis: Elizabeth Hackett, Katelyn Connolly, Tyas Suci, Heather Wilcox, Tanya Sheikh, Mike Tenaglia, and especially Tim Tenaglia. Finally, I want to thank all of the parents who took the time to share their experiences in adopting their children. Your words help to put a human face on the numbers and the issues.

Part I

An Introduction to International Adoption from Eastern Europe

1

Adoptions from Eastern Europe to the United States

International adoptions to the United States are not a new phenomenon. Officially, they date back to the post-World War II period. However, the adoption of children from Eastern European countries by Americans is a relatively new phenomenon, beginning in 1990. Despite its recentness, Americans have embraced orphans from Eastern Europe, and Russia in particular, as their own in numbers that are striking for modern times.

Between 1990 and 2005, 71,665 adoptees from Eastern Europe joined American families. Almost 66 percent of these adoptees came from a single country: Russia. Almost 25 percent came from four other countries: The Ukraine (8.7 percent), Romania (7 percent), Kazakhstan (6.2 percent) and Bulgaria (3 percent). The remaining 9.2 percent came from more than a dozen other Eastern European countries including Albania, Armenia, Azerbajian, Belarus, Estonia, Hungary, Latvia, Lithuania, Moldova, Poland, the Republic of Georgia, Tajikistan, and Uzbekistan. Children from Eastern Europe accounted for 31.5 percent of all inter-country adoptees entering the United States between 1990 and 2005.

This book is about policies and practices involving the adoption of Eastern European children by Americans since 1990. Building on a foundation of quality empirical research, my own and that of others, my major objective is to explore what works, what does not, and to draw implications for change in adoption policies and practices. High-quality, empirical research on adoptive parents and their children is essential to a clearer understanding of why adoption policies and practices that may have worked when placing healthy newborns do not work well when placing children from this new, and growing, population of potential adoptees.

A second major objective is to frame adoption policies and practices from a sociological perspective. Sociologists bring a unique perspective to bear on issues because they explore and use structural and contextual variables to analyze and explain phenomena. By examining adoption policies through a sociological lens, I can identify and discuss important issues and concerns expressed by the parents I surveyed. I can also identify patterns of issues in the published literature on older-child and sibling adoptions.

To achieve these objectives, I have organized this book around the quantitative and qualitative data I collected from a survey of more than 100 adoptive parents of children born in Eastern Europe. These data, my background as a researcher of issues in adoption from Eastern Europe, and being an adoptive parent of three Russian-born siblings, now teenagers, enable me to take a position on the issues I discuss in this book.

The thirteen chapters and epilogue are organized into four principal sections: An Introduction to International Adoption from Eastern Europe; Studying Older-Child and Sibling Group Adoptions from Eastern Europe; Interventions and Policy Shifts; and Producing Positive Changes for the Long Run.

The U. S. Government's Definition of European Countries

Beginning in its earliest tables, the INS included as part of Europe, countries we would now consider in either Central or Eastern Europe. These countries include, for example, Greece, Turkey, Czechoslovakia, Yugoslavia, Hungary, Lithuania, Poland, and the U. S. S. R. Thus, Eastern Europe is a rather amorphous entity and some may disagree with which countries should be included. For purposes of discussing trends in Eastern European sending countries, I will begin where the official U. S. records do.

Between 1957 and 1964, Greece was a major sending country of international adoptees to the United States. During those years, 1,268 Greek children were adopted into families in the United States. Adoptees from Greece continued to join American families annually between 1964 and 1986 (N = 927). Beginning in 1990, however, Greek adoptees to the United States arrived only intermittently and in very small numbers. Totals for 1990 (N = 16), 1994-96 (N = 25), 1998-2000 (N = 12) and 2003 (N = 3) reflect this trend.

Data indicate that Poland also began sending children for adoption to the United States as early as 1957. Between 1957 and 1969, 319 Polish children were adopted by Americans. Adoptions of Polish children to the United States have continued at a steady pace since then. During the 1970s, they totaled 156 children. Between 1980 and 89, Americans adopted 446 Polish children. The total then almost doubled to 766 adoptees in the 1990s. In the six years between 2000 and 2005, the total number of inter-country adoptees from Poland to the U. S. reached 437 children.

Although Poland has been a consistent sending country, to date, having sent fewer then 2,000 children to the U. S. for adoption since 1957,

Poland does not fall into the category of a major sending country. The principal Eastern European sending countries of adoptees to the United States include Russia, the Ukraine, Romania, Kazakhstan, and Bulgaria. Because 91.8 percent of the Eastern European adoptees to the U. S. came from these five countries, and most came from Russia alone, my analysis focuses on Russia first; the four other major European sending countries next; and the remaining smaller Eastern European sending countries combined.

Russia

According to U. S. government records, between 1957 and 1963, only two children from the U.S.S.R. joined American families as adoptees. These records also show a marked absence of adoptees to the United States from the Soviet Union until 1991. In 1991 and 1992 combined, Americans reportedly adopted 444 orphans from the Soviet Union. Subsequently, the numbers of Russian adoptees to the United States began to rise dramatically. According to table 1.1, between 1993 and 2005, 47,215 Russian children entered American families through adoption.

Table 1.1

Russian Adoptees to the United States by Sex and Age, 1993-2005

		Sex		Age[a]		
Year	Total	% Male	% Female	% <1	% 1-4	% 5+
1993	695	45.00%	55.00%	21.00%	57.00%	22.00%
1994	1324	49.00%	51.00%	22.00%	56.00%	22.00%
1995	1684	49.00%	51.00%	26.00%	53.00%	21.00%
1996	2328	52.00%	48.00%	20.00%	61.00%	19.00%
1997	3626	49.00%	51.00%	28.00%	51.00%	21.00%
1998	4320	52.00%	48.00%	36.00%	47.00%	17.00%
1999	4250	50.00%	50.00%	39.00%	44.00%	17.00%
2000	4210	49.00%	51.00%	30.00%	51.00%	19.00%
2001	4210	48.00%	52.00%	23.00%	57.00%	20.00%
2002	4904	49.00%	51.00%	27.00%	53.00%	20.00%
2003	5134	49.00%	51.00%	30.00%	50.00%	20.00%
2004	5878	50.00%	50.00%	30.00%	48.00%	22.00%
2005	4652	50.00%	50.00%	20.00%	51.00%	29.00%
Total	47215					
Average %		49.50%	50.50%	27.00%	52.00%	21.00%
N=		23369	23846	12748	24552	9915

a. Age of nine adoptees unknown

Source: U.S. C.I.S., Immigrants Admitted as Orphans by Sex, Age, and Region and Selected Country of Birth (Table 14, 1986-1991 & Table 15, 1992-2002 & Table 10, 2003-2004, Table 12, 2004)

An independent, reputable source, the International Social Science Resource Center for the Protection of Children in Adoption (ISS/IRC), reported that Americans first adopted Russian orphans in 1992 (N= 145). In the next year, the number of Russian adoptees more than quadrupled (to N = 695). The numbers of Russian adoptees to the United States began to grow dramatically throughout the rest of the 1990s, peaking at 4,491 adoptees in 1998. By 1999, the ISS/IRC reported that Americans had adopted a decade total of 17,991 Russian orphans. The discrepancy between the INS and the ISS/IRC data sources are that the latter were obtained from sending countries. Still, the ISS/IRC data only underestimates the 1990s decade count by 236 children.

Other Major Eastern European Sending Countries

Between 1990 and 2005, Americans also adopted 24,450 children from other Eastern European countries. Seventy-three percent of these adoptees came from four sending countries: The Ukraine, Romania,

Table 1.2
Ukranian Adoptees to the United States by Sex and Age, 1993-2005

Year	Total	Sex		Age[a]			
		% male	% female	% <1	% 1-4	% 5+	Age Unknown
1993	248	48.00%	52.00%	30.00%	56.00%	14.00%	0.00%
1994	163	51.00%	49.00%	35.00%	45.00%	20.00%	0.00%
1995	5	40.00%	60.00%	20.00%	40.00%	40.00%	0.00%
1996	10	40.00%	60.00%	0.00%	40.00%	60.00%	0.00%
1997	65	51.00%	49.00%	15.00%	68.00%	17.00%	0.00%
1998	168	42.00%	58.00%	18.00%	66.00%	16.00%	0.00%
1999	307	46.00%	54.00%	14.00%	69.00%	17.00%	0.00%
2000	645	51.00%	49.00%	20.00%	67.00%	13.00%	0.31%
2001	1227	55.00%	45.00%	19.00%	63.00%	18.00%	0.00%
2002	1093	54.00%	46.00%	8.00%	60.00%	32.00%	0.00%
2003	691	49.00%	51.00%	1.00%	69.00%	30.00%	0.00%
2004	772	48.00%	52.00%	no info	62.00%	0.09%	38.00%
2005	841	50.00%	50.00%	no info	53.00%	no info	47.00%
Total	6235						
Average %		48.00%	52.00%	16.00%	58.00%	23.00%	7.00%
N=		3171	3064	674	3853	1017	691

a. Age of 691 adoptees unknown. Total % for age categories do not add up to 100% because of missing data.

Source: U.S. C.I.S., Immigrants Admitted as Orphans by Sex, Age and Region and Selected Country of Birth (Table 15, 1993-2002 & Table 10, 2003-2004 & Table 12, 2005)

Kazakhstan, and Bulgaria. The majority of these adoptees came from two principal countries: The Ukraine (34.9 percent) and Romania (28.2 percent). The data in table 1.2 points out that over 6,000 adoptees came from the Ukraine.

Table 1.3 shows that just over 5,000 adoptees came to the U. S. from Romania between 1990 and 2005.

Table 1.3
Romanian Adoptees to the United States by Sex and Age, 1990-2005

Year	Total	Sex		Age[a]		
		% male	% female	% <1	% 1-4	% 5+
1990	90	37.00%	63.00%	50.00%	41.00%	9.00%
1991	2552	46.00%	54.00%	56.00%	39.00%	5.00%
1992	145	51.00%	49.00%	32.00%	54.00%	14.00%
1993	88	50.00%	50.00%	9.00%	63.00%	27.00%
1994	197	39.00%	61.00%	13.00%	57.00%	30.00%
1995	260	45.00%	55.00%	12.00%	70.00%	18.00%
1996	554	49.00%	51.00%	8.00%	84.00%	8.00%
1997	558	47.00%	53.00%	3.00%	85.00%	12.00%
1998	388	45.00%	55.00%	10.00%	76.00%	15.00%
1999	887	52.00%	48.00%	19.00%	67.00%	14.00%
2000	1103	50.00%	50.00%	21.00%	64.00%	15.00%
2001	781	53.00%	47.00%	26.00%	55.00%	19.00%
2002	169	42.00%	58.00%	1.00%	60.00%	39.00%
2003	197	45.00%	55.00%	5.00%	66.00%	19.00%
2004	58	38.00%	62.00%	no info	83.00%	9.00%
2005[b]	0	0.00%	0.00%	0.00%	0.00%	0.00%
Total	5043					
Average %		49.00%	51.00%	16.00%	67.00%	16.00%
N=		2470	2573	819	3398	821

a. Age of 5 adoptees unknown. Total % for age does not equal 100% because of missing data.
b. Romania placed a moratorium on foreign adoptions except for cases of relative adoption.

Source: U.S. C.I.S., Immigrants Admitted as Orphans by Sex, Age and Region and Selected Country of Birth (Table 14, 1986-1991 & Table 15, 1992-2002 & Table 10, 2003-2004 & Table 12, 2005)

According to table 1.4, just over 4,400 adoptees came to the United States from Kazahkstan between 1998 and 2005.

Table 1.4
Kazak Adoptees to the United States by Sex and Age, 1998-2005

		Sex		Age		
Year	Total	% male	% female	% <1	% 1-4	% 5+
1998	54	33.00%	67.00%	59.00%	26.00%	15.00%
1999	108	42.00%	58.00%	57.00%	35.00%	7.00%
2000	392	39.00%	61.00%	44.00%	48.00%	8.00%
2001	664	43.00%	57.00%	38.00%	48.00%	14.00%
2002	801	44.00%	56.00%	34.00%	43.00%	23.00%
2003	819	48.00%	52.00%	33.00%	41.00%	24.00%
2004	824	48.00%	52.00%	35.00%	42.00%	22.00%
2005	755	48.00%	52.00%	42.00%	37.00%	21.00%
Total	4417					
Average %		44.00%	56.00%	38.00%	44.00%	18.00%
N=		1244	1594	1061	1257	20

Source: U.S. C.I.S., Immigrants Admitted as Orphans by Sex, Age, and Region
and Selected Country of Birth (Table 15, 1998-2002 & Table 10, 2003-2004 & Table 12 2005)

Table 1.5 shows that almost 2,200 adoptees came from Bulgaria.

Table 1.5
Bulgarian Adoptees to the United States by Sex and Age, 1992-2005

		Sex		Age[a]		
Year	Total	% male	% female	% <1	% 1-4	% 5+
1992	90	47.00%	53.00%	16.00%	65.00%	19.00%
1993	126	43.00%	57.00%	1.00%	57.00%	42.00%
1994	101	44.00%	56.00%	0.00%	48.00%	52.00%
1995	108	44.00%	56.00%	1.00%	60.00%	39.00%
1996	157	46.00%	54.00%	0.00%	76.00%	24.00%
1997	137	54.00%	46.00%	0.00%	75.00%	25.00%
1998	147	45.00%	55.00%	1.00%	75.00%	24.00%
1999	213	43.00%	57.00%	1.00%	67.00%	32.00%
2000	207	42.00%	58.00%	2.00%	52.00%	26.00%
2001	288	49.00%	51.00%	1.00%	71.00%	28.00%
2002	261	47.00%	53.00%	2.00%	74.00%	25.00%
2003	196	44.00%	56.00%	1.00%	79.00%	20.00%
2004	112	51.00%	49.00%	no info	80.00%	13.00%
2005	29	45.00%	55.00%	no info	66.00%	no info
Total	2172					
Average %		46.00%	54.00%	2.00%	70.00%	28.00%
N=		998	1174	35	1527	593

a. Age of 17 Bulgarian adoptees unknown
Source: U.S. C.I.S. Immigrants Admitted as Orphans by Sex, Age and Region and Selected Country of Birth (Table 15, 1992-2002 & Table 10, 2003-2004 & Table 12, 2005)

As table 1.6 shows, the remaining 6,583 adoptees came to the United States from a variety of other Eastern European countries.

Table 1.6
Other Eastern European Adoptees to the United States
by Sex and Age, 1990-2005[a]

Year	Total	Sex[b]		Age[c]		
		Male	Female	<1 year	1-4 years	5+ years
1990	78	53.00%	47.00%	45.00%	41.00%	14.00%
1991	151	42.00%	58.00%	34.00%	42.00%	25.00%
1992	606	48.00%	52.00%	28.00%	52.00%	20.00%
1993	328	44.00%	56.00%	28.00%	48.00%	24.00%
1994	540	44.00%	57.00%	20.00%	52.00%	28.00%
1995	586	47.00%	53.00%	26.00%	49.00%	25.00%
1996	489	48.00%	52.00%	29.00%	45.00%	26.00%
1997	495	48.00%	52.00%	15.00%	56.00%	29.00%
1998	340	50.00%	50.00%	21.00%	54.00%	25.00%
1999	364	52.00%	48.00%	14.00%	63.00%	23.00%
2000	325	46.00%	54.00%	15.00%	55.00%	19.00%
2001	420	47.00%	53.00%	21.00%	57.00%	22.00%
2002	519	48.00%	52.00%	29.00%	52.00%	19.00%
2003	584	45.00%	54.00%	36.00%	41.00%	20.00%
2004	492	46.00%	52.00%	15.00%	50.00%	20.00%
2005	266	42.00%	56.00%	8.00%	37.00%	48.00%
Total	6583					
Average %		47.00%	53.00%	24.00%	50.00%	24.00%
N=		3082	3478	1540	3311	1622

a. The countries in the category include Albania, Armenia, Azerbajian, Belarus, Estonia,Hungary, Latvia, Lithuania, Moldova, Poland, the Republic of Georgia, Tajikistan, Uzbekistan, and unknown republics.
b. Gender of 17 adoptees unknown.
c. Age of 110 adoptees unknown. Total percentages do not add up to 100% because of missing data.

Source: U.S. C.I.S., Immigrants Admitted as Orphans by Sex, Age and Region and Selected Country of Birth (Table 14, 1990-1991 & Table 15, 1992-2002 & Table 10, 2003-2004 & Table 12, 2005)

Age and Gender Breakdown of Eastern European Adoptees

Beginning in 1986, the INS/CIS reported data on age and gender breakdowns of "immigrants admitted as orphans." Patterns and variations in the data are described for the countries discussed above.

Adoptees from Russia

As figure 1.1a shows, on average, the gender breakdown for Russian-born adoptees to the United States through 2005 was nearly equal: 51.5 percent females to 49.5 percent males. Although yearly breakdowns show some gender discrepancies, with the exception of 1993, the gender distribution typically varied less than 5 percent in favor of females in any single year. However, in 1996 and 1998, the percentages of Russian-born male adoptees exceeded female adoptees by 4 percent.

Figure 1.1a
Russian Adoptees to
the United States by Sex, 1993-2005

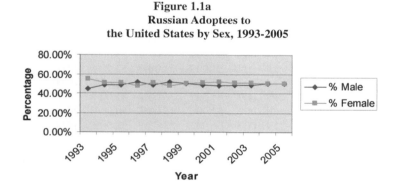

Relative to adoptees from other countries, Russian adoptees to the United States were far more likely than those from Asia, South America, and Central America to arrive in their new families beyond infancy. Figure 1.1b shows that between 21 percent (1993) and 39 percent (1999) of Russian adoptees were infants when they joined their American families. The modal age range for Russian adoptees was between one and four years old (52 percent of adoptees). Between 1993 and 2005, an average of twenty-one in 100 Russian adoptees to the United States were five years old or older. Thus, in regard to age at adoption, Russia stands in marked contrast to China and especially to Korea. Infants under one year old were the majority of adoptees from both Asian countries.

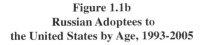

Figure 1.1b
Russian Adoptees to
the United States by Age, 1993-2005

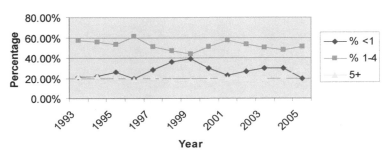

In the other Eastern European countries, the pattern of female to male preponderance is clear. This pattern varies in average percentage, however, from 3 percent for Romanian adoptees, to 6 percent for adoptees from the minor sending countries, included in aggregate fashion, to 8 percent for Bulgarian adoptees, and 12 percent for Kazak adoptees.

Adoptees from the Ukraine

The Ukraine was the only major Eastern European sending country that showed an aggregated average that slightly favored males. As figure 1.2a shows, however, the gender gap for seven of these thirteen years (1993, 1995, 1996, 1998, 1999, 2003, and 2004) favored females. Percentages in favor of female adoptees from the Ukraine varied from 20 percent in 1995 and 1996, to 2 percent in 2003. In 2005, the gender distribution of male and female adoptees from the Ukraine was equal.

Figure 1.2a
Distribution of Ukranian Adoptees to
the United States by Sex, 1993-2005

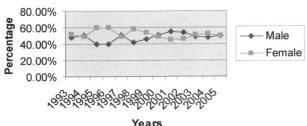

Figure 1.2b
Distribution of Ukranian Adoptees to
the United States by Age, 1993-2005

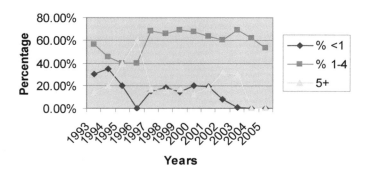

As figure 1.2b shows, the clearest trend in ages of Ukrainian adoptees to the U.S. was one to four years old. After first being observed in 1993, this trend persisted from 1997 through 2005. The likelihood of an infant born in the Ukraine being adopted by an American family peaked in 1994 (35 percent), and declined thereafter.

Adoptees from Romania

In 1990, a Romanian female was 1.7 times as likely as a Romanian male to be adopted to the U.S. The gender gap favoring female Romanian adoptees varied from 26 percentage points (in 1990) to gender balance (in 1993 and 2000). In ten of the fifteen years between 1990 and 2005, female adoptees outnumbered males.

Figure 1.3a
Distribution of Romanian Adoptees to
the United States by Sex, 1990-2005

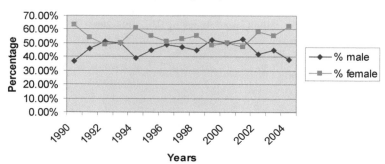

As figure 1.3b shows, between 1992 and 2005, on average, adoptees to the United States from Romania tended to be between the ages of one and four when they were adopted. In only two years (1990 and 1991) were at least 50 percent of Romanian adoptees to the United States infants.

Figure 1.3b
Distribution of Romanian Adoptees to
the United States by Age, 1990-2005

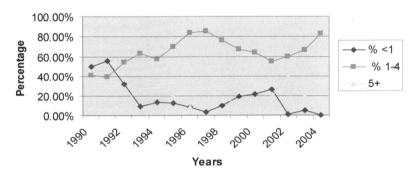

Adoptees from Kazakhstan

As figure 1.4a shows, female adoptees from Kazakhstan outnumbered males in all years. The gender gap was largest in 1998 (34 percent in favor of females), but showed a decline over time to 4 percent in favor of females from 2003 to 2005. Figure 1.4b shows that Kazak adoptees to the United States were most likely to enter their new families as infants

Figure 1.4a
Distribution of Kazak Adoptees
to the United States by Sex, 1998-2005

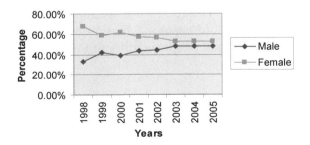

only in 1998 and 1999. In subsequent years, the percentages of older adoptees, especially those aged one to four years, increased and infant adoptions from this country dropped below 50 percent.

Figure 1.4b
Distribution of Kazak Adoptees to
the United States by Age, 1998-2005

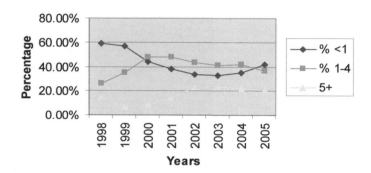

Adoptees from Bulgaria

In every year between 1992 and 2005, except for 1997, 2004 and 2005, adoptees from Bulgaria to the U. S. were more likely to be female than male. The gender gap for adoptees from this country varied from a high of sixteen percentage points in favor of females (in 2000) to a low of two percentage points (in 2001 and 2004) in the same direction.

In regard to age distribution, as figure 1.5b shows, Bulgarian adoptees to the United States most likely joined their new families when they were past infancy. The child's age at adoption generally fell into the one to four years old category. Beginning in 2001, increasing percentages of Bulgarian adoptees fell into this age category.

Figure 1.5a
Distribution of Bulgarian Adoptees to
the United States by Sex, 1992-2005

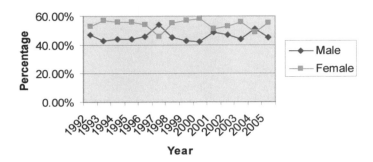

Figure 1.5b
Distribution of Bulgarian Adoptees to
the United States by Age, 1992-2005

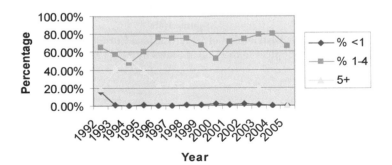

Adoptees from Other Eastern European Countries

The data in figure 1.6a indicate that, between 1990 and 2005, on aver-age, females from other Eastern European sending countries outnumbered males in all but two years – 1990 and 1999. The gender gap varied from a high of 16 percent in 1991, to parity in 1998. With the exception of 1990 and 1999, when male adoptees exceeded female adoptees by 4 percent, the trend in gender disparity was in the direction of more female than male adoptees.

Figure 1.6a
Distribution of Other Eastern European
Adoptees to the United States by Sex, 1990-2005

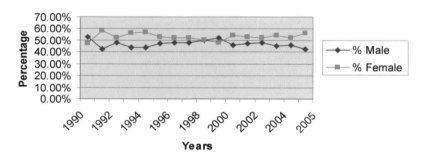

Figure 1.6b
Distribution of Other Eastern European
Adoptees to the United States by Age, 1990-2005

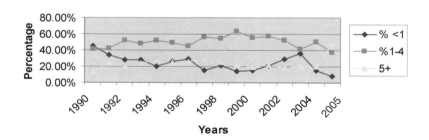

Adoptions to the United States from Russia and Eastern Europe during the 1990s in Global Perspective

With the worldwide 1990s decade total for Russian children adopted outside their birth country standing at 22,756, the ISS/IRC data reveal that, during the last decade, Americans adopted 83 percent of the Russian orphans sent worldwide for adoption. During the 1990s, Americans also adopted 87 percent of the children sent from Poland for adoption worldwide; 77 percent of the Ukrainian adoptees worldwide; 44 percent of the Romanian adoptees worldwide; and 33 percent of the Bulgarian adoptees worldwide.

2

Understanding What Motivates Americans to Adopt a Child or Children Internationally

Three principal variables impact on adoption trends, both within and across national boundaries: attitudes toward adoption in the socio-cultural context in which family formation occurs or expands; the availability of potential adoptees in a prospective adopter's own country; and the ease or difficulty of adopting available children, either domestically or internationally. In regard to the first variable, the United States is a society where attitudes toward adoption vary by race, ethnicity, and social class as well as over time. Historical evidence indicates that, in the United States, "informal" adoptions among relatives, close friends, or neighbors have been replaced by formal arrangements requiring intermediaries. A myriad of laws require the involvement of judges, social workers, and others who have a vested interest in regulating adoption—the process, the likelihood, and the outcome. Adoption has, thus, moved from the personal to the public realm.

Although practiced on a limited basis in the early decades of the twentieth century, domestic adoptions of non-relative children increased in popularity in the United States after World War II. Out-of-wedlock motherhood continued to be stigmatized well into the 1960s. Domestic adoptions in the United States reportedly peaked in 1970 and became viewed as the "legitimate" social response to the problem of illegitimacy. However, between 1973 and 1995, domestic adoptions declined.

In this chapter, I examine the social, political, demographic, and economic forces that have shaped Americans' opportunities to adopt domestically. Understanding the forces that motivate Americans to adopt more children internationally than people in any other country in the world will help to answer a commonly asked question about why they went to another country to adopt when there are so many children in need of families in this country.

Sometimes friends or relatives ask an adoptive parent this question. More often, this question comes from strangers who see an interracial or trans-cultural family on the street or in a store. Some people are just interested. Others are oddly insensitive, asking hurtful or hostile questions often in front of the child or children. It seems that, despite its popularity, international adoption is a phenomenon misunderstood by some and decried perhaps by many.[1]

A number of phenomena have transformed the face of both domestic adoption and international adoption by Americans over the last several decades. Some of these phenomena push prospective adopters out of the traditional/infant domestic adoption market. Others pull them into the international adoption market. Some factors operate as independent variables (causes) and others as mediating/contextual variables. The critical dependent variables (effects) are the opportunities for children who need and want families to be matched with adoptive parents who can manage their needs and for people who desire to parent a child or children to achieve that goal.

The Push Factors

The most important "push" factors include the widespread availability of effective birth control to women, beginning in the 1960s and the legalization of abortion in the United States in 1973. Both of these changes resulted in fewer healthy newborns and infants available for domestic adoption. Added to these two changes is the declining stigma attached to illegitimacy after the 1960s, resulting in the trend toward teenage mothers keeping their children rather than placing them for adoption.

The birth rate is also a push factor. In the United States, as in other developed countries, the birth rate has declined, especially among the middle classes. The lower birth rate combined with increasing opportunities for women to pursue post-secondary education and careers in a post-industrial society results in delayed marriage and delayed childbearing among this segment of the female population. Women who defer childbearing into their late thirties and beyond are at a greater risk for infertility problems. When infertility problems occur, the first option typically encouraged by medical personnel and pursued by many couples/singles is finding a way to produce a biological child. The availability of medical coverage to experiment with this option makes choosing this recourse possible for financially-secure women and couples. Meanwhile, a woman's so-called "biological clock" is ticking. Because of the increased demand for a newborn, relative to the numbers of healthy newborns available, the cost of a private adoption of a "healthy" white infant in the United States has increased dramatically.

When one considers adoption, the model of the "desirable" child —a healthy infant of the same race as the prospective parents, and of the potential parents—a married couple in their thirties, is the image of the adoptive family that comes to mind. This "traditional" model works against (pushes out) the increasing number of prospective adopters who are older, part of a couple who both work, single people, and those who live non-traditional lifestyles but desire to be parents. This model also works against the children likely to be available for adoption by most families in the United States (minorities, non-infants). The likelihood of a long wait for a domestic adoptee also pushes many prospective parents out of the domestic adoption market.

Although advanced computer technology and the Internet are ways to advertise older children available for adoption[2] and to market singles or couples as prospective parents to pregnant teens,[3] the discriminatory and hierarchical nature of adoption policies in the United States and the frustratingly long wait to adopt a child in state custody has also pushed many prospective adopters out of the domestic market. Concerns about the long-term challenges of adopting a special needs child or children may also be a factor.

The Pull Factors

In addition to the factors that push prospective adoptive parents out of the domestic adoption "market," a variety of "pull" factors encourage couples and singles to choose to adopt internationally. These factors include the increased opportunity for international adoptions of infants from Korea, China, and Central America; the increased affluence of individuals and couples seeking to adopt newborns or infants. Even if they do not arrive as infants, children who are available for international adoption outside their birth country are typically younger, on average, than the potential adoptees available in the child welfare system in the United States. In 2005, for example, 40 percent of the children adopted internationally were under one year old and 44 percent were between one and four years old and 16 percent were age five years or older. That same year, only 2 percent of children who were adopted domestically from foster care were under one year old. The majority (52 percent) of the domestic adoptees were six years old and older.[4]

Older, childless couples and individuals may be attracted to international adoption because of the possibility of adopting two or more children simultaneously and the opportunity to state a preference for a child/children of a particular gender or ethnic background. Clearly, major "push factors" also include the somewhat looser criteria regarding the age, marital status, and, in some countries, the sexual orientation of the adopting parent(s); the relative speed of most international adoptions (six to eight months) as compared to the prospect of waiting several years to adopt an infant privately or a child or children in state custody; the opening of new countries to inter-country adoption in the 1990s.

Since the early 1990s, Russia, the Ukraine, and other Eastern European countries have offered a pipeline to Caucasian children. During that time, the plight of large numbers of children living in orphanages in Eastern European countries captured America's attention. The media brought home stark images of abandoned children and of the social problems that forced these children into often bleak, institutional settings and into the care of non-relatives hired to provide for their basic needs. The combination of socially responsible attitudes toward parenting, which motivate some people to choose to parent children already born rather than to produce more children, and humanitarian concerns about offering an orphaned child significantly improved life chances over the opportunities the child would typically have in his/her birth country also enter the picture.

Another pull factor is the belief, held by many prospective adopters, that the child/children offered to them—and, indeed, that most children available from a particular country—is/are either healthy or have correctable medical problems/conditions or short term developmental delays which good food, proper medical attention and lots of love will rectify in about six months.[5] Finally, people are motivated to adopt internationally because they believe that the child's/children's birth parents are not likely to try to reclaim him/her/them.

The Changing Characteristics of Prospective Adopters and Adoptees

Collectively, these many changes have influenced dramatically the characteristics of those interested in adopting, how they might go about adopting, and the characteristics of the children available for adoption.

Prospective Adopters

In recent years, those who are interested in adopting tend to be more educated, more affluent, and older (40 plus). Many prospective adopters are married but a notable number are single. Some are gay or lesbian. For reasons of both relative size in the population of the U.S. and finances, whites comprise the large majority of those non relatives (of children) seeking to adopt (them).

The Pool of Children Available for Domestic Adoption

Who are the children typically available for adoption in the United States? Clearly, the number of healthy newborns available for adoption domestically in recent years has dropped dramatically. Many couples and singles wish to adopt healthy infants or toddlers, but soon find a scarcity of both in the United States, except among children of color. Unfortunately, placement philosophies which have required, or strongly preferred, racial matching of African American children with African American adoptive parents have taken their toll in discouraging many whites from adopting children of a different race in domestic adoptions, preventing these waiting children from finding a stable, loving home at the earliest possibility.

So, on average, children who are available for domestic adoption tend to be non infants who have more problems and issues than did the pool of available children 25 or so years ago. Some of their family circumstances, like poverty and family dysfunction, are common across geographic boundaries. Family dysfunction—including problems of pre natal drug and/or alcohol exposure—has increased the number of drug- and alcohol affected infants, children who have been neglected, physically and/or sexually abused, those over two years of age, and sibling groups. Many available children have witnessed or experienced family violence, extreme deprivation, and malnutrition.

Once viewed as unadoptable, these children now comprise a large portion of the adoption pool of children typically available especially to couples and singles, age forty and older. Known as "special needs" in this country, many of these children and sibling groups languish in the system for years without a permanent place to call home. According to a recent AFCARS (Adoption and Foster Care Analysis and Reporting System) Report, 115,407 children were available and waiting to be adopted on December 31, 2005.[6] This number included children under age sixteen whose biological parents' rights had been terminated and for whom adoption was a goal. Eighteen percent of the children who exited foster care during fiscal year 2005 were adopted. This population of adoptees was comprised of more minority (36 percent black Non-Hispanic and 15 percent Hispanic) than white children (40 percent) and six percent more males than females (53 percent versus 47 percent, respectively). As of September 30, 2005, the median age of a child waiting to be adopted from the foster care system was 8.4 years old and the mean age was 8.6 years. Seventy-four percent of these children were living in foster care. Twenty-one percent of them had lived in foster care continuously for at least three years and another 21 percent for five or more years. The median wait to be adopted of a child in foster care was 30.7 months. The mean wait was almost 41.6 months.

Of course, "healthy" infants are still available domestically. However, they usually get adopted through independent or lawyer-assisted placements and through expensive private agencies that only a relatively small percentage of people can easily afford.

The Children Typically Available for International Adoption

The children available for international adoption come to more developed, richer countries from less developed, poorer ones. Their lives have been severely affected by poverty, politics, and/or family dysfunction. For one or more of these reasons their birth parent(s) cannot or will not raise them.

Some waiting children are infants who are taken care of by their birth families or by a foster family until they are adopted. Such may be the experience of newborns and infants adopted from South and Central American countries and from Korea.

Others may be older "street kids" abandoned by their families and who, at some point, find themselves in an institutional setting where they become available for adoption. In Russia, for example, some children who become available for adoption may have been left in maternity hospitals by birth mothers unable to care for them and, later, are moved to orphanages. Others may have been abandoned. Still others may have been removed from birth parent(s) because of extreme abuse and/or neglect often resulting from parental alcohol and/or drug abuse, family violence, or other problems. Some children available for international adoption have been exposed to radiation, lead, or have experienced the trauma of war.

Many of the children adopted internationally, especially those adopted from Eastern European countries and from China, have lived in orphanage settings. Some available children have lived in an orphanage all their life.

Children are sometimes in orphanages because of the fallout effects of government policies gone to extremes. These include the population policy that was initiated under former President Ceausescu in Romania, forcing women to produce more children than they could care for or support, and China's one child policy, motivated by concerns about over population and the threat of starvation, if population continued to grow unchecked. The latter policy had the effect of requiring couples, especially those living in cities, to have only a single child. Most parents hoped for a boy. So, if the child was a girl, she ran a high risk of being abandoned or given up for adoption.

Concluding Statement

In sum, there are both benefits and costs to adopting a child or children internationally.[7] Understanding why Americans decide to do so in such large numbers when there are many children who need good homes in this country requires that we understand the diverse factors which both pull Americans toward international adoption and push them away from the domestic adoption of children in state custody. The many social and demographic forces which have occurred over the last several decades have combined with political and economic factors and the policies and practices of domestic adoption to make the opportunity to adopt domestically less likely for certain categories of prospective adopters. Whether formal or informal, current adoption policies and practices in the U. S. discriminate against individuals and couples who have certain social or demographic characteristics: Those age forty and older, a married woman working full time, a single woman or man, and homosexuals.

Throughout the history of domestic adoption, cross-racial adoptions (of black or racially mixed children by whites) were either not considered or were actively resisted by black social workers and members of the black community. However, on January 1, 1997, President Clinton enacted a change in the law. Through U.S. Special Needs Children, H.R. 3448, the barriers to interracial adoption were removed. The new law states: "No person can be denied the opportunity to become an adoptive or foster parent on the basis of race, color or national origin of the person, or of the child involved."[8] How this law actually plays out in the current domestic adoption "market" needs to be researched. Its effect remains to be seen because those in control of adoptions may still be able to find barriers other than race to exclude many whites from adopting across racial lines.

Also, with the opportunity to adopt minority children domestically being pitted against the availability of white orphans in Russia and other Eastern European countries, older and minority "waiting children" in the

United States are placed at a disadvantage. The fact also remains that a cumbersome legal system still regards biology as ownership, thus resulting in many children not being released for adoption by the courts (i.e., parental rights terminated) until after they have been severely abused and neglected for some time.

Notes

1.   McKelvey, C. A. and J. Stevens. 1994. *Adoption Crisis: The Truth Behind Adoption and Foster Care*. Golden, CO: Fulcrum Publishing.
2.   Mirabella, M. 1996. "Brazil's Older Orphans Seeking Homes in the Web." *CNN Worldview*, Transcript #260 5 (September 19).
3.   Cobb, N. 1996. "Infants through the Internet; Some would-be Parents Scan Cyberspace for a Match." *The Boston Globe* (April 28).
4.   International adoption data is for fiscal year 2005. USCIS, Table 12. Immigrant Orphans Adopted by U.S. Citizens by Gender, Age, and Region and Country of Birth: Fiscal Year 2005.
       Adoption and Foster Care Analysis and Reporting System (AFCARS) data submitted for the Fiscal Year 2005, 10/1/04 through 9/30/05. Available at http://www.acf.hhs.gov/programs/cb/stats_research/afcars/tar/report13.htm
5.   Such beliefs are typically based on informal statements from agency personnel or their facilitators in the sending countries.
6.   U.S. Department of Health and Human Services Administration for Children and Families, Administration on Children, Youth and Families Children's Bureau Adoption and Foster Care Analysis and Reporting System (AFCARS) web address: http://www.acf.hhs.gov/programs/cb/stats_research/afcars/waiting2005.pdf
7.   See Hollingsworth, L. and V.M. Ruffin. 2002. "Why Are So Many U.S. Families Adopting Internationally? A Social Exchange Perspective." *Journal of Human Behavior in the Social Environment*. Vol. 6, No. 1, pp. 81-97.
8.   *ODS News*. 1996. "Income Tax Credit and Ban on Race Discrimination in Adoption Now U. S. Law." (October), p. 1.

3

Similarities and Differences in
Issues Relevant to International
and Domestic Adoption

One or several of the push-pull factors described in the previous chapter may encourage would-be adopters to go the international, rather than the domestic, adoption route. Prospective adopters who explore domestic adoption are realistically concerned about many things. These include the number of children actually available for adoption in the United States, their characteristics—especially age and gender, and the time frame involved in completing an adoption. They are also concerned about their own characteristics especially, age, marital status, and/or sexual orientation being perceived by gatekeepers as disqualifying factors. With the increasing emphasis on "open adoptions" in private, domestic adoptions, there is also the fear (nearly always unfounded) of a domestic birth mother, or father, suing to reclaim an adopted child. Because of the frustrations, delays, and uncertainties of adopting domestically and with the willingness of Eastern European countries to place orphans with adoptive parents in other countries, agencies and facilitators specializing in inter-country adoptions began to spring up virtually overnight.

In this chapter, I examine eight issues which individuals and couples who plan to adopt an older child or a sibling group need to understand and which agencies placing such children need to acknowledge. However, issues in the international adoption of children, especially older children, overlap with some of the important issues involved in the domestic adoption of the children most likely to be available for adoption. Some of the issues that may be associated with both younger and older child adoptions here are similar to those of children available for adoption from some Eastern European countries. These issues include, for example, the risk of pre-natal exposure to alcohol and/or drugs, family violence, neglect, physical and/or sexual abuse, and significant emotional and behavioral problems. Areas of difference are in the experiences associated with institutionalization as opposed to family care, the severity of malnutrition, the quality of physical health, the higher risk of certain diseases, and physical disabilities of some children available for inter-country adoption, and language differences between many of the adoptive parents and the non-infant children they adopt.

The Research on Recent International Adoptees

Reports on recent international adoptees began with investigations of Romanian children and started to appear in the cross-disciplinary literature in the mid-to-late 1990s. The cadres of researchers who are interested in the most recent wave of international adoptees include Americans,[1] Canadians,[2] and the British.[3] Currently, empirical articles on children born in Russia, as a major category of adoptees, and on older inter-country adoptees, including sibling groups, are virtually non-existent in the published, social science literature.

The existing professional literature on recent international adoptees can be organized primarily into one of the following categories, although some reports contain overlapping objectives. These categories include: investigations of adoptees' physical health, reported by medical professionals;[4] outcome variables for children adopted from orphanages;[5] parental outcomes such as stress from parenting difficult children;[6] and policy and/or practice issues,[7] or possible interventions.[8]

However, other research on international adoptees is also relevant to the discussion of issues involved in adopting a child or children who has certain kinds of early experiences. That research is integrated with the discussion of the eight issues which follow.

The Issue of the Deleterious Effects of Orphanage Living on Children's Health, Behavior, and Development

Many of the children adopted internationally, especially those adopted from Eastern European countries such as Romania, Russia, the Ukraine, and Poland—as well as from China, have lived in orphanage settings. Some children available for inter-country adoption have lived in an institutional or orphanage setting all their lives.

Pediatrician Dana Johnson describes the orphanage setting and the experiences of children who have lived in them in clear and poignant terms:

An orphanage is a terrible place to raise an infant or young child. Lack of stimulation and consistent caregivers, sub optimal nutrition and physical/sexual abuse all conspire to delay and sometimes preclude normal development. All institutionalized children fall behind in large and fine motor development, speech acquisition and the attainment of necessary motor skills. Many never find a single individual with whom to complete a cycle of attachment. Physical growth is impaired. Children lose one month of linear growth for every three months in the orphanage. Weight gain and head growth are also depressed. Finally, congregate living conditions foster the spread of multiple infectious agents. Intestinal parasites, tuberculosis, hepatitis B, measles, chicken pox, middle ear infections, etc. are all found more commonly in institutional settings.[9]

Despite the fact that the research on the effects of orphanage living on American children dates back to the 1940s,[10] Americans have little knowledge of and even less direct experience with orphanages. Thus, when they imagine what life in an orphanage may be like, the nostalgic "Boys Town" image may come to mind.

Unfortunately, that image is dated and would be unrealistic even in the United States today—never mind in a developing, or less affluent, country. Although orphanages do vary in conditions and in quality of care provided to the children who live in them, they are deprived environments that are not adequate alternatives to growing up in a stable, loving family.

Too few people who adopt children from orphanage settings understand the culture or social structure of orphanages. Placement professionals do not emphasize this point either. In fact, what orphanage life is like is often down played. Although orphanages may be able to provide a relatively safe, more structured environment for children who come from dysfunctional, chaotic families, even the best orphanages are not set up to provide the level of verbal and tactile stimulation which infants and young children need. Neither are orphanage staff able to provide consistent, long term interaction with an adult with whom children can connect emotionally and who will be there to hold and cuddle them and can be counted on to fulfill their other needs. According to Bowlby (1951), normal development is contingent on attachment to a mothering figure. Orphanage-raised children have rarely had such a consistent figure before being adopted.

The Issue of Physical Health Problems

Although the research on some of the children adopted internationally by Americans during the 1990s is still the early stages, statistics about medical and other problems have appeared in some published sources. For example, in an article in *Newsweek Magazine*, Bogert described certain patterns of risk that were emerging in Romanian and Russian adoptees.[11] Bogert cited statistics that indicated that children adopted abroad are 1,000 times more likely to carry tuberculosis than are American children. As compared to American children, those adopted from Romania were also reported to be forty to fifty times more likely to have Hepatitis B. Fetal alcohol syndrome was also reported to be showing up in Russian adoptees.

A study of 129 adoptees published in The Archives of Pediatric and Adolescent Medicine a year later, Pediatrician Laurie Miller and her colleagues documented some similar patterns of problems in the foreign born adoptees that the team of physicians and affiliated staff assessed.[12] All of the children they studied had arrived in the United States between 1989 and 1993. The children's median age was twelve months. The staff studied the children about six weeks after their adoption, using detailed developmental and medical assessments. These adoptees came from twenty-two countries—most commonly from Romania, China, Paraguay, and South Korea. The assessment results indicated that 50 percent of these adoptees had developmental and widespread medical problems, some of which were not detected (or perhaps not revealed to the U. S. agency or the adoptive parents), before the children had arrived in the United States. Problems identified in this group included hepatitis, malnutrition, intestinal parasites, rickets, and previously undiagnosed heart disease. The most compelling and thought-provoking statement the authors made was about the likelihood of reversing severe delays. The authors stated that, for example, the effects of malnutrition on the developing brain during the crucial first two years of life are unknown at present.

A 2002 report from Russia's Health Ministry provides some shocking health statistics. This report states that no more than one in three Russian newborns and only one in ten teenagers are "healthy."[13] Health problems afflicting this population include tuberculosis, heroin addiction, alcoholism, abuse of other drugs, and a fast-growing HIV epidemic. In April of 2005, MOSNEWS.com released an article, entitled "13,000 Russian Children Are HIV-Positive." This statistic is attributed to Olga Sharapova, a senior official from the Health and Social Development Ministry. Sharapova states that most of the HIV-infected children are homeless and orphans.[14]

Concerns about the increasingly unhealthy and projected shrinking size of the Russian population are mounting. Nearly half of Russian expectant mothers are malnourished. "Babies in Russia are born smaller and sicker today than in the past."[15]

Programs aimed at promoting good health, preventing disease, and replacing abortion as the major form of birth control have low priority in Russia right now. Potentially successful treatment and prevention will require a multi-level approach and the involvement of collaborative efforts. As Massey points out, these efforts will need to come from constituencies both inside and outside of Russia. Those outside of Russia include European and American allies and volunteers.

Problems in Establishing Close Relationships

More than fifty years ago, Bowlby explored problems in attachment of children separated from their mothers.[16] Consistent with Bowlby's research, twenty years ago, Wolkind and Rutter reported that children who are institutionalized during the first year of life are likely to show disturbances in social relationships and to develop a style of interacting with others which may work, and be considered appropriate, within the institutional setting but which may not work well outside of it.[17]

Geraghty also speaks to this point. She reports on an interview she conducted with Ronald Feldman, a former Deputy Director of Boys Town during the 1970s. Feldman talked about some of the myths and realities of orphanages. He made several important points that apply to children who have lived in institutional settings, either in the United States or in other countries. Focusing on the issue of behavior, Geraghty reports that Feldman commented:

> Kids comply in institutions.... But they don't know how to generalize those positive changes to an open community that is not so highly structured.[18]

These are important issues about which both adoptive parents and professionals who treat formerly institutionalized children need to be aware.

In talking about policy issues and the broader picture, Feldman stated that lawmakers in this country who may be consider reinstating orphanages as a means to deal with the problems of poverty and child abuse, need to recognize the other problems which institutional living creates, such as the reinforcing of aggressive and antisocial behavior and the high price tag they carry (as high as $75,000 per child at the time the article was written). Feldman suggested that money could be better spent on preventative programs that could work through community centers. Such programs and services should focus on helping at-risk families before they fall apart, by providing educational programs for adults and recreational sports programs for children. Preventing family crises before they happen, Feldman believes, would result in "... less child abuse, less neglect, healthier neighborhoods and healthier children."[19] This comment is reminiscent of Jane Adams' concept of the many functions of the settlement house.

The Impact of Abuse and Older Age at Placement on a Child's Behavior and Emotional Issues

In the early 1990s, Verhulst and his colleagues published a series of articles about the later behavioral/emotional problems of children adopted internationally by Dutch parents in the 1970s.[20] These researchers report the results of an epidemiological study they conducted, examine problem behavior in relation to age at placement in the home, and look at psychiatric disorders the children have. The children in their sample were adopted between January 1, 1972 and December 31, 1975, and were ten to fifteen years old when the study took place. Adoptees came from a variety of countries including Korea, Columbia, India, Indonesia, and Bangladesh.

The data that Verhulst and his colleagues collected are based on parents' self reports of their children's competencies and behavioral/emotional problems. The sample consisted of 2,138 adoptees.

Although these researchers did not study the recent wave of international adoptees, their conclusions are potentially relevant. Verhulst and his associates reported that children who come from seriously damaging early environments are at risk for developing conduct problems and depression later in life.[21] The factor that best predicted later problems was early abuse.

Age at placement was also related to later problems in children twelve to fifteen years old: age at placement was found to be associated with delinquent behavior and depressive symptoms. The age of the child at placement and the presence of physical problems also were reported to have an independent association with the child's level of later maladjustment.

Verhulst and his associates conclude that the early experiences/factors which place children at risk for behavioral/emotional problems are neglect, abuse, and the number of changes of caretaking/placements. Of these three variables, the best predictor of later maladjustment was early abuse. This conclusion is a very important one for policy makers, adoption agency facilitators who place children, and foreign adoption facilitators/officials to take seriously:

These findings underscore the importance of reliable and detailed information that parents should obtain about the background and behavior of the child in the pre-adoption period. Severely damaging early experiences put a child who is eligible for adoption at risk for developing problem behaviors. Knowledge of these influence early recognition of deviant behavior and may enhance early interventions and support. [22]

In sum, according to Verhulst and his colleagues (1990b, p. 104, 1992, p.518) and others whose results they cite, adopted children may experience an elevated risk for future problems such as alcoholism,[23] antisocial personality[24] and schizophrenia[25] through increased genetic vulnerability. These problems result from inadequate pre and post natal care, malnourishment and stress experienced by the birth mother both before and after the child's (often illegitimate) birth, and negative environmental influences, including separation from the birth mother, dysfunctional family relationships, poor parent child relationships, and interruptions or discontinuities in care giving prior to the child's adoption. These negative environmental influences may include nutritional deprivations, lack of adequate stimulation, linguistic delays, lack of affection, and lack of opportunities for developing attachments. Other causal factors include the child's concerns about the biological parent(s), the relationships and expectations in the adoptive family, and the stresses which the adoptive family may be experiencing.

The Risk of Future Problems

In a recent article, Groza and Ryan agree that experiencing adversity or trauma early in life can lead to behavior problems at a later age. They also state that a longer history of institutionalization is associated with more behavior problems.[26]

The Issue of the Number of Children Placed in a Family
at the Same Time

While placing more than one child in a family at the same time can be challenging and stressful for the new parents, the degree of challenge and the level of stress depend not only on how many children join the family at the same time but also on other stressors and the availability of stress reducers. Other stressors include the age and pre-adoption history of the child/children—both the pre-natal history and the history of experiences from birth to adoptive placement, the presence of emotional, psychological, and/or physical health problems. Such problems may be manifested in children as depression, anger, anxiety, panic on separation from the new parent(s), poor impulse control, aggressiveness, difficulties attaching to the new parent(s), and poor relationships with peers.[27] Stress reducers are resources to which parents have access. For example, having access to a steady network of family, friends, and professionals who understand the child's needs and offer to help by providing respite is an important stress reducer. Access to community resources like pre-school and after-school programs, the YMCA/YWCA, the Boys and Girls Club, athletic leagues, church-affiliated youth programs, and appropriate types of summer camps can make a big difference in both the child's and the family's stress levels. Groza and Ryan identify the following mitigators of stress for the parents of a child who has behavior problems: (1) having accurate information about a child's pre-natal and pre-adoption history; (2) having information about known or anticipated behavioral challenges or problems; (3) having resources to help parents understand and manage their child's behavior. Such resources may include personal and professional help and support.[28]

In a study of special needs domestic adoptees, Leung and Erich identify sibling-group adoption as an important variable that is related to significantly lower family functioning.[29] These researchers developed a seven-variable model that accounted for a total of 68.63 percent of the total variation. Three variables alone accounted for over 52 percent of the total variation: sibling adoption (25.3 percent), number of each child's behavior problems (17.08 percent), and contacts with the law (10.52 percent). The remaining four variables accounted for less than 16 percent of the total variation: spouse or partner support (5.36 percent), child's age at adoption (4.27 percent), relative support (3.73 percent), and school support (2.33 percent).

The findings of research on sibling placement in the same adoptive home are inconsistent. Boer and Verhulst[30] did a follow up investigation of 399 adoptees in the same sample of children first discussed by Verhulst and others. The children Boer and his colleagues studied were placed in adoptive homes with one or more siblings. The follow up was conducted about ten years after placement.

These researchers reported that the children placed with siblings were not at higher risk of disruption. Neither did they show more problem behaviors than children placed alone. However, these researchers also point out that there are both advantages and disadvantages to separate as well as to joint placements and the results of other studies of single vs. multiple placements to the same family and the risk of disruption/dissolution are inconclusive—that is, results are mixed. These researchers also recognize that the absence of formal dissolution of an adoption does not necessarily signal adoption success.

Adoption Agencies and Facilitators: Issues of Licensing, Reputation, Quality, and Accessibility

If an adoption agency is licensed, it is, at least in theory, subject to regulation at the state level. Adoption facilitators and entities that may "look like agencies" are not licensed.

Licensing is important at least in the sense that there is a government body which keeps records on complaints against agencies and whether or not the complaints are resolved. On the other hand, even licensing and the risk of complaints do not serve as serious deterrents to unethical practices on the part of some agencies. Only anecdotal information may be available about the ethical standards of facilitators.

Although private domestic adoption agencies and international adoption agencies may refer to themselves as non profit, human service agencies, in fact, they typically operate as businesses. The fact that a business owner describes him or herself as a "non-profit" entity does not mean that the business makes no money. A non-profit agency or business does not have stockholders. Such a business also has no accountability to any one but their funding sources. In order for a business to call itself "non-profit," its assets (including earned income) (A) must equal its liabilities (B) plus its equity (C). The two sides of the equation cancel each other out: $A = B + C$. A "no profit" balance sheet may be maintained through moving assets around, into non-liquid assets, or out of the business.

If one views private adoption agencies as businesses, then it follows that the children the business places are its product or commodity. Healthy infants and children are in the highest demand. Yet, as I documented earlier through the available empirical research, many of the available children, especially in Eastern European countries, would fit the definition of special needs placements. From a financial standpoint, it is in an agency's best interest to place as many children as possible. One way of placing as many children as possible is to gloss over or omit important information about the child's health or pre-adoption history or fail to tell prospective parents about the risks and likely problems of the child/children they will adopt.[31] Another way to increase the number of children placed, and to maximize fees, is to "stretch" prospective parents to take on more children than they really want or can handle—for example, to accept a sibling group of three children when they expressed initial interest in adopting two children.

Therefore, entities operating as international adoption agencies may gloss over or omit information about known problems because honesty is not the most profitable policy and because, as of this writing, no law or government agency serves as a sufficiently menacing watchdog to ensure it. Conservative placement philosophies and prejudices may operate in inter-country adoptions just as they do domestically, resulting in decisions to place a child or children with many and/or serious problems in the families regarded as least desirable or lowest on the ranking scale (i.e., couples and singles over forty, homosexuals, those not in the best of health, etc.). Such decisions may be supported or even required by some orphanage directors and/or officials in sending countries. At other times, agency staff may be operating under the misguided beliefs that adoptive parents do not want to know about a child's past or that, somehow, past traumas and present problems will miraculously disappear in a new family environment. None of these approaches is in the child's best interests and certainly not in the best interests of the functioning of the adoptive family system

Some adoption agencies have been around for many years and have established reputations to protect. Others come and go when the going gets tough and the complaints or lawsuits start coming in. Although they may be licensed in a given state, that state probably maintains little control over the practices of international adoption agencies (unless numerous, blatant violations come to light) or their fee structure.

Moreover, it is not uncommon for people to work with adoption agencies which may not be in their home state and which, in fact, may be hundreds or even thousands of miles away. In such cases, all of their contact with the agency will probably be via telephone and mail. This is especially true if their home study is completed by a local agency and not the agency that will facilitate the adoption. If there are problems at or with the agency, the matter of geographic distance will make it impossible to know first hand what is really going on at the agency, to advocate effectively for the child's/children's needs, or to force the agency to provide needed services.

Distance creates a level of anonymity that may encourage some agencies to engage in shoddy treatment of dissatisfied clients. Also, since some of the children's problems may not show up right away, agency staff and foreign facilitators and officials may pass off children with serious medical, but more likely serious emotional, psychological, or other problems, as "healthy." Disreputable individuals may feel that the adoptive parents will be too far away to reach them when problems do show up or that the agency or facilitator will be long gone so why should they worry.

The Financial Costs of International Adoption

When supply is low and demand high, the cost of adoption increases. This is true of both private domestic as well as international adoptions. Private agencies hold out the promise of dreams fulfilled—for a price.

Focusing specifically on international adoption, the costs of adopting a child or children can be considerable. First, fees vary by agency and sending country. Fees also vary over time and may change without notice at the discretion of the agency. For these reasons, it is difficult to offer figures. However, a "ballpark figure" of at least $30,000 per child for adopting a single infant or young toddler is not unrealistic. Agencies may reduce the fee somewhat when sibling groups are adopted simultaneously but the cost may still be considerable. Travel, passport and visa costs, fees to in-country employees for their services, lodging and meals, and other expenses must also be figured into the total cost of an international adoption when children come from a country which requires that pre-adoptive parents must travel to the prospective child's country and make more than one trip.

Not only do officials and bureaucrats of the sending country make money on adoptions, but so also do the locals who are hired as facilitators, escorts, translators, drivers, host families, etc. International adoption has most certainly fueled the underground economies of many impoverished and third world countries. The U.S. government has also gained financially by the thousands of foreign adoptions that it processes annually. For example, The Bureau of Citizenship and Immigration Services (B.C.I.S.) clearance fees and proof of citizenship fees have increased the latter sharply, over the last decade.

There are other costs involved in international adoption from some countries. These costs may include the uncertainty of the political climate in sending countries which can result in delays, changing policies, extra trips to the sending country, foster care costs, the possibility of the loss of an identified child, and so on. Of course, in recent years, federal tax incentives to adopt have been put in place. However, they are one-time incentives and may not begin to cover the long-term costs of the services a special needs child will require.

In sum, people who adopt internationally often do so with high hopes of adopting a healthy child or children, or one(s) with correctable medical problems, and at considerable expense. In addition to up front agency fees, there are many other expenses involved in adopting overseas: fees for B.C.I.S. clearance, travel expenses to/from/within the child's country for adoptions which must be completed in the birth country, or for the child to be brought to the United States, travel visas for the parents who adopt in country (required by some countries), exit visas for the child/children required by the United States, a medical exam acceptable to the U.S. government before a child will be granted an exit visa, fees for documents going to and coming from the child's country, passports, facilitator's fees and expenses, living expenses in the child's country, fees to drivers in each city, costs of gifts brought to distribute at the orphanage, etc., costs of readoption in the United States, and proof of citizenship for the child/children.

Of course, on the pro side, recent tax incentives at the federal level may be viewed as at least partially offsetting the initial financial costs of adoption, either domestic or international. However, the tax benefit may be claimed only in the year the child was officially adopted. At this writing, federal tax incentives are the same for a healthy newborn as for an older child with serious, long-term special needs. Future financial and other costs involved in raising both children, however, are likely to be very unequal. Tax incentives are not retroactive to families that adopted before the law came into effect even though they may have unknowingly adopted a child or children with special needs. Although financial assistance has been available to those who adopt special needs children domestically in the form of state subsidies, these subsidies appear to have dried up, at least in some states. This situation stands in opposition to recent federal incentives to states to place older children expeditiously. Now states get the incentives, not families who take on the onerous task of parenting one or more special needs children.

Concluding Statement

So, it seems reasonable to conclude that a sizeable number of the children who are available for adoption internationally—specifically older children who have lived in orphanage settings for long periods of time and/or who have come from abusive or neglectful early environments—have experienced significant traumas and/or delays at, or exceeding, the levels of those experienced by many of the non-newborn children available for adoption in the United States and have some problems from which they may not recover. The range of such problems includes, for example, some permanent ones [like fetal alcohol syndrome (FAS) or fetal alcohol effects (FAE), retardation or brain dysfunction, penetrating head trauma

and its effects on functioning at various levels], some possible permanent or clearly long-term ones (such as Hepatitis B, severe malnutrition,
pre-maturity and low birth weight), serious emotional and/or behavioral
problems, developmental delays, and attachment problems.

For troubled families, the costs of adopting are very high and may
be permanent. These couples and individuals feel that they have been
grossly misinformed or inadequately prepared about their children's real
problems and long term prospects for improvement.

An internationally adopted child's prognosis for doing well in adoptive families depends on many factors. Among the most important are:
the country from which he/she is adopted, its risk factors, and adoption
policies, that is, who (age, health, etc.) gets to be adopted outside the
country; the child's early experiences in the birth home and orphanage;
his/her age at the time of adoption; and whether s/he was adopted prior
to living, or never having lived, in a orphanage setting. If s/he did live in
an orphanage, the length of time spent there, social structure and culture
of the orphanage are important factors.

Unfortunately, many of the children offered for external adoption
may not be healthy either medically or emotionally—especially if they
are children who have come from violent, abusive, dysfunctional families; or who have experienced war close up; or if they have lived in an
institutional setting from birth or for a long period of time. Chances for
problems in attachment to the new parent(s) are high as are the likelihood
of behavior problems in interpersonal relations both inside (i.e., problems
with intimacy, accepting limits) and outside of the family (i.e., problems
initiating and sustaining healthy relationships with peers and adults).

Dr. Andrew R. Adesman, a child development expert, is one of a growing number of international adoption doctors/counselors making their
services available to families who are considering international adoption.
He agrees that pre-adoptive families who plan to go this route need to be
cautious. In an article which appeared in *The New York Times* in 1996,
Dr. Adesman, the Chief of Developmental and Behavioral Pediatrics
at Schreider Children's Hospital in New Hyde Park, NY, was quoted
as stating that people who are considering adoption in Eastern Europe
and China should be aware that a child whose developmental delay is
attributed to the unstimulating environment of an orphanage may have
deficits that are broader and more difficult to remedy than reported.[32] At
that time, Dr. Adesman singled out Eastern Europe and China as having
developed less accurate evaluation procedures for distinguishing between
children who have normal and those who have abnormal development

than countries like Korea, India, and those in Latin America. He pointed out that, in order to evaluate a child's situation and risk factors, it is critical that accurate health records and assessments of the child's development be obtained. He added: It is also desirable to obtain information about the child's biological parents and "the circumstances surrounding labor."[33]

Individuals or couples who have adopted a child with few or no unanticipated problems of a serious nature comprise many of the supporters of international adoption, along with directors and staff of placing agencies who operate internationally. Among the critics and advocates for reform are a vocal number of families, adoption spokespersons, researchers, and media professionals who report the stories that few people want to hear and even fewer want to tell. In a 2001 Moscow Times article, reporter Deborah Hastings talks about several families who adopted troubled children from Russia and the frightening turn their lives have taken because of violent and unpredictable behavior their adopted children evidenced. None of these families were prepared for what they got. Hastings states:

> It has taken a decade for Americans to realize that hidden in a deluge of children adopted from Eastern Europe are untold numbers of violently and profoundly disturbed youngsters… No one knows how many of these disturbed youngsters now live in the United States… No central agency monitors them…Dispairing and isolated, most adoptive parents of severely disturbed children speak candidly only to others like themselves.[34]

When families with seriously troubled children speak to others, including to parents who have adopted children as young infants or children who do not exhibit serious or extreme problems, the former are defamed and effectively silenced. How might people do this? If the "other" does not know the adoptive families who have troubled children personally, they may say that their statements are exaggerated or that such problems only occur in a very small percentage of adoptees. If they do know the family, they may label the adopters as "bad parents" or as "anti adoption" and proceed to shun them, while at the same time defaming them to others. Either way, the effect is demoralizing for families who are relegated to living lives of quiet desperation and abuse at the hands of children who have not attached to them.

In chapter 4, I explore the process of international adoption from Eastern European countries as described by the parents I surveyed. I also explore the variables which predict satisfaction with their decision to adopt their child or children internationally.

Notes

1.   See, for example, R. Goldberg 1997. "Adopting Romanian Children: Making Choices, Taking Risks." *Marriage and Family Review.* Vol. 25 (1/2), pp.79-98. and 2001. "The Social Construction of Adoptive Families: A Follow-up Study of Adopting Romanian Children." *International Review of Sociology.* Vol. 11, No. 1, pp. 89-101; V. Groze and D Ileana. 1996. "A Follow-up Study of Adopted Children From Romania." *Child and Adolescent Social Work Journal.*, Vol. 13, No. 6, pp. 541-565; S. Cermak and V. Groza. 1998. "Sensory Processing Problems in Post-Institutionalized Children: Implications for Social Work." *Child and Adolescent Social Work Journal*, Vol. 15, No. 1 (February), pp. 5-37.

2.   See, for example, S. Marcovitch, L. Cesaroni, W. Roberts, and C. Swanson. 1995. "Romanian Adoption: Parents' Dreams, Nightmares, and Realities." *Child Welfare.* Vol. 74 (Sept./Oct.), pp. 993-1017; S. J. Morison, E. W. Ames, and K. Chisholm. 1995. "The Development of Children Adopted From Romanian Orphanages." *Merrill-Palmer Quarterly.* Vol. 41, pp. 430-441; H. Mainemer., L. C. Gilman, and E. W. Ames. 1998. "Parenting Stress in Families Adopting Children From Romanian Orphanages." *The Journal of Family Issues.* Vol. 19, No. 2 (March), pp. 164-180; E. Ames, S. J. Morison, L Fisher, and K. Chisolm 2000. "Some Recommendations from a Study of Romanian Orphans Adopted to British Columbia" in International Adoption: Challenges and Opportunities, T. Tepper, L. Hannon, and D. Sandstrom, Editors, pp. 33-39.

3.   See M. L. Rutter, and others on the English and Romanian Adoptees Study Team. 1998. "Developmental Catch-Up, and Deficit, Following Adoption After Sever Early Global Privation." *Journal of Child Psychology-Psychiatry.* Vol. 39, No. 4. pp. 465-476; and M. L. Rutter, J. M. Kreppner, and Thomas G. O'Connor. 2001. "Specificity and Heterogeneity in Children's Responses to Profound Institutional Privation." *British Journal of Psychiatry.* Vol. 179. pp. 97-103.

4.   See L. C. Miller, M.D., M. T. Kiernan, M. I. Mathers, and M. Klein-Gitelman. 1995. "Developmental and Nutritional Status of Internationally Adopted Children." *Archives of Pediatric and Adolescent Medicine.* Vol. 149, No. 1 (January), pp. 40 44; D. Johnson, M. D. 1997. "Adopting an Institutionalized Child: What Are the Risks?" *The Post*, Issue #9 (January February), pp. 1-3.

5.   The research in this category includes studying the impact of early deprivation and other factors—such as length of time in orphanage, age at adoption, and psychological privation, on various dependent variables. Examples of the dependent variables are physical and cognitive functioning, IQ, and emotional, behavioral or other problems of the child/children observed and reported to researchers by adoptive parents. See Marcovich and others 1995; Morison and others 1995; Groza and Ileana 1996; Cermak and Groza 1998; Rutter and others 1998. Some of the surveys in this category have been designed and conducted by adoption agencies. See, for example, D. Claus and S. Baxter. 1997. "Post-Adoption Survey of Russian and Eastern European Children: Completed by Rainbow House International." http://www.rhi.org/ANews/SurveyResults1997.html .M. Essley and L. Perilstein. 1998. "Good News on European Adoptions." Unpublished Manuscript, Cradle of Hope Adoption Center, Silver Spring, MD. See P. Price. 2000. "FRUA's Health & Development Survey." *The Family Focus.* Vol. 1-3. and

6.   Mainemer et al. 1998.

7.   K. J. Herrmann and B. Kasper. 1992. "International Adoption: The Exploitation of Women and Children." *AFFILIA*, Vol. 7, No.1 (Spring), pp. 45-58; A. K. Johnson, R. L. Edwards and H. Puwak. 1993. "Foster Care and Adoption Policy in Romania: Suggestions for International Intervention." *Child Welfare.* Vol. 72,

No. 5 (September-October), pp. 489-506; L. A. Serbin, 1997. "Research on International Adoption: Implications for Developmental Theory and Social Policy." *International Journal of Behavioral Development*. Vol. 20, No.1, pp. 83-92; S. Zeppa. 1998. "'Let Me In, Immigration Man': An Overview of Intercountry Adoption and the Role of the Immigration and Nationality Act." *Hastings International and Comparative Law Review*. Vol. 22, No.1 (Fall), pp. 161-185.Ames and others 2000.

8.   S. L. Judge. 1999. "Eastern European Adoption: Current Status and Implications for Intervention." *Topics in Early Childhood Special Education*. Vol. 13, Issue 4 (Winter), pp. 244-252.

9.   Johnson, M. D., 1997, page 2.

10.   See the following three articles: W. Goldfarb. 1943. "Effects of Early Institutional Care on Adolescent Personality." *J.Exptl. Educ*. Vol. 12: 106-129; 1944. "Effects of Early Institutional Care on Adolescent Personality: Rorschach Data." *Am. J. of Orthopsychiatry*. Vol. 14: 441-447; W. Goldfarb. 1945. "Psychological Privation in Infancy and Subsequent Adjustment." *Am. J. of Orthopsychiatry*. Vol. 15: 247-255. R. A. Spitz. 1946. "Hospitalism." in Anna Freud et al. Eds. *The Psychoanalytic Study of the Child*. Vol. 2. New York; International Universities Press, pp. 52-74.

11.   C. Bogert, et al. 1994. "Bringing Baby Back." *Newsweek*. (November 21), pp. 78-79.

12.   L.C. Miller, M.D., M. T. Kiernan, M. I. Mathers, and M. Klein Gitelman. 1995. "Developmental and Nutritional Status of Internationally Adopted Children." *Archives of Pediatric and Adolescent Medicine*. Vol. 149, No. 1 (January), pp. 40-44.

13.   "Russia on the Ropes," *Parade Magazine*, December 15, 2002.

14.   See Mosnews.com, 4/14/05. http://mosnews.com/news/2005/04/14/hivchildren.shtml

15.   S. M. Massey. Highlights of Policy Brief: "Russia's Maternal and Infant Health Crisis: Socioeconomic Implications and the Path Forward." http://psp.iews.org/highlights.cfm?view=detail&id=33

16.   J. Bowlby, 1951. Maternal Care and Mental Health. Geneva: World Health Organization.

17.   S. Wolkind and M. Rutter. 1985. "Separation, Loss and Family Relationships." In *Child and Adolescent Psychiatry: Modern Approaches*. M. Rutter and L. Hersov, Eds. Oxford: Blackwell Scientific Publications, pp. 34-57.

18.   M. Geraghty. 1995. "The Myths and Realities of Orphanages." *The Chronicle of Higher Education* (January 6), p. A5.

19.   Ibid. p. A5.

20.   See the following four articles by F.C., Verhulst, M.D., M. Althaus, and H. J. M. Versluis Den Bieman: 1. 1990a. "Problem Behavior in International Adoptees: I. An Epidemiological Study." *The Journal of the American Academy of Child and Adolescent Psychiatry*. Vol. 29, No. 1 (January), pp. 94-103. 2. 1990 b. "Problem Behavior in International Adoptees: II. Age at Placement." *The Journal of the American Academy of Child and Adolescent Psychiatry*. Vol. 29. No. 1 (January), pp. 104-111. 3. 1900c. "Problem Behavior in International Adoptees: III. Diagnosis of Child Psychiatric Disorders." *The Journal of the American Academy of Child and Adolescent Psychiatry*. Vol. 29, No. 3 (May), pp. 420 428. 4. 1992. "Damaging Backgrounds: Later Adjustment of International Adoptees." *Journal of the American Academy of Child and Adolescent Psychiatry*. Vol. 31, No. 3 (May), 518-524.

21. Ibid.
22. Verhulst and others, Ibid, 1992, p. 523.
23. C. R, Cloninger, M. Bohman, and S. Sigvardsson. 1981. "Inheritance of Alcohol Abuse." *Archives of General Psychiatry*. Vol. 38, pp. 861-868.
24. B. Hutchings and S. A. Mednick. 1975. "Registered Criminality in the Adoptive and Biological Parents of Registered Male Criminal Adoptees." In *Genetic Research in Psychiatry*. R. R. Feve, D. Rosenthal, and H. Brill, Eds. Baltimore: Johns Hopkins University Press.
25. S. S. Kety, D. Rosenthal, P. H. Wender, and F. Schulsinger. 1976. "Studies Based on a Total Sample of Adopted Individuals and Their Relatives." *Schiz. Bulletin*. Vol. 2, pp. 413-428.
26. V. Groza and S. D. Ryan. 2002. "Pre-Adoption Stress and Its Association With Child Behavior in Domestic Special Needs and International Adoptions." *Psychoneuroendocrinology*, (Vol. 27, No. 2), pp. 181-197.
27. Ibid.
28. Ibid.
29. P. Leung and S. Erich. 2002. "Family Functioning of Adoptive Children With Special Needs: Implications of Familial Supports and Child Characteristics." *Children and Youth Services Review*. Vol. 24, No. 11, pp. 799-816.
30. F. H. Boer, J. M. Versluis-den Bieman and F. C. Verhulst. 1994. "International Adoption of Children With Siblings," *American Journal of Orthopsychiatry*. Vol. 6-4, No. 2 (April), pp. 252-262.
31. Doing this is illegal in domestic adoptions and is unethical in international adoptions. Agencies which belong to the JCICS include open disclosure as part of their ethical standards.
32. J.T. McQuiston, J. T. 1996. "Doctor Helps Couple Avoid Adoption Trouble." *The New York Times* (July 13), Section 1, p. 25.
33. Ibid.
34. Hastings 2001 (February 9), p 2 of 9, retrieved online from http://www.gay.ru/english/life/family/exported.htm on 7/30/02.

Part II

Studying Older-Child and Sibling Group Adoptions from Eastern Europe

4

Parents Speak About the Process of International Adoption and Their Satisfaction-Dissatisfaction with Their Decision to Adopt Internationally

This chapter is divided into two main parts. In Part I, I look at respondents' answers to ten important questions about the process of adopting and the agency or agencies with which they worked to adopt internationally. Their answers give the reader a good idea of what the process of international adoption was like for them. In Part II, I report respondents' satisfaction-dissatisfaction with their decision to adopt their child or children internationally (perceived outcome). Potential predictor variables of perceived outcome fall into three main categories: adoptees' characteristics and issues, post-adoption issues and needs, and agency performance.

Part I. About the Process of Adopting Internationally

Did respondents typically work with a licensed agency to locate their child/children?

Most respondents (94 percent) reported that they did work with licensed agencies to adopt some or all of their children. The remaining respondents said that they had done an independent adoption.

Did most respondents work with a placing agency located in their home state?

No, fewer than half did. What explains this pattern? States require prospective adopters living within their geographical limits to use a licensed social worker in their home state to do their home study. However, states do not place restrictions on where the placing agency is located. Therefore, it is fairly common for families interested in arranging an international adoption to work with a facilitator or placing agency located outside their home state. Sometimes prospective adopters hear about an out-of-state agency from a friend or acquaintance or from "surfing the net." Many agencies have web sites where they post pictures of children who are available for adoption. This is a low-cost, passive way through which agencies can recruit prospective adoptive parents located anywhere. Sometimes agencies are more active in marketing their services. For example, agencies may send staff great distances to large adoption conferences in order to recruit families for waiting children who have already been identified for the agency by their facilitators in the sending countries. The practice of using different agencies to do the home study and to locate the child/children was evident for many of the adoptive parents in this study. Fewer than four in ten respondents (37 percent) report using the same agency to both do their home study and to locate their child/children. Of the adopters who worked with a licensed agency to locate their child/children, 45 percent said that they worked with an agency in their home state but nearly the same number (46 percent) used an out-of-state agency.

Did most respondents who worked with a licensed placing agency investigate the agency's track record with the state licensing board?

No. Just under half (49 percent) said they did. However, most respondents who did investigate their agency's track record described their efforts as either somewhat careful (48 percent) or very careful (43 percent).

Why didn't more respondents check their agency for any unresolved complaints?

The reasons given by respondents who did **not** check out their agency through the state licensing board before selecting the agency tended to fall into two categories, one negative and the other positive: 36 percent said that they did not have time and 21 percent said that they had references from other adoptive parents. Respondents who did **not** check out their agency's track record seemed to rely on informal references: most (78 percent) respondents reported that they talked to other parents before they chose an adoption agency. These respondents (42 percent) typically talked with between three and four adoptive parents.

How much information did the placing agency provide to respondents about the referred child/children?

Respondents said they were most likely to get only basic information about the child's height and/or weight or about the birth parents' ages and circumstances at the time the child entered the orphanage, if known. When it came to information about their child's birth or his/her medical history, respondents report that the information they got was sparse at best. Most respondents' answers indicated that they had received very little/ limited (32 percent) or no (45 percent) birth information about their child or his/her medical history. Information was even less likely to be provided about the birth parents' medical history.

Did respondents think that the information they received was either accurate or complete?

About half (52 percent) of the respondents believe that the information they received about their child's/children's health was accurate. However, almost as many respondents (41 percent) said that the information they got was *not* accurate and an additional eight percent said that the information was accurate for one child they adopted but *not* for another.

Responses as to the completeness of the information received were another matter: the majority of respondents (65 percent) said that the health information they received about their child or children was *not* complete. Four percent said that it was complete for one child but *not* for another. The remaining 31 percent said that they felt the information the agency had provided was complete regarding what was known.

Did respondents wish they knew more about their child or children before the adoption?

Generally, yes. I asked respondents an open-ended question about whether there was information they wished they knew about their child/ children before they adopted. Sixty-four percent of them answered yes. There were things they wished they knew. These respondents identified what they wished they knew. The content of the "wished-for" information was coded for first, second, and third mentions.

Respondents' first-mentioned wished-for information was almost evenly split between more information about the (1) child or children they had adopted and (2) his/her/their birth parents. The kinds of information respondents wished they had about their children included more medical/ health information, information about institutional effects, attachment disorder, developmental history/milestones, delays, needs, habits and food preferences. Regarding the birth parents, they wished they had more information about family history and family life and about the birth parents themselves. Second and third mentions focused largely on wishing to have more information about the child/children. Wishing "information" is not the same as wishing to have "contact" with the child's birth parent(s).

How much pre-adoption preparation did respondents receive from their agencies?

Pre-adoption preparation varied from none to a "fair amount." A large minority (44 percent) of these parents said that they had received none. The remaining respondents reported getting various amounts of "preparation" from very little (1-5 hours [20 percent]), to some (6-10 hours [16 percent]), to a fair amount (defined as 11 or more hours [20 percent]). When asked whether or not the agency they used provided information on two important pre-adoption issues: the known effects of institutional living and the effects of early trauma on a child's development and behavior, respondents were more likely to answer negatively than positively. Forty-nine percent said that their agency had *not* provided information on institutional effects and 56 percent said that the agency had *not* provided information on the effects of early trauma. An additional 6 percent and 8 percent respectively said that the information they did get was too little or insufficient.

The importance of adequate pre-adoption preparation cannot be emphasized enough. Getting an adequate understanding about both institutional effects and possible early traumas before they adopt an older child from Russia and Eastern Europe is a very important issue because the large majority of children adopted from Russia and Eastern Europe have spent at least some time in orphanage settings. Recall that 92 percent of these adoptees whose parents participated in my study did and that half of them had lived in an orphanage setting for at least two years. Also, more than a few children go to orphanages from a prior neglectful and/or abusive home as did about one-third of the adoptees in this study. As research by Verhulst and his colleagues showed, parents who adopt children internationally—especially children with pre-adoption histories of abuse and neglect need to be very well prepared for what life will be like after the child/children enter the family.[1]

Did respondents need post-adoption services or support?

Yes. Just over half (51 percent) of the respondents said that they did need such services or support. I asked respondents if their agency had either offered them the services of a professional or had put them in touch with someone who provided post-placement services for their child or family. Seventy-five percent of the respondents who said that they needed such services also said that their agency had *not*.

According to fourteen parents, the services their agency provided included meeting with a social worker employed by the agency or suggesting referrals for psychological services to an adoption specialist or to an international adoption clinic. About two thirds (66 percent) of the respondents said that their agency/facilitator did *not* provide, or put them in touch with, a support group.

Did respondents think that the agency/facilitator they used should have done better?

Generally, yes. Almost seven in ten (68 percent) of the respondents stated that they thought the agency or facilitator they used should have done a better job for them. Parents identified what the agency or facilitator could have done better. Combining the first through third mentions, answers fell mainly into three categories: (1) better preparation, guidance/coordination/communication; (2) more accurate/complete information about their child/children and their early history including life in the orphanage; and (3) more realistic/honest perspectives about adopting their child/children.

Part I Summary

Parents' responses to the questions in this part reveal that the large majority of these adoptive parents worked with a licensed agency to locate their child/children. However, fewer than half of them worked with a placing agency located in their home state. Parents reported that the information they received about their referred child/children was often sparse—especially birth information and/or medical history. The majority (65 percent) reported that the health information they received was incomplete. Moreover, about four in every ten respondents believed that the information they did get from their placing agency was inaccurate. Not surprisingly, almost two thirds of these parents said that they wished they knew more about their child/children before the adoption took place.

Regarding pre-adoption preparation, most reported receiving none (44 percent) or very little (20 percent). What was lacking from their pre-adoption preparation too often involved information about the known effects of institutional living (49 percent got no information) and early trauma on a child's development and behavior (56 percent got no information). The majority of respondents (68 percent) thought that their agency or facilitator should have done a better job for them. Just over half needed post-adoption services or support.

Part II. About Respondents' Satisfaction-Dissatisfaction WithTheir Decision to Adopt a Child or Children Internationally

Satisfaction with the decision to adopt is a commonly asked question in some fashion in adoption surveys conducted by parent organizations[2] or by/for adoption agencies. Self-reported satisfaction in questionnaire surveys also tends to be high. For example, in the survey conducted for eighteen agencies, The Cradle of Hope Adoption Center reported parental satisfaction at 97.5 percent.[3] Although not nearly as high as the Cradle of Hope figure, when respondents rated their overall satisfaction with their decision to adopt their child or children internationally, almost eight in ten respondents answered positively. Most respondents reported being either very satisfied or satisfied. However, a notable minority of respondents expressed either feeing "so so" or dissatisfied with their decision to adopt one or more of their children internationally.

To look at the issue of satisfaction with the decision to adopt their child/children internationally, I examined more than thirty variables as possible predictors of variations in satisfaction. Of these variables, twenty-three turned out to be strong to moderately-strong predictors of differences overall satisfaction. Potential predictor variables fall into one of the following categories: Variables connected with the adoptees, with post-adoption needs, with agency performance or with an "other" issue. The percentages I report below are based on using satisfaction as the dependent variable and the other variables as predictors of satisfaction. I computed the percentages of satisfied respondents who had a particular agency experience—for example, needed post-placement services versus did not need services; adopted a child with a particular characteristic—for example, a boy vs. a girl or a particular medical or other condition; or who had a particular personal characteristic—for example, being single or divorced vs. being married at the time they completed the questionnaire. Next, I compared the percent differences for predictor attributes/categories that show the largest differences in satisfaction.

I report percentage differences here rather than measures of statistical correlation because the latter are appropriate only for random or probability samples. These percentage differences should be interpreted as suggestive of a correlation or lack thereof and not as definitive measures of association.

Differentiating Between Satisfaction and Dissatisfaction

One variable stands out as the major predictor of satisfaction versus dissatisfaction: the likelihood of respondents saying that they would adopt their child, if they knew then what they know now about their child's issues and needs. Saying that they definitely or probably would make the same decision to adopt, if they knew then what they know now about their child's issues and needs, distinguishes between satisfied and dissatisfied adopters by a wide margin. Not surprisingly, all of the respondents who answer yes definitely report being satisfied. The large majority of those who say that they probably would make the same decision also describe themselves as satisfied. The average of these two categories is 98 percent.

In contrast, saying that they probably or definitely would *not* make the same decision predicts dissatisfaction with the decision to adopt a particular child. Although fewer in number than parents who describe themselves as satisfied, all of the respondents who say they definitely *would not*, and more than 90 percent of those who say they probably *would not*, make the same decision describe themselves as dissatisfied. The average of these two categories is 95.5 percent. It is interesting to note that a small number of satisfied respondents who say they definitely would not (N=1) or probably would not (N=2) make the same decision make a point of saying that they do not regret their decision to adopt their child. Only one of the dissatisfied parents who says she probably would not make the same decision also says she does not regret adopting her child. It follows that respondents who say they considered disrupting the adoption were much more likely to be dissatisfied than satisfied.

Strong Differentiators of Satisfaction

In this section and the next, I focus on the variables that predict differences in the percentages of respondents who report that they are very satisfied or satisfied with their decision to adopt their child/children internationally. Twelve variables fall in the grouping of strong differentiators of satisfaction. The delta values for variables range from 41 percent to

24 percent. Predictor variables fall into the following categories: characteristics and issues of the adoptees, post adoption issues and needs, and agency performance.

Characteristics and Issues of Adoptees

According to table 4.1, respondents' overall satisfaction appears to be most strongly correlated with the type and number of non-physical problems the child/children they adopted had. Parents who adopted a child they reported to have no behavioral, emotional, or psychological problems or only one of these problems are more than 40 percent more likely to express satisfaction than those who adopted a child who has all three of these types of problems. Respondents who adopted one or more girls are 27 percent more likely to report being satisfied than those who adopted one or more boys. Age of the child at adoption does not show a consistent pattern of differences in satisfaction among respondents. The largest difference in satisfaction is between respondents who adopted a child aged twenty-five to thirty-six months old and those who adopted a child aged forty-nine to sixty months old. The former are 28 percent more likely to be satisfied than the latter (See table 4.1).

Table 4.1
Differences in Respondents' Satisfaction on
Characteristics and Issues of Adoptees

% Difference	Variable	Category	% Satisfied	Number
41%	Presence of problems behavioral, emotional, or psychological problems	NONE ONE of these problems ALL THREE	94% Satisfied 93% Satisfied 53% Satisfied	(48) (13) (20)
27%	Gender of Adoptee(s)	One or more girls One or more boys	91% Satisfied 64% Satisfied	(42) (21)
28%	Age of Child at Adoption	25 to 36 months old 49 to 60 months old	90% Satisfied 62% Satisfied	(26) (8)

Post-Adoption Issues and Needs

Table 4.2 shows that respondents who say they did *not* need post-adoption support or services from/through their agency are 38 percent more likely to say they are satisfied than are those who say that they did need support or services. Adoptive parents who report that they did *not* wish more information pre-adoption are 26 percent more likely to report satisfaction than those who say they wish they did have more information before making the decision to adopt their child/children (See table 4.2).

Table 4.2
Differences in Respondents' Satisfaction by
Post-Adoption Issues and Needs

% Difference	Variable	Category	%Satisfied	Number
38%	Needed Post-placement support or services from their agency	NO	98% Satisfied	(59)
		YES	60% Satisfied	(36)
26%	Whether or not respondents wished to have more information before making the decision to adopt other children	NO	96% Satisfied	(46)
		YES	70% Satisfied	(51)
				(21)

Agency Performance Variables

As table 4.3 indicates, adoptive parents who were required to participate in at least eleven hours of pre-adoption preparation are 29 percent more likely to be satisfied than are those who report getting no pre-adoption preparation. Adoptive parents who believe that the information they got was accurate are also 29 percent more likely to be satisfied than those who do *not* believe the information was accurate. When respondents got detailed information, they are 28 percent more likely to report satisfaction than those who got no information. Respondents who report that their agency did provide this information are 27 percent more likely to be satisfied than are respondents who say that the agency did *not* provide it.

Respondents who report that the agency they used provided information about the effects of institutional living on a child's development and behavior are 25 percent more likely to be satisfied than those who said their agency did *not*. This variable is closely related to respondents' overall satisfaction with the agency or agencies they used. Adoptive parents who gave their agencies a high versus a low rating differed in satisfaction. Those parents who say that, prior to adopting, the agency/ agencies they used could not have done anything better are 25 percent more likely to be satisfied than are those who think that their agency/cies could have done something better for them. Finally, respondents whose agencies provided a moderate amount of birth information about their child/children are 24 percent more likely to be satisfied than those whose agencies provided no birth information about their child/children (see table 4.3 on page 57).

Part II A Summary

The strongest predictors of satisfaction-dissatisfaction are the presence of behavioral and mental health problems in the adopted child/children (Delta = 41 percent); whether or not respondents needed post-adoption support or services from/through their agency (Delta = 38 percent); amount of time respondents spent in required pre-adoption preparation (Delta = 29 percent); accuracy/inaccuracy of the information the placing agency provided about physical and emotional health, etc. of the adoptee(s) (Delta = 29 percent); amount of medical information the placing agency/person provided about the adoptee(s) (Delta = 28 percent); and age of the child at adoption (but not in a linear fashion). Parents who express the most satisfaction are those who adopted a child between twenty-five and thirty-six months old. The next most important variable is whether or not the agency provided information about the known effects of early traumas on a child's development and behavior (Delta = 27 percent).

The two strongest predictors of differences in satisfaction focus on child issues in relationship to information *not* provided to respondents in advance of their making the decision to adopt a specific child/children. These variables include the state of adoptees' behavioral and mental health and the need for post-adoption support and/or services. Obviously, these two variables are related as are the other predictors identified above: accuracy/inaccuracy of information (physical and emotional health, medical) provided or not provided to them by the placing or home study agency (cies) in advance of their decision to adopt the referred child.

Table 4.3
Differences in Respondents' Satisfaction by
Seven Agency-Performance Variables (Pre-Adoption Stage)

% Difference	Variable	Category	% Satisfied	Number
29%	Amount of time the home study agency required respondents to spend in pre-adoption preparation.	11 or more hours NONE	96% 67%	(25) (34)
29%	Accuracy of the information the placing agency gave Rs about the physical and emotional health, etc. of the child/children they adopted.	Believe info was accurate DID NOT believe info was accurate	93% 64%	(55) (27)
28%	Amount of medical information the placing agency/person provided about the child/children.	Detailed info NO info	89% 61%	(16) (19)
27%	Whether or not the agency provided information about the known effects of early traumas on a child's development and behavior.	YES NO	95% 68%	(39) (43)
25%	Whether or not the agency provided information about the effects of institutional living on a child's development and behavior.	YES NO	92% 67%	(49) (37)
24%	Amount of birth information placing agency provided about the child/children's birth	A moderate amount NONE	92% 68%	(11) (36)
25%	Rs' overall satisfaction with the agency/agencies they used.	HIGH LOW	95% 70%	(35) (49)

Moderate Differentiators of Satisfaction

Ten variables fall into this category. Their Delta values range from 20 percent to 14 percent. Tables 4.4 – 4.6 present a summary of the predictors in this category.

Agency-Related Variables

Although there is no reported difference in satisfaction between respondents who talked with other adopters before choosing an agency and those who did not, among those who did talk with other adoptive parents, the number of parents they spoke with mattered. Table 4.4 shows that adopters who report talking with five or more adoptive parents before they chose an agency are 19 percent more likely to say they are satisfied than those who report talking to only one or two adoptive parents. Parents who received even a moderate amount of information are 18 percent more likely to report being satisfied than are those who received very little information. When respondents believe that the information the placing agency provided about their child's physical and emotional health,

Table 4.4
Differences in Respondents' Satisfaction by
Three Agency-Related Variables (Pre-Adoption)

% Difference	Variable	Category	%Satisfied	Number
19%	Number of adoptive parents with whom Rs talked before they chose an agency and adopted their child/children.	FIVE or more ONE or TWO	88% 69%	(21) (18)
18%	Amount of other information the placing agency provided about the child/children.	Moderate amount Very little	91% 73%	(20) (16)
14%	Completeness of information the placing agency provided about the adoptees' physical and emotional health, etc.	ALL known info INCOMPLETE Info	91% 77%	(31) (54)

and so on, was complete—that is, that all known information was provided to them, they are 14 percent more likely to express satisfaction with their decision to adopt their child/children internationally than when they do *not* believe the information they got was complete (see table 4.4 on page 58).

Post-Placement Issues and Needs of Adoptees

As reported earlier, generally, parents whose children did *not* need post-adoption services are more likely to be satisfied than those whose child/children did. Table 4.5 indicates that, when a child needed any of the listed services, the best predictor of parental satisfaction was arranging for speech therapy. The high percentage of parental satisfaction may be due to the several things: speech therapy is often provided by the school and/or covered by insurance. Parents may see their child progress relatively quickly. Arranging for psychological services was the worst predictor of satisfaction. This result may be due to several factors: the difficulty and frustration associated with finding a therapist who is knowledgeable in the issues of post-institutionalized children; the long-term nature of such therapy; and the lack of noticeable changes in the child's functioning at home, in particular. The difference between the reported satisfaction of respondents whose child or children needed speech therapy and those whose child/children needed psychological services is 18 percent (see table 4.5 on page 60).

Other Variables

As table 4.6 reports, respondents who were *not* burdened with having to pay for services out of pocket are 20 percent more likely to be satisfied than those who did. Interestingly, those who adopted either one child or three or more children are about 16 percent more likely to express satisfaction than those who adopted two children. Respondents then aged thirty-nine or younger are 20 percent more likely to report being satisfied than are respondents then in their forties and 14 percent more likely to be satisfied than adopters in their fifties (see table 4.6 on page 61).

Part II B Summary

Seven of the ten variables in this grouping are similar in the strength of their predictive value. They range from a percentage difference of 20 percent (payment for post-placement services out of pocket), shown in table 4.6, to 17 percent (presence of any problems), shown in table 4.5. Three variables in this grouping show percentage differences of 14

Table 4.5
Differences in Respondents' Satisfaction by
Three Children's Post-Placement Needs and Issues

% Difference	Variable	Category	% Satisfied	Number
19%	Child/Children's need for post-placement services.	NO	96%	(22)
		YES	77%	(75)
18%	Types of services child/children needed.	Yes: Speech Therapy	75%	(50)
		Yes: Psycho-logical Services	57%	(28)
17%	Presence of ANY of the five categories of problems at the time Rs completed the questionnaire.	NO	89%	(32)
		YES	72%	(44)

percentage points or less: completeness of information provided by the placing agency; whether respondents would or would not make the same decision to adopt their first child; and respondents age at completion of the survey.

Other Variables Examined as Possible Predictors of Differences in Satisfaction

Some variables which one might assume would matter did not. For example, variables that did not distinguish between respondents' reported satisfaction include whether or not the agency or facilitator placing the child or children was located in the respondent's state of residence, or provided information about the child's birth parents' age and circumstances. Helping respondents obtain needed services and putting them in touch with an adoptive parents support group also did not distinguish reported satisfaction. Whether or not adopters had birth or other adopted children in their home before they adopted internationally showed some difference (9.4 percent) as did marital status (9.5 percent). Respondents who had no children were more likely to be satisfied with the child they

Table 4.6
Differences in Respondents' Satisfaction by
Four Other Variables

% Difference	Variable	Category	% Satisfied	Number
20%	Adoptive parents paid for services their child/children needed out of their own pockets	NO YES	87% 67%	(39) (35)
16%	Number of children adopted	ONE THREE or more TWO	85% 86% 70%	(48) (12) (35)
14% to 10%	Respondent's age at completion of the questionnaire.	30s 40s 50s	88% 78% 74%	(21) (62) (14)
14%	Whether respondents WOULD or DEFINITELY WOULD NOT make the same decision to adopt their first child.	Definitely Would Definitely Would NOT	85.6% 100% Dissatis-fied	(80) (8)

adopted than those who did. Single and divorced adopters were more likely to be satisfied than married adopters.

The direction of these differences is logical. Childless respondents may not have had the same expectations as did respondents who already had children. Also, although potentially stressful, indeed, single parenthood has its benefits. One benefit is that decisions can be made more easily when one, rather than two parents, makes them. A second benefit is that the child with a single parent cannot "split staff" to get his/her way as children with two parents often try to do.

Interpreting the Meaning of Satisfaction and Dissatisfaction

How can satisfaction be interpreted? The largely positive claim of satisfaction may be due to a number of factors. For example, parents' reference may be to the achievement of the long-awaited personal goal of becoming a "parent," or to the change in social role from being "single" or a "couple" to being a "family" (i.e., more socially acceptable). In some cases, the response may tap into issues which the respondent is hoping will be temporary (i.e., related to the child's "adjustment") or into the unwillingness of some parents who dearly love their challenging child to say they are dissatisfied with the gap between the family life they expected and the life they got.

How can dissatisfaction be interpreted? Based on both the quantitative and qualitative responses parents gave, parents indicated that their formerly well-functioning family had become more dysfunctional. I asked these respondents whether they had considered disrupting the adoption of the child/children in question. Eighty-two percent (N = 23) of them said that they had considered disrupting the adoption of the child/children in question. Of those who had considered disruption, about one in three of these respondents said they had considered disruption very seriously and 22 percent said somewhat seriously. Subsequent to the completion of the questionnaire survey, disruptions did take place in at least two families. In these cases, family functioning and the marital relationship were overwhelmed by long-term stress.

Research conducted recently on domestic and international adoptees parallels and reinforces the patterns I observed in my study. In a study published in 2004, in *The Child and Adolescent Social Work Journal*, Egbert and LaMont identified twelve child, family, and agency related variables which are significantly correlated with preparation to parent a special needs child. Their dependent variable, the extent to which the parent felt prepared for the realities of adoption, was self-reported, based on a seven-point scale.

Of the twelve statistically significant variables that Egbert and LaMont[4] identify, six are related to the child, three to the agency, and three to the adoptive family. Emotional, sexual, and physical abuse or neglect of the child significantly predicted adopters' feeling less prepared to parent a special needs child. Having a child who exhibited emotional and behavioral concerns since adoption was also a factor. Parents' overall relationship with the agency, Department of Children and Family Services (DCFS), was the second most important predictor of parents feeling prepared to parent a special needs child. Support from the placing agency both before and after the adoption also mattered.

In the next chapter, I describe three scenarios that I have created to provide a context for understanding the experiences the parents in my study describe. I use the analogy of a trip whose anticipated destination is Paris.

Notes

1. Verhulst and others, Ibid, 2002.
2. Price, P. 2000. "FRUA's Health & Development Survey." *The Family Focus*. Vol. VI-3.
3. Cradle of Hope Adoption Study Center. 1998. "Adoptions from Eastern European Orphanages Overwhelmingly Successful." (March). http://www.cradlehope.org/surv/html.
4. Egbert, S. C. and E. C. LaMont. 2004. "Factors Contributing to Parents' Preparation for Special-Needs Adoption." *Child and Adolescent Social Work Journal*, Vol. 21, No. 6 (December), pp. 593-609.

5

Embarking on the Journey of a Lifetime: Breathing Life into the Data Through Case Narratives

This chapter serves as the transition from my reporting on the experiences of the full sample of adopted parents to focusing on a smaller number of parents who wrote in more detail about their Eastern European adoption journeys. These parents tell the reader what the adoption process was like for them. Through their words, readers learn about the variables that shape adoptive family well being—for better or worse.

As a researcher, I believe that it is important to look at a rich data source in the fullest and most creative way possible. For this book, that means bringing parents' narratives together with the quantitative data. Giving voice to their words is vital to the reader's understanding of the issues that serve as challenges to traditional adoption policies and practices. Respondents' words also help to put human faces on the numbers and issues I discuss here.

These case narratives illustrate what works and what does not in the way Eastern European adoptions have been handled. They also illustrate why and in what direction international adoption policies and practices need to change.

Creating, or Adding to a Family through Adoption

The parents in my study all traveled to their child's or children's birth countries to adopt them and bring them home. In this section of the chapter, I speak of a figurative trip rather than the actual trip they made.[1]

Comparing adoption to a much-anticipated journey is an analogy to which most people can relate. This is not just any journey. This will be the journey of all journeys, the trip of a lifetime. For that reason, I chose Paris as the desired destination. Although Paris is a real city, the destination "Paris," as I use it in this analogy is, of course, a subjective state of being. I chose Paris, the "city of lights" and of love, because Paris is a special city—beautiful, and full of life. I find it difficult to imagine that most people would not want to go to Paris at least once in their lifetimes, if they could. Of course, like every large city, Paris has its share of problems. Still, it is the "experience that is Paris" that most people remember.

The case narratives that appear in chapters 7 – 9 fall into one of the four scenarios I describe below.

Scenario 1A: Adopters Who Have Arrived in Paris. Some people plan a trip to Paris and end up in the heart of Paris. They have spent years perfecting their mastery of the French language. They have studied the customs and have packed their suitcases with the appropriate clothes. They land at the airport. On their way into the city, they begin to see some of the well-known landmarks for which Paris is so famous. Before long, they realize that Paris is everything they imagined and more. They have a wonderful time and have stored up many positive memories of their marvelous trip. As their case narratives show, the first five families in chapter 7 have arrived in Paris.

Scenario 1B: Adopters Who Have Arrived in an Unrecognizable Part of Paris. Paris is a very large city. Some of the people who plan a trip to Paris arrive there, but they do not see familiar landmarks they expected. The taxi from the airport has apparently dropped them off in the outskirts of the city. They wonder what they are doing here and how long it will take them to get to their hotel in the heart of Paris. They hope it will be soon. They look around for someone from whom to ask directions, but no one they meet understands what they are asking. It is getting dark and they are beginning to worry. As their case narratives show, the other families in chapter 7 have arrived in an unfamiliar part of Paris.

Scenario 2: Bewildered Adopters Who Have Not Even Arrived in France. Some people plan a trip to Paris but their flight is detoured to a completely unanticipated location. They disembark from the plane and look around. The scenery is so different from what they expected. They are obviously not in Paris. They soon discover that they are not even in France. They do not speak or understand the native language. However, a few friendly inhabitants come along and try to help them get settled. The travelers wonder how long they will need to stay. They try to adapt to this unexpected country. They hope that, maybe some day, they will get to Paris.

For some of these travelers, the trip has been an ordeal. It is the unknown that worries them most. What will happen next? The case narratives of adopters in chapter 8 fit with scenario 2.

Scenario 3: Adopters Who Have Lost Hope of Ever Finding Their Way to Paris. Some people plan a trip to Paris. They board a plane that they think will take them to Paris. But, instead of Paris, they end up in a strange and unexpected place. They look around and see that the plane has left them in the middle of a vast, isolated locale. There is no airport, just an empty field. There are no friendly inhabitants. The people they approach appear to be hostile and not at all interested in helping them to get to Paris. The travelers are dressed for warmer weather than they find here. They do not know where to find shelter from the harsh elements. Their luggage is still on the plane that has taken off for some other destination. They stand and stare in bewildered fashion. They feel completely alone. Worst of all, they have no idea how they will survive until the plane that dropped them off returns for them. They are not even sure if it will return. They fear that they will not even have a fighting chance to survive, never mind to get a glimpse of Paris. The case narratives in chapter 8 fall into scenario 3.

The analogy of a trip speaks effectively to the experiences of people who adopt an older child or children from troubled pre-adoptive backgrounds and/or years of institutional living. These parents all expected to arrive in Paris. Some do. Others do not get to see the Paris of their dreams right away, but they hope that they will eventually. Some parents have not even landed in France. Others feel abandoned in an unknown, desolate location. They no longer even think about seeing Paris. Their biggest concern is surviving and getting back home.

There are no more powerful words than those which come from people's own pens and hearts—words that reflect their deepest feelings. To give the reader the distinctive flavor of the scenarios in this analogy, I use the words and experiences of twenty-eight adoptive mothers and couples who participated in my study. I chose to highlight the experiences and perceptions of these adoptive parents in the three chapters that follow.

Many of the parents wrote comments to the open-ended questions in the questionnaire. Their comments sum up where they felt things were with their adopted child/children at the time they participated in that survey.

Their words paint a picture of any prior expectations they had about the child/children that they would adopt and about family life after adoption. In essence, their often-unsolicited, verbatim comments also provide valuable insights into their experiences in building, or adding to, their families by adopting internationally from Russia and/or other Eastern European countries.

In order to view respondents' comments in context, I also include information about their marital status, the presence and ages of any birth or prior adopted children in the family, some pre-adoption background about their internationally adopted child or children, and details about the adoption process, including some information about the agencies that did their home studies and located their children.

Outsiders looking at their comments may see these parents' lives differently than they themselves do. However, in order to understand their post-adoptive experiences as an insider would, the reader must accept their statements as valid and go from there.

How I Organized the Parents in Chapters 6-8

I organized the sub-sample of respondents into one of the three chapters. I used as criteria, first, their satisfaction with their decision to adopt one, or more, of their children internationally and second, the content of their concluding statements, when present.

In chapter 6, I share case narratives of respondents who described themselves as very satisfied or satisfied with their decision to adopt their child or children internationally. The first four respondents, Anne, Barbara, Claudia, and Donna, have arrived at the destination they expected. The next four respondents, Frances, Grace, Irene, and Karen, have not arrived in the heart of Paris right away, or even by the time they completed the questionnaire. However, among those who are still not there, they hope that the Paris of their imaginings is not too far away.

In chapter 7, I offer case narratives of adopters who typically rate themselves in the middle, or "so so," category of satisfaction. Meredith through Joan talk about issues and problems of at least one child they adopted internationally.

In Chapter 8, I focus on ten respondents whose comments are reflective of some or a lot of dissatisfaction. These parents, Patricia through

Zoe, talk about their adopted child or children and family life in straight-forward language. Taken together, the parents who share their stories in the next three chapters illustrate very well the four scenarios I described earlier in this chapter.

Prior to participating in the questionnaire survey, I promised respondents "anonymity of identity." However, because it is important for the reader to see these parents as real people, I needed to name them. So, I created fictitious first names for each parent. Any resemblance to an adoptive parent with the same first name or who is similar in other ways is purely coincidental. Although the names I use are fictitious, the facts and words that I include here are a faithful rendition of the content of these respondents' questionnaires.

Ozzie and Harriet: The Ideal Family?

In chapter 6, Irene, one of the parents who speaks in more depth, says that before she adopted her two sons from Russia, she expected family life to be "a regular *Ozzie and Harriet* life." Her reference to the 1950s sitcom about the Nelson family is interesting because many families in the 1950s watched this show regularly and could identify with the Nelson family. Many children of that era probably thought that other people's lives, if not their own, were like life in the Nelson family. And, unlike the Cleaver family of the *Leave it to Beaver* TV show that also portrayed family life on television during the same era, everyone knew that the Nelsons were a real family.

The Nelson family consisted of two parents, Ozzie and Harriet, and two children, sons David and Ricky. Ozzie worked. Harriet kept house and raised her sons. The whole family sat down together for dinner every night. Ozzie and Harriet got along well and with their sons. The brothers got along well with each other. Viewers got glimpses of interaction at the dinner table and elsewhere in the home.

Conversation among all members was abundant and pleasant. Lots of smiling went on. Life was not without its challenges but the positive messages the viewer got were many: family mattered. Problems could be solved by working together. Being part of a loving, close-knit family was, without question, a good thing.

When many of the children who grew up in the 1950s think about a model or "ideal type" of a family, they think of the Nelsons. But how many families—biological or adoptive, look like or really are like the Nelsons?

Are Adoptive Families Different From Biological Families?

The answer: yes and no. The obvious difference is in how they are formed. Adoptive families may also differ from biological families in physical characteristics: skin pigmentation, hair color, and shape and color of eyes. These differences may provide clues to a child's origins. However, as the numbers of bi- and multi-racial families have increased, unless both parents are present, strangers can't be sure whether or not a child is adopted.

Regardless of how they are formed, families in contemporary society are quite diverse. For example, some birth children are raised by a birth mother and father, others by a mother or father. Many children live in blended families where they have blood ties to some members and social kinship connections to others. Others may have two parents of the same sex, one biological and that person's partner. In some families, one or both grandparents is/are the principal parental figure(s).

Like biological children, adopted children are raised in diverse types of families. The model of a young white, married, childless couple adopting a newborn is no longer normative in American society. People of all races adopt. Older, childless couples adopt. Single professionals and divorced parents adopt. People with disabilities adopt. Children of all ages need parents. Some children only get a "forever family" when they are eight, or twelve, or fourteen years old.

Creating a family is not only exciting, it can also be stressful. Adopting children close in age to each other and at the same time other may bring a couple closer together. However, going from being a single person or a childless couple to a family of three, four, or more can also result in a build up of stress which threatens, or tears apart, relationships. Successful as well as troubled families happen—regardless of how a family is formed. The point is that sometimes they come about because of the operation of social forces over which parents and the children have little control or understanding.

Getting the Insider's View

In reading chapters 6 through 8, I encourage the reader to note what these parents choose to emphasize. Also consider whether they report that their child/children demonstrated or was/were diagnosed as having problems at the time they joined the family and subsequently. I asked respondents to classify the types of problems that their child or children could have experienced into one or more if the following categories:

health-related (including physical, psychological, and emotional/mental health), behavioral, and/or other. Note that some children have few or no reported problems. Others have many. As a way to pull the case narratives across chapters together, at the end of chapter 8, I discuss the issues and patterns that emerge from the case narratives in chapters 6, 7, and 8.

How different is the sub-sample of parents in their expectations of what their children and family life would be like? Do satisfied parents have realistic expectations and dissatisfied parents unrealistic ones? To shed light on the answers to these questions, I include each respondent's verbatim response to the following two questions: Prior to adoption, what, if any, expectations did you have about the child (children) you planned to adopt? Prior to adoption, what expectations, if any, did you have about what family life would be like after adoption?

Note

1.   Credit needs to be given to Emily Perl Kingsley, "Welcome to Holland," for first using the idea of a trip planned for one destination, but which ends up in another.

6

Case Narratives of Satisfied Adopters

Anne, Barbara, Claudia, and Donna share their positive adoption outcomes. These respondents describe themselves as very satisfied with the adoption of their child/children. These parents are good examples of adopters who have arrived in the heart of Paris.

Scenario 1A: Adopters Who Have Arrived in Paris

Anne and her husband adopted two healthy infants, a boy and a girl, from Russia in the late 1990s.

The adoptions of these unrelated children took place about fourteen months apart. The ages at adoption of the first child was 8 ½ months and of the second child, ten months.

Case Narrative 1: Couple View Their Children as Gifts from God

In addition to being an adoptive parent, Anne is also a stepmother to two almost grown children from her husband's first marriage. When Anne completed the questionnaire, she was in her mid to late thirties. Her husband was then in his mid to late forties. Their first child had been living with them for about nineteen months and their second child, for five months. At that time, the older child was just under 2½ years old. The younger child was about fifteen months old. Neither child had lived in his/her birth home. Anne reports that their first child had no problems upon arrival in the family. Their second child had been exposed to tuberculosis in Russia. This child's physical problem was being treated through medication and was expected to resolve after six months of treatment. The couple worked with a licensed placing agency outside their home state. Anne states that she checked out the agency's track record with the licensing bureau in that state "somewhat carefully" and talked with three to four parents who had adopted through the agency. She spoke with the agency director, facilitator, lawyer, and administrative assistants. The information the couple received from the agency about their children was accurate but not complete. She says: "Current measurements were not given for our son. The info was as accurate as a 'snapshot' can be for that moment in time when our children were examined." She states further that, before they made the decision to adopt their son, she wishes she had his current measurements "to determine whether his growth was within normal range—would have made the decision easier. We asked for them but the orphanage never provided them to the agency." Although they were neither required to do any pre-adoption preparation nor got information about institutional effects or early trauma from the agencies they used, Anne comments that she and her husband "were very happy" with their agency's performance. "We felt it was our job to prepare ourselves and research effects of institutionalization, etc." Prior to adopting, Anne expected that the children "would be God's choice for our family." She expected family life to be "almost exactly like the family life we would have had if we had had our children biologically." In closing, Anne states "...We feel so very blessed to be parents to our two Russian children. They are so very precious to us. We consider them to be miraculous gifts from our Heavenly Father. We can't imagine life without them..."

In October of 1997, Barbara, a single woman, adopted a girl at age twenty-six months from Russia.

Case Narrative 2: Mother and Daughter Are a Good Match

When she completed the questionnaire, Barbara was in her mid fifties. Her daughter was almost five years old and had been home for about two years and nine months. Prior to being adopted, she had lived in an orphanage most of her life. Barbara reported that her daughter had no problems at the time of her adoption. This single mother worked with a licensed placing agency located outside the state in which she lived. Before choosing an agency, Barbara called twenty to thirty agencies and talked with a representative at each one. She also talked with a couple of adoptive parents. Barbara says that she completed more than eleven hours of pre-adoption preparation. However, she received "very little" information from the agencies she used either about the effects of orphanage living or early traumas on children's development and behavior. The information she received about her daughter was complete but "not accurate in that United States medical doctors at the International Clinic dismissed most of the neurological words on [the] report as meaning-less." Barbara states that the agencies she used did a good job in referring this specific child to her. Barbara expected the child to be healthy and she was. Barbara reports that she had no prior expectations about family life after adoption. She concludes: "I was very fortunate. My little girl is healthy, intelligent and has a great personality. We are a good match. The process happened so quickly—six months from the day I decided to adopt till I was in court in Russia—that I didn't have time to worry about all the things that could have gone wrong and the possibility of getting an ill or emotionally damaged child. My biggest problem was our own INS and how difficult they were to deal with."

Case narrative 3 introduces Claudia, a divorced mother of one daughter, determined to add a second daughter to her family, this time through adoption.

Case Narrative 3: Adoptive Mother's Family is Happy and Functions Well

Claudia was in her early forties when she participated in my research. In late 1995, Claudia adopted a girl nearly seven years old from Bulgaria. Her adopted daughter had lived with Claudia and her biological daughter for almost four years. The child was nearly eleven years old then. Claudia's biological daughter was then eight years old. The adopted daughter had lived in an orphanage for her whole life. According to Claudia, the problems her child had prior to her adoption involved her physical health only—severe iron deficiency and hernias. Those problems were treated and/or repaired either immediately [iron deficiency] upon her arrival in the United States or within eight months [the hernias]. Claudia worked with a licensed placing agency not located in the state where she lived. She checked the agency out "somewhat carefully" and spoke to one parent who had adopted through them. She says that the information she got about her daughter was "as accurate as it could be." She was not required to do any pre-adoption preparation and got no information about either institutional effects or early trauma from the home study agency she used. Claudia expected that life with a second child would be "more fun—and it is." Her adopted daughter has done very well. Claudia sums up her story by saying: "We are all happy and function well as a family."

In case narrative 4, Donna, a married woman, shares her experiences in adopting two siblings from Romania in April of 1996. The children were: two years, five months; and twelve months old when they were adopted.

Case Narrative 4: Already Parents, Couple Adopts Siblings

Both Donna and her husband were in their mid thirties when she completed the questionnaire. Their biological son was then eight years old. Their Romanian children were five years and ten months old and about four years old respectively. The latter had lived in their American family almost 3 ½ years. The older child lived in the orphanage until being adopted. The younger child lived in the birth home for three weeks before entering the orphanage. Donna learned that the children's birth parent[s] relinquished their parental rights. The older child had an intestinal parasite [ghiardia]. The younger child had strabismus and borderline sensory integration problems in relation to clothing textures and lumps in food. This child needed occupational and physical therapy. At the time she completed the questionnaire, Donna reports all of these problems as resolved. In adopting their children, the couple worked with a licensed placing agency that was not located in their home state. Donna reports that she did check out the agency's track record "somewhat carefully" and spoke with at least five families who also adopted through the same agency. She believes that this agency provided mostly accurate and mostly complete information about their children. The couple hired an independent source to re-translate the information their agency provided. They found only minor discrepancies in the medical information. The home study agency they used did not require the couple to do any pre-adoption preparation and only provided "minor detail" on both the effects of institutional living and early traumas on a child's development and behavior. When asked what she thought her home study agency could have done better prior to their decision to adopt their children. Donna says: "They could have educated prospective parents about all potential problems post-institutionalize[d] children faced. Parents could be given reading lists and source guides. Luckily, we had done this for ourselves." She adds: "It worries me that other couples may not have the information I found on my own. There are excellent sources of information available but not readily offered to prospective parents." Before she adopted, Donna says, "I read everything I could get my hands on about institutionalized children. I 'talked' with people online who had adopted from Romania. I subscribed to adoptive newsletters and magazines. I think my expectations were realistic." Donna says that she "anticipated the developmental delays and expected that the older child and maybe the younger child would need early intervention services. I planned for the worst, figuring the reality had to be better. [It was!]" Donna concludes: "I don't think most prospective parents are educated properly. Advice offered in standard parenting books does not always hold true for PIC [post-institutionalized children]. Many of these prospective parents have no experience with children. Often, parenting problems are confused with the adoption process. Post-institutionalized children need their own parenting guidelines. I believe our experience turned out so well because we had thoroughly prepared ourselves."

Part IA Concluding Statement

The families in this part of the chapter consist of two couples, a single woman, and a divorced mother. These respondents adopted a total of six children. Both couples adopted two children each. The single and divorced women adopted one child each. Only one of the respondents, Donna, adopted siblings, both children at the same time. These four respondents describe positive adoption outcomes. They also describe themselves as very satisfied with the adoption of their child/children. Referring back to the analogy, these parents have "arrived" in the heart of Paris.

There are six variables that contribute to the arrival of these families in the heart of Paris: Young age of the child/children at adoption; child's lack of serious problems at adoption; good fit between parent(s) and child; good match between parents' pre-adoption expectations and the post-adoption reality respondents encountered; pre-adoption preparation; and, for, two respondents, previous parenting experience. Although I will discuss them separately, when they appear in combination, these variables should be considered as having additive value [that is, $A + B + C.... + F$ = total value] in predicting post-adoption success.

In regard to the first variable, age, at adoption three of the children were infants between 8 ½ months and twelve months at adoption. Two others were twenty-six and twenty-nine months old. The seven-year-old was adopted into a family in which a birth child was already present.

In regard to the second variable, absence of serious problems, most of the children either had no problems when they arrived in their adoptive families or had problems that had resolved by the time the respondent participated in the phase I questionnaire. These adoptees either had no problems upon arrival in their new families or had physical problems that had been resolved. None of the adopters in this part reported that the child/children had a pre-adoption history of abuse or exhibited serious emotional or behavioral problems in their home.

The third variable, the "goodness of fit" between adopter and adoptee, may be the key to post-adoption success. Certainly, the power of this variable should not be underestimated. Personality characteristics, similarities in interests between parent and child, having a sense of humor in common, for example, can help the attachment process immensely. The parents in this section all believed that the child/children they adopted "fit well" into their new families. Their perceptions of a good fit with their child/children translated into perceptions that the adoption was very successful.

Similarly, these parents either had positive pre-adoption expectations [i.e., adopting the child/children was God's will; believing that the child would be healthy], realistic expectations, or no expectations about the children before they adopted them. In every case, the post-adoption reality either matched or exceeded these respondents' expectations.

The fifth variable, pre-adoption preparation, was also an important predictor of perceptions of post-adoption success. All of these respondents felt prepared before they adopted. Although only Barbara, a single woman, was required by her agency to complete pre-adoption preparation, Donna and her husband and Claudia had previous parenting experience before they adopted internationally.

Finally, previous parenting experience was probably a help to two of the adopters. Both Claudia and Donna were parents of a biological child before they adopted. Previous experience is especially helpful when subsequent children in the family fall within the "normal" range of milestones and behavior. Having another child already in the family may also work to the new child's advantage. The biological child can help to cue the adopted child about how to behave and what will be expected of him or her as a family member. If the first child is older, the cuing and support s/he provides may help the adopted child navigate the school experience more easily and effectively.

Scenario IB: Adopters Who Have Arrived in an Unrecognizable Part of Paris

The four respondents in this section also describe themselves as either very satisfied or satisfied with their adoption outcome. However, their experiences after the child/children they adopted entered their families were not idyllic at the start and, for some adopters, life was described as still not easy. Referring back to the analogy, these are the people who arrived in an unrecognizable part of Paris.

In December 1993, Frances, a single woman, adopted a fifteen-month-old girl from the Ukraine.

Case Narrative 5: After a Difficult First Year, Adopted Daughter Began to Thrive

Frances was in her mid to late thirties when she completed the questionnaire. Her daughter was then about 5 ½ years old and had been home for more than four years. The child had lived in the orphanage all her life prior to being adopted. Frances reports that her daughter had behavioral and physical health problems when she entered her family. Her daughter was born prematurely [two pounds at birth] and still had low weight. At age fifteen months, she could not walk, stand alone, or sit up. She would only take food from a bottle. Her eyesight was poor. Frances reports that her daughter did not like to be touched, bathed, or to have her hair washed. Frances arranged for her daughter to receive early intervention services for about one year. She also received occupational therapy once a week. The child needed glasses to correct astigmatism, amblyopia, and strabismus. Frances worked with a licensed placement agency located outside the state in which she lived. She says that she did not check out the agency's track record through the state licensing board but that she did speak with at least five adoptive parents who had adopted a child from the same agency. She had a lot of contact with the agency director and also spoke with the social worker on staff. Frances worked with a different agency to do her home study and reports that she completed six to ten hours of pre-adoption preparation. However, neither the home study nor the placing agency she used provided information either about the known effects of orphanage living or about the impact of early traumas on children's development and behavior. Regarding the information she received about her daughter before she adopted her, Frances says: "Diagnoses were inaccurate [perinatal encephalopathy], tons of information missing." When asked whether she thought her agency could have done anything better prior to her decision to adopt her child, Frances says: "Very much so! They painted an idyllic picture of how easily, quickly a child would catch up developmentally." She says that her daughter needed post-placement services. Frances sought these services out herself—her agency offered none. She comments further about the local [home study] agency she used: "They should have been proactive in helping newly adoptive families get all the info/support necessary." Regarding Frances' prior expectations about her daughter she states: "Apart from my hope that she be physically, emotionally, and psychologically healthy, I had no other expectations of her." About family life, Frances says: "I imagined money would be tighter [It is!] and that I would be more busy/tired [I am!] and that I would be having a lot of fun [I do!]."Although Frances' daughter had a difficult first year home, Frances describes her daughter as "a happy, healthy child and the delight of her life."

In October of 1995, Grace and her husband adopted a girl age seven years three months from Bulgaria.

Case Narrative 6. Older Couple Adopts a Child Who Had Lived Whole Life in Orphanage

At the time she completed the questionnaire, both Grace and her husband were in their early to mid fifties. Their daughter was then ten years and nine months old and had been in their family for about 3 ½ years. As soon as she entered her adoptive family, Grace says that her daughter exhibited hyperactivity, engaged in angry outbursts and yelling on a regular basis, rocked and banged her body against walls, and was hyper-vigilant. The child also had difficulty tolerating noise and "certain touches," and wet her bed regularly. She was also undernourished at the time she was adopted and had a hernia. To locate their daughter, the couple used a licensed agency in the state where they lived. The same agency also did their home study. Grace reports that she and her husband completed eleven or more hours of pre-adoption preparation and that she had contact with a variety of staff at the agency, including the director and the facilitator in charge of adoptions. She says: "I demanded answers from someone throughout the process. The training program for people adopting older children lasted three weeks. Still, the agency staff knew very little [like nothing!] about adopting older children from orphanages in Eastern Europe." Grace states that the agency also did not know anything about the child she and her husband adopted. When asked what she thought their agency should have done better prior to their decision to adopt, Grace says: "They should have demanded more specific background from [the] orphanage or [the] Bulgarian agency they worked with about my child." This family needed post-placement services for their child. Grace reports that she called the social worker who did the older-child pre-adoption preparation often during the first two to three months after her daughter was in their family. The couple was able to obtain psychological services for their daughter and some support for themselves through the agency. Grace points out that the agency had "no group remotely adequate for Eastern European children." She says she learned about possible issues and resources for her child through the Parents Network for the Post-Institutionalized Child rather than from her agency. What did Grace expect her child to be like? She says she expected "only that she would be a child with the needs of a child." Grace also says that she to be "a lot more interesting! As difficult as it has been at times, it has been worth every minute and every hug from our daughter."

In June of 1996, Irene and her husband adopted two brothers, aged three and four years old, from Russia.

Case Narrative 7. Adopting Older Children Was an Eye-Opening, Exhausting Experience

At the time she completed the questionnaire, Irene was in her early fifties. Her husband was in his early forties. The boys had been in their family for about three years and were then ages seven and six respectively. The children were removed from the birth home because of neglect and/or abuse and had lived for several years in an orphanage. The older child was reported to have no problems at the time of adoption. The younger child displayed symptoms of attachment disorder and Attention Deficit Hyperactivity Disorder (ADHD). Irene and her husband worked with a licensed placement agency located outside the state in which they lived. They also talked with three to four parents who had adopted a child similar to theirs. Irene thinks that the information they got about the children was accurate, although not complete. She says that they "needed more information on behavior and abilities plus family history." Before they made the decision to adopt their children, she says she wished she had more information about "behavior and delays." The home study agency the couple used did not require any pre-adoption preparation. The couple did receive some information about the impact of orphanage living, but none on the effects of trauma on a child's development and/or behavior. Irene says that "more literature and access to various resources" would have been helpful. Irene describes her pre-adoption expectations about the children as follows: "They would be full of adventure—wide-eyed—loving." She expected family life to be "full of excitement—watching our sons grow and discover—a regular *Ozzie and Harriet* life." The couple discovered that parenting children who have a pre-adoption history of neglect and abuse is far more challenging than many people assume. Irene concludes: "Adopting older children has been eye-opening and at times exhausting. They come with their own hidden problems and fears that they don't understand and can't control. If adoptive parents were made more aware of potential problems instead of mentioning them in passing, the parents could be better prepared and hopefully be less frustrated."

In October of 1995, Karen and her husband adopted a boy from Bulgaria who was then five years, nine months old. The couple already had a biological son at home.

Case Narrative 8. Couple's Struggle to Get Services for Adopted Son Was Not as Successful as Expected

At the time she completed the questionnaire, Karen and her husband were both in their early forties. Their adopted son was 9 ½ years old and had been in their family just over 3 ½ years. Their biological son was then 11 ½ years old. Prior to being adopted, their Bulgarian son had lived his whole life in an orphanage setting. After he arrived in his new family, he displayed several problems: auditory processing problems, sensory integration disorder, and problems paying attention. Karen described her adopted son as very immature for his age and developmentally delayed. None of the problems identified above had resolved by themselves. The couple worked with the same licensed agency to do both their home study and to locate their son. Karen says that she did not investigate the agency's track record with the state licensing board but she did talk with three or four parents who had used their services to adopt. Although Karen says that she is satisfied with the decision to adopt her Bulgarian son, she does not think that the agency provided either accurate or complete pre-adoptive information about him. She comments: "Our son was described to have 'normal' development. The information was too scarce. We did not know what to expect." Although she and her husband did complete at least eleven hours of pre-adoption training, the concentration was on abuse and FAS. She says: "I wish we knew more about neglect and malnutrition. There should have been specialized classes on the effects of institutionalization, how to recognize the common issues & how to seek help." Their adopted son needed a variety of services, including speech therapy, therapy for sensory integration disorder, tutoring, and psychological services, to help his address his issues. There was also a need for family counseling. Karen reports that they paid for the major portion of the cost of the services. Karen states that her pre-adoption expectations were "that he would be healthy, need help with language acquisition; that he might need counseling for issues [without any understanding of what they might be]." Once in the family, she "expected the two kids to play happily together." [She] "thought we'd have shared family activities." Her concluding comments make her frustrations at the lack of services for her adopted son clear: "I still don't feel that after 3+ years of seeking help for our son that he has been able to get his needs met. His school recognized that he has some needs but nothing 'severe enough' to qualify for help. Our health insurance does not adequately cover services… It is deeply frustrating to have brought a child for evaluations, have some of his needs recognized but then not receive help. I don't feel that most health professionals or school personnel are familiar with the needs of post-institutionalized kids. I've done my best to educate them, but it hasn't been enough. It is as if they are stuck in their preconceived notions plus prejudices, their familiar knowledge.

Part 1B Concluding Statement

The adopters in this part describe themselves as either very satisfied or satisfied with their adoption outcome. However, their experiences after the child or children they adopted entered their families were not idyllic at the start and, for some, life is still not easy. Referring back to the analogy, these are the people who arrived in an unknown part of Paris. After some tough going, Frances and Grace seem to have arrived in the heart of Paris. Irene and Janet have discovered that the road they are on is still filled with bumps and detours.

Three respondents are married. The fourth is a single woman. Taken together, these respondents adopted a total of five children. None of these adopters had a birth child in the home before adopting internationally.

One of the three couples adopted two children. The other two couples and the single woman each adopted one child. The adoptees ranged in age at time of adoption from fifteen months old to seven years, three months old. Four of the five adoptees were age three or older when they were adopted.

What common threads do these adoptive families share and how do they compare to the adopters whose experiences are described in case narratives 1-4? The respondents in this section share four common threads. First, they adopted children who were older at adoption than were the adoptees described in part IA. The children described in the part 1B case narratives ranged in age from fifteen months to just over seven years old. They had a real median age of four years old as compared to an interpolated median of nineteen months old for the adoptees in part 1A.

Second, more adoptees in part IB had more serious and longer-term problems than did the adoptees in part 1A. On the plus side, however, three out of four of these parents had some pre-adoption preparation. Among those who got pre-adoption preparation, three parents spent at least eleven hours in "training" to adopt their child/children. Third, only one of these families had a biological child at home before adopting. In the case of children who have challenging behavioral or emotional issues when they enter their new family, the absence of other children in the home can be a plus in the sense that these parents are able to focus their time and energies on meeting the needs of their adopted child/children. Finally, when help was needed, these parents knew that they had to be proactive in getting it.

7

Case Narratives of Families Who Typically Feel "Caught in the Middle"

This chapter presents the case narratives of ten adoptive families. Although some of the respondents report that they have experienced or continue to experience challenges and stress, they tend to make closing comments that are more positive than negative in outlook.

Scenario 2:
Bewildered Adopters Who Have Not Even Arrived in Paris

Meredith and her husband went from being a childless couple to adopting one child from Russia and from there, became the parents of three children when they adopted two more children, siblings also from Russia, to their family simultaneously.

Case Narrative 1: Couple Finds Managing the Mix of Three Adoptees the Great Stressor

The couple adopted their daughter and sons in two separate adoptions completed about two and a half years apart. At the time of their adoptions, the children were ages four years, eleven months old; four years, ten months old; and three years, four months old. Meredith rated her satisfaction level as very satisfied with the adoption of their first child, but as so so with the adoption of their second and third child. When Meredith completed the phase I questionnaire, she and her husband were in their mid to late forties. Their first child had been in their family for just over five years. The second and third children had been home for about 2 ½ years. The children were then ages ten years, almost 7 ½ years, and almost six years old. Their first child had lived in the birth home for more than four years and became available for adoption after the father's death, when the birth mother relinquished her rights. The second child lived in the birth home for more than three years before moving to an orphanage. The court terminated parental rights. The third child spent about three years in an orphanage prior to being adopted and had lived in the birth home. Meredith states that all three children had correctable physical health problems, and behavioral problems, related to having Attention Deficit Disorder/Attention Deficit Hyperactivity Disorder (ADD/ ADHD). One child also has cognitive difficulties. For the adoption of their second and third children, Meredith and her husband used a licensed agency that she describes as "very new." She states that they did not get any pre-adoption preparation. The couple also did not get any information about the effects of orphanage living and early traumas on children's development and behavior. Meredith says that she does not think that the information they received about these two children was either accurate or complete. About the agency's effort, she states: "We think that they could [have been] more thorough. Initially, they gave us the wrong birth date for one child and the wrong name of another. We don't know what to believe or pass on to the kids about their histories." Prior to making their decision to adopt, Meredith thinks that the agency should have provided "more formal info on the children's health, development plus behavior. [The agency should have] given us more info on the orphanage routine, etc. They could (have) advise(d) us on the issues of bringing together 3 special needs kids and what to consider before making the decision." When asked about the couple's prior expectations about the children, Meredith's expectations are no different from those of many pre-adoptive parents. About the children: "We expected them to be average (hopefully) in most arenas including relationship building." Similarly, they expected family life…"to be busier, fuller, fun plus work. What we did not plan on was a very sick adoptive mom who has found it necessary to continue working full time and stress on the marriage." In closing, Meredith comments: "Overall, we are happy with our family and, at least to date, we are not dealing with serious issues… Managing the mix—especially the ADHD has been the great stressor."

The motivations behind people's decision to adopt can be personal as well as altruistic. Case narrative 2 is an example of the latter. Nora and her husband already had four biological children in their family.

Case Narrative 2. Parents of Four Biological Children Adopted Because They Felt the Need to Help at Least One Child

Nora and her husband adopted a girl aged three years, five months from Romania. When Nora completed the questionnaire, she and her husband were both in their early forties. Their adopted daughter was eleven years, eight months old and their biological children were seventeen, fourteen, ten, and seven years old. Their adopted daughter had lived all her life in an orphanage. Once home, she began to exhibit a variety of behaviors. Nora states that her daughter did what she wanted, even though she knew her behavior was wrong. She "pushes you." Nora describes the child as having a short attention span and being easily distracted. She rocked herself for comfort, was frightened by loud noises such as thunder and fireworks. She also liked to "show off" especially in front of others (which this author assumes refers to non-family members). Health wise, this child was described as a carrier of hepatitis B and had *H.pylori*. This child was reported to still have problems at the time of the Phase I questionnaire. However, Nora did not provide any details about services this child needed. The couple used a local social worker to do their home study. They were not required to do any pre-adoption preparation and were not advised about possible effects of orphanage living and early traumas on children's development and behavior. They hired a Romanian-American woman located in a western state to facilitate the adoption. Nora rates her level of satisfaction with the decision to adopt this child internationally as "so so," although she states that she probably would have adopted her even if she knew in advance about her needs and problems. Regarding her prior expectations about this child, Nora states that they "had no idea it would be this difficult." About family life, she expected it to be "much easier to get along with [this] child, more pleasant, not as difficult with behavior problems. We had no idea what we were getting into but felt [the] need to at least help 1 of these children…"

Olivia and her husband already had children in their family before they adopted their Russian son, at eighteen months old, in the summer of 1994.

Case Narrative 3. None of the Child Development Books Published Gave This Couple Insight into Their Adopted Son's Development

Olivia says that her son had lived in an orphanage all his life prior to his adoption. She also says that he was a hepatitis B carrier but that the agency the couple used to locate their son did not provide neither accurate nor complete information about his physical health. They only found out about him being a Hepatitis B carrier after they returned home and had him examined here. The couple worked with a licensed agency located in the northeastern state where they lived. The same agency did their home study and placed their son. Olivia reports that they had checked the agency out "somewhat carefully" and talked with three to four other parents who had worked with the same agency. She says that they were not required to complete any pre-adoption preparation. The couple felt that they needed post-adoption services and support from or through their agency. However, Olivia says that the agency did not put them in touch with anyone who provided these services. They feel that their agency should have done a better job checking their son's health before they offered them the referral. She adds that she probably would not have agreed to accept a child who was a hepatitis B carrier, if she had known about this condition in advance. Her prior expectations focused around possible emotional issues: "I expected that things would be a little smoother and worried about attachment issues. Attachment has not been a problem. What has been unusual in their experience is that his development varied widely and was complicated by his extremely enthusiastic personality. He was like a super-charged toddler. Even now at 5 ½ [years old], it's hard to know what is his innate personality and what, if any, of his behaviors are due to ongoing developmental issues. He was evaluated [as part of a study of Eastern European adoptees] for sensory integration issues and shows some deficits. How to respond is not clearly indicated."

Case narrative 4 introduces Paula and the two infant boys she and her husband adopted five months apart from Russia in 1996 and 1997.

Case Narrative 4: Agency Insisted Children Were Healthy and Normal and Needed Only Food, Love, and Medical Treatment

Each boy was seven months old when he was adopted. At the time Paula completed the questionnaire, her first son was a little over three years old and her second son was about two years and nine months old. Paula was then in her early forties and her husband was in his early fifties. The couple adopted their first child from an orphanage. The other child was in a premature baby hospital until the couple adopted him. Paula points out that she and her husband only learned his location the night before they met him in Russia. Their first son has problems in three categories: physical (Pervasive Development Disorder(PDD)/Autism), behavioral (self-stimulating and PDD/Autistic characteristics), and emotional (problems with reciprocity and engagement that this parent attributes to early institutionalization). Their second son has cerebral palsy. The couple worked with a licensed placing agency in a mid-western state. Although they were not sure why, the placing agency insisted that Paula and her husband use another agency to do their home study. Paula says that she checked into the placing agency's record of placements "somewhat carefully." She also talked with three to four parents who had adopted children through the same agency. Paula had contact with the adoption agency's director, the facilitator in charge of inter-country adoptions, and other staff involved in the process. When asked whether the information the placing agency provided about her children was accurate and/or complete, Paula replied no to both. She commented further that the agency provided no information about the physical and emotional health for their first child and incomplete information about their second child "in light of what was available." Paula stated that her placing agency neither required nor provided any pre-adoption preparation despite the fact that their contract said that they would. The so-called preparation the couple got consisted of a "dossier list... period." She wishes that they had provided information about what to expect after the boys joined their family. In addition to providing "no preparation at all for parents," Paula says that the agency "glossed over [the] realities of institutional life." What did Paula expect about the children and family life before she adopted? She says she expected "a typical family existence with typical health problems and development along normal lines for the children with education in Catholic schools; then college." She thought there would be "normal kid problems and joys; regular education; maybe sports; typical middle-class life." In her closing comments, Paula gives examples of what should constitute unethical behavior on the part of a placing agency: "bribes; withholding information; non-humanitarian efforts; lack of preparation for families; requiring acceptance\declination of [the] referral ' on the spot;' and no post-adoptive support."

In case narrative 5, the reader meets Laura, a single woman, who adopted a twenty-two-month old girl from Romania.

Case Narrative 5: Woman Was Told Her Daughter Was Healthy… But Tests Done in the U. S. Confirmed That She Had Multiple Problems

At the time she completed the questionnaire, Laura was in her early fifties. She did not say how old her daughter was then. The child had lived in an orphanage most of her pre-adoption life. It appears that she lived with her biological family for less than one month prior to parental rights being terminated. Laura states that what little information she got about her daughter before the adoption took place was either "useless history" or "wrong." Sometime after their arrival home, Laura took her daughter to an international adoption clinic that helped her to recognize the myriad problems her daughter actually did have. She says that she was told the following about her daughter: that the child has "ADD with hyperactivity, impulsive type" and "oppositional defiant disorder"; and is "non-complaint" and "not articulate about emotions" (but very explicitly clear on emotions at home, according to Laura). The child has learning disabilities, Central Auditory Processing Disorder, visual perceptual problems, and Sensory Integration Disorder. A genetic illness was discovered two years after the adoption and, more recently, the probability of Fetal Alcohol Effects. Laura states that she probably would not have adopted this child if she had known in advance about her many problems. She says: "I asked for as healthy a child physically, emotionally, [and] mentally [as] possible given that I was a single parent, also [a child] not over 15 months. I was pushed over and over again and enervated by her myriad of problems. The level of 'high risk' was NOT ever acknowledged." Laura worked with a licensed placing agency in the New England state where she lived at the time. That agency also did her home study. Laura says that she checked out the agency "very carefully" and talked with at least five parents that had adopted through the agency before she decided to work with them. The agency required Laura to do very little pre-adoption preparation, did not share information about the effects of early traumas and orphanage living on a child's development and behavior. Laura reports that about two years into the adoption, she contacted her agency for help and support. According to Laura, the agency did not follow up with the family to see how they were doing. There was no response to her correspondence even after six weeks had passed. The agency provided "no references, books, or recommendations for any kinds of services." Laura describes her expectations about her daughter prior to the adoption as "easier to manage. Not needful of so many services… Less stress!!!" She thought that family life would be "less full-time, more rewarding, and less anxious about what's going to happen to this child over the long haul." Laura adds: "I spend 90% of my time on her ... I've been told [that the child could be] suicidal or sociopathic – high likelihood. Not exactly what I had fantasized." In her closing comments, Laura says: "NO AGENCY SHOULD BE ALLOWED TO EITHER NOT DEAL WITH SINGLES OR SO OBVIOUSLY MAKE THEM WAIT LONGER FOR LESS HEALTHY CHILDREN. THERE'S UNBELIEVABLE DISCRIMINATION against both straight and gay singles."

Maureen and her husband, already parents of a biological child, decide to adopt two brothers, aged five and seven years old, from Russia. They completed the adoption of their sons in 1998.

Case Narrative 6: Agencies Should Research More History on the Kids They Refer

The brothers had been in their adoptive family for about eighteen months when Maureen completed the questionnaire. The couple's biological daughter was then eighteen years old. Maureen and her husband were then both in their early forties. About the boys' pre-adoption history, Maureen says that her sons had lived in their birth home, but were later abandoned by their mother. Their father had died. The boys were brought to an orphanage where they lived for a year. They were moved to a different orphanage and lived there for two years prior to their adoption. Maureen states that both boys had many problems that became obvious after they arrived home. Both had severe tooth decay and tooth loss, bowed legs, rickets, and a parasite. Both boys had hearing problems and needed hearing aids. They were unable to give and take affection. They were controlling and prone to rages and tantrums when they did not get their way. The boys lied, were sneaky, and had no remorse when they were caught doing something wrong. Maureen describes her sons as having Reactive Attachment Disorder (RAD) and Attention Deficit Disorder (ADD). Maureen and her husband, who lived in California, worked with a licensed placing agency located in a southern state. Before choosing this agency, she says that she checked the agency's record "somewhat carefully" and spoke with three to four parents who had adopted through them. Regarding pre-adoption preparation, Maureen states that they received only a few hours worth. Maureen reports that the placing agency provided "no birth records, no psych testing & no knowledge of (the) 1st year of orphanage life and possible alcohol exposure." There was also no mention of the existence of an older sibling. The agency required the couple to do very little pre-adoption preparation. Maureen says that the agency should have educated them about Reactive Attachment Disorder, informed them about parenting techniques appropriate for managing children with this psycho-logical disorder, and taught them about sibling issues. The family needed support and services after the adoption but the agency did not help them in finding either. Maureen says that if she had known how long the boys had actually lived in orphanages, about RAD, and about "how siblings close in age mix up each other to escalate things, I may not have looked at them." About her prior expectations regarding the children, Maureen states: "There would be many therapists to choose from to deal with their problems." About her prior expectations about family life, Maureen was optimistic: "More loving, give and take, calmer, fulfilling, bio sibling would have [a] good relationship with the boys, & fun."

Nancy and her husband, a then childless couple, adopted a brother and sister from Russia simultaneously in March of 1998.

Case Narrative 7: Couple Was Terrified at Their Older Child's Post-Adoption Behavior

At their adoption, the children were thirty-three and twenty-two months old. At the time Nancy completed the questionnaire, the children had been in the couple's family for about two and one half years. They were then five years and four months and four years and four months old. Nancy and her husband were both in their early forties at this time. Nancy reports that both children had lived in an orphanage all their lives. The older child had Post-Traumatic Stress Disorder (PTSD), Attachment Disorder, and severe developmental delays. That child needed a variety of post-adoption services including speech therapy, special education, counseling, and other therapeutic interventions. The younger child had no long-term problems. The couple worked with a licensed adoption agency located in the Midwestern state where the couple lived. The same agency did their home study. Nancy says that she did not check out the agency's track record of successful placements and talked with only one other parent who had used the same agency. She states that the agency did not provide either accurate or complete information about one of the children. The older child had "huge problems which were not indicated" (in any records). Nancy also says the agency they used did not require, or provide, any pre-adoption training for the couple. Once at home, the couple realized that their older child had problems. Nancy refers specifically to head banging, acting out, abuse, dissociation, attachment issues, and "huge developmental delays." Nancy says that this child's problems were so troubling that she had considered disrupting the adoption, although "not very seriously." What is clear is that, if she had known about the child's problems in advance, she probably would not have agreed to the adoption. According to Nancy, their agency did nothing to help the family regarding needed post-placement services. She says that they did not find an adoptive parents' support group through the agency, but she describes this support group as "clueless—a cheerleading group." She adds that she got help from other social agencies that the couple found themselves. Nancy feels that the agency could have done better: "There are a ton of resources in this town—they told us of none [emphasis put on none]." Did Nancy have any prior expectations about the children? She says: "None really—just siblings 5 and under—healthy—we were pretty busy professionals. Stress 'were.'" When asked about her expectations about what family life would be like, Nancy says: "Busy, but fun. Much of the last two years have been a nightmare."

In the fall of 1997, Owen and her husband, parents of a biological son, decided to adopt a brother and sister from Russia.

Case Narrative 8: Not Once Did Facilitator Ask Couple If They Were Sure of Their Adoption Decision

The siblings were then six and five years old. The couple's biological son was in his teens at the time Owen completed the questionnaire. She and her husband were in their mid to late forties then. About the children's pre-adoption history, Owen states that the children had lived in their birth home until their parents relinquished their parental rights. The children entered an orphanage setting where they lived for about two years prior to being adopted. Both children had behavioral, psychological, and emotional problems which had not resolved at the time Owen participated in my study about 3 ½ years after their adopted children had joined their adoptive family. Their problems included Oppositional-Defiant behavior, stealing, telling lies, anger, frustration, and fear. Both children were diagnosed as having Reactive Attachment Disorder. They needed speech therapy, special education services, medication, and RAD therapy and individual counseling. The children and the parents also participated in family counseling. Although she has never considered disrupting the adoption, Owen does indicate that she probably would not have chosen to adopt children with the issues and needs her children have, if she had known more about them in advance. The couple worked with a facilitator, not an adoptive agency, to locate their children. Both the facilitator and the couple resided in the same Western state. Owen does not say how they decided on this facilitator. She does say that she did not check out the facilitator's track record of placing children or talk to any other parents who had. Owen states that the Russian facilitator did not provide the couple with any pre-adoption preparation. The home study agency they used expected them to do a small amount of pre-adoption preparation. Although the home study agency did not handle Russian adoptions, the social worker that worked with the couple did share information about the effects of early traumas and orphanage living on a child's development and behavior. About their home study agency, Owen says: "... I am pleased with our home study agency – they have the resources available, answer questions willingly and publish an excellent newsletter. However, they don't handle Russian adoptions." Owen says that the post-adoption support they got came through their home study agency- not the facilitator. Through the agency, they got a referral "for a wonderful therapist specializing in adoptions & RAD." About the Russian facilitator, Owen says "I think the Russian facilitator is more concerned with ongoing business and keeping up appearances for that. I notice that we & our traveling companions have never been added to the reference list. We were not thrilled with the facilitator." What prior expectations did Owen have about her Russian children? She says that she "expected anger, confusion, testing of limits, curiosity, food hoarding, language diffi- culties, happiness, laughter, fun. Even though our home study social worker talked about older children difficulties and that it would be compounded with two children, I expected it to be short term—less than a year." What expectations did Owen have about what family life after adopting would be like? She wrote: "I knew that our older son would feel displaced and a loss of privacy. I expected that we would feel frustration, anger & regret. But I expected to feel happy to have these kids to introduce new things to, that they would take pleasure in joining our fun family and that the fun and laughter in our family would increase."

In February of 1997, Peggy, a single woman, adopted a boy from Russia, when he was five years old.

Case Narrative 9: Son Had a Pre-Adoption History of Sexual, Physical and Emotional Abuse

At the time Peggy completed the questionnaire, her son was close to eight years old. She was in her early fifties. Her son spent his first two years in his birth home. However, because of abuse, parental rights were terminated. He was placed in an orphanage, where he lived for thirty-seven months until his adoption. Peggy says that she learned nothing about her son's background from the orphanage staff. She got only information about his health status from the orphanage doctor. At the time he entered Peggy's home, her son was diagnosed with a variety of problems including PTSD, RAD, and Sensory Integration Disorder. He had been sexually abused and was prone to severe tantrums. There was evidence of stomach ulcers, parasites, bacterial infections, and a hole in one eardrum. The boy also had low motor skills and was unable to write. The child needed a variety of post-adoption services: speech therapy, special education, surgery for the hole in his ear, treatment for *H.pylori*, and medication. Peggy reports: "Seven therapists could not help him." He only began to talk about the abuse he experienced in his birth home after he went on medication. Peggy had to pay for many of the services her son needed because he did not qualify for any medical assistance. She says: "I am broke due to the severity of his needs." To facilitate the adoption, Peggy used a licensed agency in the southwestern state where she lived. The same agency completed her home study. Peggy says that she checked out the agency "very carefully" and spoke with one other adoptive parent who had worked with the same agency. She feels that the agency did not provide either accurate or complete information about his physical and emotional health. They also did not tell Peggy that her son had a sister and brother and where they were. She states that the agency should have told her about the fact that he was taken away from his birth parents and why his mother was put in jail before she made the decision to adopt her son. Peggy reports that she received no pre-adoption preparation from her agency. Once home, her son was abusive and refused to sleep. Peggy says that she "asked [her agency] for support and got none." Peggy also approached her agency because her son needed post-adoption services. After two years, a therapist was provided by the agency. In regard to services and referrals for services, Peggy states that one thing her agency could have done better was to "provide written documentation as to known services needed by other older kids from Russia & how to get in touch with these people." Peggy admits that she probably would not have adopted her son, if she had known in advance about his many problems. What were Peggy's prior expectations about this child? She says, "Only happiness mixed with anticipation of that fact that it would not be easy, but still a manageable situation." Did Peggy have any prior expectations about what family life would be like? Her answer: "No expectation as to the difficulties we have had and others. No information was shared regarding issues you would encounter."

Mark and Joan, a married couple, already parents of a biological daughter, adopted a 5 ½-year-old boy from Romania in July of 1997.

Case Narrative 10: In Retrospect, Couple Disagrees About the Decision to Adopt Their Romanian Son

At the time Mark and Joan answered the questionnaire, their son was almost nine years old. Their daughter was just entering her teen years. Joan and Mark report that they were then in their late forties and early fifties. This child was left at the orphanage a day or two after his birth and lived his entire life in an orphanage setting prior to his adoption. The couple reports that, prior to agreeing to adopt their son, their agency had told them nothing about his birth parents, early history and experiences, development or mental health. They got a brief videotape. Someone from the agency also visited him at the orphanage "a couple of times prior to adoption." Mark and Joan say that, after arriving in their home, their son exhibited a variety of problems. He had behavioral problems and psychological issues including impulsivity, seeking immediate gratification, lack of fear, stealing, and lying. He also was easily distracted, had a poor sense of time, and had a mild facial tic. The couple states further that their son had a confused sense of "gender identification." Mark and Joan described him as "overly attracted to women's things, makeup, etc." They also state that he needed to be the "center of attention" in games and with playmates. According to his parents, this child knows how to manipulate others and "can be a 'little con man.'" "Their son had only one physical health problem: intestinal worms. His other problems consisted of "poor memory, subnormal physical stamina, and needing lots of sleep." He also had difficulty understanding what he reads and "getting" the plots of television programs and videotapes made for children his age. Joan and Mark state that their son needed services like English as a Second Language(ESL) "but (the) school never offered—[we were] told several times 'there are others worse off.'" He also needed tutoring, chiropractic care, nutritional services, and counseling. The child did meet with therapists, but his parents report that he got "no help since none [of the therapists he saw were] familiar with this group of children [i.e., foreign orphans]." His parents gave him phonics instruction themselves and paid for the other services that he needed "out of pocket." The couple lived in a north central state at the time of their son's adoption. They worked with a placing agency also located in a north central state but not in the state where they lived. Mark and Joan say that they checked the agency's track record "somewhat to very carefully." They also talked with two other parents who had used the same agency. However, the children the other parents adopted were younger. The couple talked with the agency director and the facilitator in charge of foreign adoptions. They do not know about any of the staff's "background." Mark and Joan make clear that the agency did not provide them with an English translation of Romania's policy for out-of-country adoptions. The agency also failed to provide either accurate or complete information about this child. Before they made the decision to adopt their son, Mark and Joan say that they wish they had information about "the daily ritual of orphanage life: food, care givers, how well these kids speak their native language, schooling, play things, interaction with [the] 'outside world.'" They also wish they knew about the "family background of [his] parents, their health, age, alcohol problems." This couple was not required to do any pre-adoption preparation. They also got no information about the known effects of either orphanage living or early traumas on children's development and/or behavior. Mark and Joan state that, prior to the couple's decision to adopt this child, their agency could have provided them with information about "How to care for this child in the first weeks home—rest, diet, avoiding too much stimulation. Long-term problems with older adopted kids—e.g., sensory integration type problems and what to do about them, where to find support, help, etc." This couple needed help with all of the above issues, but they got nothing from, or through, their agency. They wrote that their agency should have provided a "list of parents with same age adoptions, a list of qualified professionals near to our home, counselors, etc." Mark and Joan rated themselves as differing in their satisfaction-dissatisfaction with the decision to adopt their son internationally. Mark described himself as satisfied. Joan said she is dissatisfied. This couple is included here because their two responses, when averaged, place them in the "so so" category. They do say that they have considered disrupting this child's adoption "somewhat seriously." They also make clear that, had they known about their son's needs and problems in advance, they would either probably not [Mark] or definitely not [Joan] have made the decision to adopt him. They add: "Our age/energy level is (a) serious consideration." What expectations did Joan and Mark have about their son prior to adopting him? They expected "that love, time, sound family life and attention to educational needs would solve most problems." What were their prior expectations about what family life would be like? They say: "tough for 6 months, fairly normal by 1 year—fairly clear sailing there after." In their closing comments, Mark and Joan focus on information and help they think their agency should have provided to them: (1) "books, articles, and web sites that can help parents understand problems, solutions to be dealt with;" (2) "lay out potential health, socialization, education problems—what to look for, what 'odd behaviors' may indicate, what to ignore, what to watch, what to 'jump on' immediately;" and (3) "How to prepare siblings + help them deal with the adoption."

Concluding Statement

The parents in this chapter consist of eight couples and two single adopters. Collectively, these respondents adopted a total of sixteen children. Just over two thirds of the adoptees are boys. At their adoptions, the children ranged in age from seven months old to seven years old. The modal age of these children at adoption was five years old.

These parents in this chapter adopted children who have many, serious problems. Yet, the large majority of them (78 percent) received no pre-adoption preparation at all and four others state that they received "very little" or a "small amount" of prior preparation. The general sentiment of these parents is that they did not receive either accurate or complete information about the child or children they adopted. They also needed post-adoption services and, with one exception, the agencies they used provided none.

8

Case Narratives of Adopters Whose Children Have Many, Serious Problems

The adopters in this chapter have struggled to understand and overcome the serious problems of the child or children they have adopted. They share their pre-adoption hopes and the post-adoption realities of their lives.

Scenario 3: Adopters who have Lost Hope of Ever Finding Their Way to Paris

Patricia and her husband adopted two unrelated boys from Lithuania. They adopted their first son in 1995, when he was fourteen months old. Their second son joined their family in March of 1998, when he was four years old.

Case Narrative 1: Adopters Said That If They Knew Even Some of the Ramifications of Adopting an Older Child from an Orphanage, They Might Have Made a Different Decision.

When she completed the questionnaire, both Patricia and her husband were in their mid to late thirties. Their first child had been home for about 4 ½ years. Their second child was in their family just over two years. The boys were about 5.8 years and just over six years old respectively at that time. Their first son had lived in the orphanage all his life prior to being adopted. Patricia reports that he had no problems upon arrival in his new family. Their second son had lived with his birth parents for his first month of life. Patricia says that his mother did not want him and that his birth father neglected and did not feed him. This child's birth father died of a head trauma. The courts in Lithuania terminated parental rights. The child entered an orphanage and lived in that setting for four years until Patricia and her husband adopted him. Patricia describes her second son as having behavioral, psychological, emotional, and physical health problems. He was oppositional/defiant, showed symptoms of attachment disorder, Post-Traumatic Stress Disorder(PTSD), and prior sexual abuse. He lacked remorse for things he did. In regard to physical health, he had an active case of Hepatitis B, celiac disease, and dental problems. He needed services to help address his many problems. The couple reports that they completed no pre-adoption preparation and got no information about the possible effects of orphanage living and early traumas on children's development and behavior. They used a doctor in Lithuania to facilitate the adoptions of their sons. Patricia does not believe that the information they got about the children was either accurate or complete. However, she speculates that the reason was that the "orphanage's records were lacking in detail" not because the doctor withheld any information. Patricia states that she is very satisfied with the adoption of her first son but is very dissatisfied with the adoption of the second son. She comments: "I wish we were told to stick to our original plan to adopt a child under 2 years old." The couple needed services after they adopted their second child. However, because they used a facilitator rather than a placing agency in the United States to locate this child, they did not get any help. Patricia comments further: "It has been a very frustrating battle of self learning…He has disrupted what was once a very happy family." According to Patricia, the couple's prior expectations about the children were reasonable: "We just wanted happy, healthy kids." She sums up their prior expectations about family life by stating: "We didn't see any reason(s) for not having a normal family life." In her closing comments, Patricia states: "I think if we knew even some of the ramifications of adopting an older child from an orphanage we would have stuck to our original plan of adopting a child who was 2 years old at the oldest. I only wish we had been better informed before we decided to take on such a huge task of trying to raise this child. Now, our first child is beginning to have issues and I really believe it is the result of living in a very stressful situation."

Case narrative 2 describes the experiences of Quinn and her husband who adopted an unrelated girl and a boy from Romania in two separate adoptions. The couple completed the adoptions in December of 1990, and March of 1992. At their adoptions the children were ages 5 ½ years and four years old.

Case Narrative 2: Our Dilemma—Do We Save One Child and Forget the Other?

At the time Quinn completed the questionnaire, she and her husband were in their early fifties. Their daughter was about fifteen years old and their son was about twelve years old. Neither child had ever lived in the birth home. Their daughter had only lived in orphanages. Their son was removed from the orphanage at age two and had lived in multiple homes until his adoption was finalized. Quinn reports that both children had many problems upon their joining the family. Their daughter was phobic and had problems sleeping. She engaged in rages. Quinn describes this child as also having Reactive Attachment Disorder (RAD), institutional autism, ADHD, and sensory integration issues. In terms of her daughter's physical health issues, Quinn identifies Fetal Alcohol Effects(FAE), regressed growth, rickets, and worms. She had scars from needle marks that Quinn believes resulted from sedating her in the orphanage. This child also has neurological impairments (possibly resulting, at least in part, from environmental pollutants like radiation fallout and lead paint on cribs). Quinn states that her son had been sexually abused, was anorexic, and was extremely sensory defensive (avoided both being touched and touching others). She also describes him as having RAD, severe PTSD, emotionally-based learning disabilities, and auditory processing problems. Both children continue to need multiple and diverse services to help address their problems. Quinn went to Romania on her own, in 1990, to arrange the first adoption. She did not work with a placing agency for the second adoption, either. Quinn states that the agency the couple used for their home study did not require them to complete any pre-adoption preparation or discuss the impact of institutional living and early traumas on a child's development and/or behavior. She states further: "The head of the agency that did our home study had 8 foreign adoptees. She knew the effects of orphanage living. She never made one suggestion about anything." Regarding the need for post-placement support or services from their agency, Quinn comments: "We needed so much help and no one helped us. For the last 10 years, we have had to learn everything thru trial and error. We have no family, friends, or even neighbors who assist or have a 'clue' as to what has gone on. Only the attachment therapist in Colorado has helped us." About Quinn's prior expectations regarding the children, she states: "That we could provide a safe, loving home." Regarding her prior expectations about family life, Quinn comments: "That there would be special moments, laughter and love to share. So far, there has only been struggle and we see no light at the end of the tunnel." Quinn reports that she was very dissatisfied with the outcome of her second child's adoption. She says that they have considered disrupting his adoption "very seriously." Quinn's closing remarks explain: "Our constant struggle is, do we save one child and forget the other? We have spent tens of thousands of dollars in trying to help our kids. Both have great potential. However, we are exhausted and we can't possibly keep our son in this special school [which costs $29,000 per year plus transportation] for the next five years. Without the school, he will never be able to earn a high school degree. Our daughter needs on-going psychological services. We need therapy to help them get through the adolescent years. We can't afford all this..."

Rhonda and her husband adopted three siblings at the same time from Bulgaria in March of 1997. The sibling set consisted of a girl, then almost seven years old, and twin boys who were almost five years old at the time of their adoption.

Case Narrative 3. They Were To Be "Normal, Healthy" Children.

At the time Rhonda completed the questionnaire, she was in her late thirties and her husband was in his early forties. The children had lived with their adoptive family for just over two years. During that time, a fourth child, a daughter, also entered their family. The girl had lived in her birth home for a while until her parents relinquished their rights. She then entered an orphanage setting where she lived almost all of her life until she was adopted. According to Rhonda, the boys had never lived in their birth home. They spent their whole life in orphanages before they were adopted. Rhonda and her husband received very little information about their children's pre-adoptive history. Their agency told them a little about the children's birth parents and said that all three children were in good physical health. Rhonda reports that her daughter had no problems after arrival in her home. However, both boys had emotional problems. One of the boys also had psychological problems. Rhonda describes the boys as lacking self-confidence. She says they were likely to bite and hit themselves. The children needed language, speech, and special education services. The couple worked with a licensed agency in a north central state to locate the siblings. The couple's home study was done by an agency located in a different north central state. Rhonda says that she checked out the adoption agency "very carefully" and talked with at least five people who had used the same agency. The placing agency required no pre-adoption preparation of the couple. Rhonda also states that the information the couple received about their Bulgarian children was neither accurate nor complete. Before they made the decision to adopt, she says that the agency should have provided "more information about institutionalized children… and not painted such a 'rosy picture'—more upfront about what to expect." The couple needed help from their agencies after they adopted but they got none. In fact, Rhonda states: "I have not heard from my agencies since I picked the children up." She also says that she "had no idea how to deal with the language barrier or the physical abuse." In retrospect, Rhonda says that she "would never adopt 3 at one time." What were Rhonda's prior expectations about the children? She states: "I thought they would be like American children after about 6 months—1 year. Wrong!" What did Rhonda expect family life to be like? She answers: "I figured we would have a 'normal' family with good and bad times."

Case narrative 5 describes the experiences of Suzanne. In July of 1997, Suzanne, a single woman, adopted two sisters from Russia. The girls were then ages ten years old and seven years old.

Case Narrative 4: RAD Issues Are Huge.

At the time she completed the questionnaire, Suzanne was in her late forties. Her daughters were about eleven years, eight months and eight years, eight months old. Both children had lived with their birth family before they entered the orphanage. The older child had probably lived in her birth home for two years. She spent eight years in an orphanage. The younger child probably lived with her birth parent(s) for about 1½ years. She spent 5 ½ years in the orphanage before she was adopted. The Russian courts had terminated parental rights because of abuse and/or neglect. Suzanne reports that both girls exhibited numerous problems after arriving in her home. These problems included sexual acting out, urinating on the floor, biting, hitting, and physical abuse of other children. They had symptoms of RAD: They were superficially "sweet/charming" to strangers. She states that they never bonded—were unable to form loving relationships. They each had several parasites. Both children were diagnosed with Reactive Attachment Disorder (RAD). Both children are receiving a variety of services. The older girl is in therapy to address her attachment issues. Suzanne reports that she worked with an agency and a facilitator based in two different states. The facilitator had been affiliated with the licensed agency Suzanne used but she is now independent. She had the most contact with the facilitator because she was local. The facilitator did not have a degree in human services. About her, Suzanne states: "… she was an idiot. I would never recommend her to anyone and have told people not to use her." Regarding the home study agency's track record, she states that she checked the agency out somewhat carefully: "They had a good track record in China; were just starting in Russia." Suzanne did talk with three or four adoptive parents who had worked with the same agency, but they had all adopted from China. She reports that she was not required to do any pre-adoption preparation by her home study agency. Neither that agency nor the facilitator Suzanne used discussed the adverse effects of orphanage living or early traumas on children's development or behavior. Prior to adopting, Suzanne says that she did a lot of research herself on the Web. Because the girls lived in two different parts of Russia, Suzanne completed the adoptions of her daughters in two different courts. She does not believe that she received either accurate or complete information about her children's physical and emotional health: "The parents were both very sick alcoholics… No mention of alcohol abuse at all. Agency actually denied any alcohol influence when asked." She says that, before she made the decision to adopt her children, she wishes that she knew "the truth about their treatment, medication, and background." After the adoption, she needed support services. She found them herself. Why didn't Suzanne go to her home study agency for help? She says "… I would not have trusted anything they said or sent anyway." What were Suzanne's prior expectations about the children? She says: "I knew things would be difficult for the first six months and had arranged for translators and school help, etc." What were Suzanne's prior expectations about family life after adoption? She comments: "I thought we be a family. RAD will not allow that. The girls' goal is to completely destroy anyone who potentially could be a 'loving force." Suzanne described her satisfaction level as ambivalent—ranging from very satisfied to dissatisfied. Her response to the question of whether she would have made the same decision to adopt both children if she knew about their needs and issues in advance was: "No, definitely not. I would have adopted one child only. The RAD issues are huge and one child is manageable. I was led to believe the girls knew each other. They didn't even know the other existed."

In October of 1991, Tracy and her husband adopted the first of two, unrelated girls, from Romania. They adopted their first child when she was three months old. Just over four years later, in December of 1995, the couple adopted their second daughter. This child was 3 ½ years old when the couple adopted her.

Case Narrative 5: Emotional and Other Stresses Resulted from the Adoption of Second Child.

At the time she completed the questionnaire, Tracy was in her late forties. Her husband was in his early fifties. Their daughters were about nine and eight years old respectively. In the questionnaire, she focuses only on the child adopted at age 3 ½ years old. It appears that this child lived all her life in an orphanage. Tracy reports that she had many problems that were noticeable upon her entry into the family. The child was immature, engaged in lying, stealing, cheating, and promiscuous behavior. Tracy describes her as behaving in a "superficial" and controlling manner, saying that it was difficult to form a relationship with the child due to the child's lack of trust. The child also had language difficulties. At the time she completed the questionnaire, Tracy states that this child still had these problems. She was receiving psychological/psychiatric and language services. Tracy reports that she was seeking, but did not yet have in place, services for the child's attachment issues. The home study agency the couple used did not require them to do any pre-adoption preparation. The agency also did not discuss any issues related to previously institutionalized children. Tracy says that she wishes they had been told about attachment disorder and other related issues before they made the decision to adopt this child. However, she is not sure that the agency that facilitated the placement "knew about these things in 1995, or even in 2000." About her prior expectations regarding her second child, Tracy stated: "That the child would be part of our family; that we would love her and that she would love us; that our other child [adopted first at age 3 months] would have a sibling and that these two would become 'friends' & 'sisters.'" About Tracy's prior expectations about family life, she responds: "We thought that life would be busy [twice as busy as before] and we were concerned that our older child, who had been the princess here for four years, might be jealous and have some adjustment problems—none of this, however, happened this way. There have been serious problems to be sure—but not of the type we anticipated." Tracy says that she is very dissatisfied with the decision to adopt the second child. Her closing comments elaborate: "Nothing much to add to this very complete survey—except to emphasize that parents must be educated about all the possible outcomes—including disruption, treatment [including residential], costs, emotional stress, etc., etc. Some parents may still choose to go ahead. I say this based on people I have met over the past couple of years, but clearly we would not have."

Case narrative 6 describes the experiences of Ursula and her husband. This married couple adopted two children domestically prior to adopting their third child, a boy, from Romania in July of 1997. Their Romanian son was adopted at three years old.

Case Narrative 6: Couple States "If Going Special Needs, We Would Have Gone Domestic."

Ursula was in her early forties when she completed the questionnaire. Her husband was in his early fifties. Their older children were then six and ten years old and their Romanian son was five years old. He was not adopted from an orphanage. Rather, he spent the first three years of his life in hospitals. He was first in a maternity hospital and went from there to a pediatric hospital. Ursula reports that this child had behavioral, psychological, emotional, and physical problems at the time he joined their family. She identifies the following behaviors: significant hyperactivity, impulsivity, and aggressive outbursts--biting, scratching, pulling hair, throwing things, screaming, screeching, spitting excessively. He rocked, banged his head against the floor, had major temper tantrums, sucked his thumb, and engaged in other self-stimulating behavior. He would wet his pants. She describes him as a very defiant child who refused to let anyone show or teach him things. He showed a very high tolerance to pain, was sensory defensive, and easily frustrated. He exhibited autistic-like behavior—staring at objects for long periods of time, playing with hands. He was delayed in speech and language skills. Ursula also states that he would approach total strangers and showed no fear of anything. Physically, he had vision problems (both near- and farsightedness) for which he needed glasses. He also needed minor dental work and to have two non-cancerous lesions removed from his tongue. He continued to have problems that required him to see a neurologist, a clinical neuropsychologist, participate in family behavior therapy, and take medication. He also sees an ear, nose and throat (ENT) doctor and a dentist. Ursula and her husband worked with a licensed agency in the state where they lived. The same agency did their home study and located their son. She reports that they did not check out the agency's record because they had used the same agency to adopt their first two children. However, they adopted their first two children domestically. Ursula did talk with three or four parents who had adopted a child from Romania through the agency they used. How similar her child was to the children adopted by these parents is unclear. The couple completed at least eleven hours of pre-adoption preparation through their agency. However, their agency only told them "very briefly" about the effects of institutional [e.g., hospital] living and early traumas on children's development and behavior. Ursula says that the agency also did not provide either accurate or complete information about their son: "Too many questions left blank & he has scars that we know nothing about." Prior to making their decision to adopt him, Ursula says that her agency should have "worried less about the paperwork & stressed more the known effects of orphanage living and early traumas on children's development and behavior. We also felt they only gave us part of the picture (he is very active) & not the reality of it all—i.e., he was truly special needs and would require a lot of time, patience, money, skills, etc." She also says that, before they made the decision to adopt their third child, they wished they had more information. They specifically wished to know about (1) their son's birth parents' religion, (2) whether he is really of Romanian origin; (3) why he was abandoned at birth; (4) if his family ever visited him; (5) whether he had siblings; (6) why he was in a hospital and not an orphanage; (7) why he was tethered to his crib; and (8) his activity level and behavior prior to being adopted. They wonder if their child was just "warehoused" or whether he had had any interactions with caring people during his first three years of life. After they adopted their son, they looked to their agency for services and support: "We called our agency repeatedly—sometimes in tears begging for help. We kept at them until they got us in contact with Dr. Ronald Federici. They offered basically no support or services from them except to meet the Romanian requirements." Ursula states her prior expectations about this child as follows: "Every child deserves a family. We expected to give extra attention to our last adoption. We knew he could have problems but we trusted our agency [after 10 years of dealing with them] to make the proper match. We never expected the problems we've encountered." Her prior expectations about family life appear reasonable: "More time directed to getting our son to learn English, catch him up on an educational level and learn how to be part of a family." Ursula describes herself as very dissatisfied with her decision to adopt this child internationally. When asked whether she would have adopted this child if she knew then what she knows now about his issues and needs, Ursula answered: "no, probably not." She provides the following explanation in closing: "If we were told about his special needs, we probably wouldn't spend a large amt. of money, go half way around the world, deal with a foreign language barrier, and not get any financial aid... If going special needs we would have gone domestic."

In November of 1997, Vivienne and Tom, a childless couple, adopted two unrelated children from Hungary— a boy age five years and a girl age twenty-three months. In their case narrative, the couple focuses on their experiences with their son.

Case Narrative 7: "Adopting Our Two Children Was a Package Deal."

Vivienne and Tom completed the questionnaire together. At that time, these respondents were in their mid to late forties (wife) and early fifties (husband). Their son was just over 7 ½ years old. They filled out the questionnaire focusing only on their son. Prior to being adopted, he had lived all of this life in an orphan-age setting. The couple reports that, upon entering their family, he exhibited multiple problems—including attachment disorder, PTSD, and ADHD. He had sensory integration issues and central auditory processing problems. Physically, he had a "tied tongue" (frenuleum attached). His problems required language therapy, speech therapy, psychological services, special education, and other services (for example, sensory integration therapy, behavioral optometry, and central auditory processing therapy). They ended up paying for many of the services this child needed themselves. Tom and Vivienne worked with licensed agencies in two different states. They put together this plan so that they could adopt from Hungary. They report that the (out-of-sate) placing agency they used was "one of the few that had a proven record of success in Hungary." They spoke with three or four other families who had adopted through that agency. They had contact with the agency director and the agent in Hungary who helped with the adoption. They state that their (local) home study agency had never set up an adoption from Hungary and usually placed infants. The home study agency was not familiar with the issues that a family adopting an older child from Hungary might face: "They did not realize our issues any more than we did." The home study agency did not require them to complete any pre-adoption preparation. The couple states: "Only cash was required."

The couple does not think that the placing agency/facilitator they used provided either accurate or complete information about their son's problems. They also state that the orphanage's monthly notes about the child were translated into English only after the adoption took place, not before. Tom and Vivienne explain how they felt pressured to go along with the adoption of their son in order to get their daughter. They state: "They were a package deal. We got them both or none; took the oldest even though [we] had second thoughts at adoption as [we] didn't want to lose [the] youngest—figured we would tough it out to work with (the) older one—didn't realize all it would entail; zero help from [the] state." What prior expectations did they have about their son? The couple states: "Some adjustment phase—deprived but able to be normal." What prior expectations did they have about family life? They mention an "adjustment phase, then normal with only adoption issues as child grew up and wondered about birth parents." Vivienne and Tom report being dissatisfied with the outcome of their son's adoption and indicate that, if they knew then what they know now about his issues and needs, they would definitely not have made the same decision to adopt him.

Case narrative 8 describes the adoption experiences of Wilma and her husband. This couple adopted two unrelated boys from Romania, both at twenty months old. They completed the adoptions in November of 1994, and in October of 1996.

Case Narrative 8: Couple Didn't Know Dissolution Was an Option.

At the time she returned the questionnaire, Wilma and her husband were in their early forties. Their sons were then about 11 ½ and 7 ½ years old respectively. Their older son had been in their family almost six years and their younger son, for four years. Wilma is not sure if either child had lived in his birth home. She believes that both children had lived in the orphanage virtually all of their lives prior to being adopted. She reports that her second son had no problems at the time of his entry into their family. However, the first son had uncontrollable fits of rage, especially at meal times. He was rarely happy or laughed. He had delays in both fine and gross motor skills and severe speech delay, diagnosed as Apraxia. He also had, and continues to have, psoriasis. He has the diagnoses of Attention Deficit Hyperactivity Disorder (ADHD) and Oppositional Defiant Disorder (ODD). He receives both psychiatric and psychological services on a monthly basis. He also receives speech therapy and special education services. He sees a dermatologist every other month to check on his skin condition. The couple worked with a licensed agency in their home state to do both their home study and to locate their sons. Wilma reports that she did not think about checking out the agency's track record and only talked with one parent who had used the same agency. She reports having contact with the director, the facilitator in charge of international adoptions, and a social worker at the agency. The agency did provide an English translation of Romania's foreign adoption policy before the couple adopted their children. The couple was required to complete no more than a few hours of pre-adoption preparation. They were not provided with information about the effects of early trauma on a child's development and behavior. About orphanage living they were told "it is nothing to worry about because they'll be just fine after a few weeks in your home." Wilma says that the information the agency provided about their first son was neither accurate nor complete. She states further that he "...should never have been eligible for adoption because his problems were so obvious and the mother left false info." When asked if she would have made the decision to adopt him if she knew in advance about his needs and issues, she says "no, definitely not." Wilma adds: "too much work, too much money, too much pain and heartache." When asked what the agency could have done better, Wilma states the following: "Told first-time parents what to look for re: delays & real behavior problems; could have told us about state agencies that provide free services." Wilma went back to her agency to ask for help and advice when her first child turned three and was diagnosed with Apraxia. She says that she got neither help nor referrals. "They said they would pray for me." Wilma also says that the agency should have suggested dissolution of the adoption and made her aware of options available through the state. What did Wilma expect about the children prior to adopting? She says: "Just that the literature from the agency said that they had 100% rate of providing 'healthy & normal' children. I just wanted healthy and normal—[child's name] is neither." What did Wilma expect about family life prior to adopting? She expected: "Raising my boys the way I was [morally and ethically] and to provide good opportunities for them. But that's one sided because all our $ goes towards [child's name] school, [child's name] doctors, [child's name] therapists, etc." Wilma describes her overall satisfaction to adopt her children as follows: very satisfied with the decision to adopt the second child, but very dissatisfied with the decision to adopt the first child. She explains her dissatisfaction further in her closing comments: "Raising a special needs child can be very expensive & heart-breaking. I wish I had post-adoption services four years ago when we realized how many problems our son has." Wilma also states, "Pre-adoption, I think there should be a law for all agencies to provide thorough background and health information on birth parents. If that info is not available, the child should not be eligible for adoption."

Case narrative 9 describes the experiences of Yvonne, who became divorced subsequent to adopting. In May of 1996, as a married couple, she and her (then) husband adopted two children, a boy and girl from Russia. The unrelated children were then five years, nine months and fifteen months respectively.

Case Narrative 9: Future Long-Term Residential Treatment Probable for Adopted Son

At that time they adopted, the couple already had a biological son. When Yvonne completed the questionnaire, she and former husband were both in the mid to late forties. The adopted children had been in their family for three years and were then ages eight years, nine months and four years, three months old respectively. Yvonne's biological son was twelve years old. Yvonne reports that her Russian son lived with his birth parents for at least two years. After their deaths, he entered an orphanage. She describes the early years in his birth home as horribly traumatic: The child "saw his mother murdered and was beaten by her and witnessed other shootings/violence. [His] mother was an alcoholic prostitute—we were led to believe otherwise as his birth parents were married and had 2 other kids— Dad died of unknown causes when child 1 was 2 years old." She also says that this child had been sexually abused in the orphanage. Her adopted son had behavioral, psychological, emotional, and other problems at the time he was adopted. He would urinate in lots of inappropriate places, smeared feces, was cruel to animals, and tried to kill his sister. He also reportedly shoplifted, stole, did damage to property. He lied and tried to manipulate others. Yvonne describes his behavior as reflecting Reactive Attachment Disorder (RAD), Oppositional Defiant Disorder (ODD), Post-Traumatic Stress Disorder (PTSD), and mood disorder. He also had "significant learning lags." She states that none of the problems resolved by themselves. He needed speech therapy, which his mother arranged, and language services that she was unable to arrange because ESL was not available in the school he attended. He needed and got special education services. This child also needed therapy for his RAD. He got therapy through intensive in-patient services in a children's psychiatric hospital in Evergreen, Colorado. Yvonne reports that most of his psychological issues were still unresolved at the time she completed the questionnaire—despite two weeks of intensive in-patient therapy and being on "lots of medication." She paid for his in-patient therapy out of pocket. Her daughter had lived in an orphanage all her life prior to being adopted. Despite coming from an institutional environment, Yvonne reports that her daughter had minimal problems at the time she was adopted. She mentions only mild sensory integration and speech difficulties. The sensory integration problem was resolved through occupational therapy. The child was getting speech therapy and was expected to continue getting this therapy for another year. The home study agency required the couple to complete between six and ten hours of pre-adoption preparation. However, this agency said very little about the effects of orphanage living and early traumas on children's development and behavior. The couple used a licensed agency in another state to locate their children. Although they did not think to check out the agency's record with that state's licensing board, they did talk to at least five others who had used their placement services. Yvonne states that the placing agency did not provide them with an English translation of Russia's foreign adoption policy. She also says that the information that the placing agency gave them about their son was neither accurate nor complete. Yvonne writes that she did not have any information about his experiences in his birth family before she made the decision to adopt him. Prior to the decision to adopt him, she says the placing agency should have "told us the truth about his early life & orphanage behavior." Yvonne reports that she is very satisfied with her decision to adopt her daughter but very dissatisfied with her decision to adopt her son. Regarding her Russian son, she says that, if she knew then what she knows now about his needs and issues, she would definitely not make the same decision to adopt him. About her prior expectations regarding the children, Yvonne states: "That they would love me." About her prior expectations regarding family life, she answers, "I expected we would be a complete family with the 3 children we always wanted. I was to be a stay at home mom to raise my kids & help them adjust but my husband asked for a divorce two months after our adoption." Yvonne says that she had considered disrupting her son's adoption "very seriously." She comments further:

"Future long-term residential treatment is probable & will not be paid for unless I relinquish parental rights."

Zoe is a married woman who was living separately from her husband at the time she completed the questionnaire. In July of 1993, she and her husband, a then childless couple, adopted a seven-year-old boy from Russia.

Case Narrative 10: Couple Seeks Permanent Residential Treatment for Son.

At the time she completed the questionnaire, Zoe was in her mid fifties. Her husband was in his early fifties. Their son was then fourteen years old. Zoe believes that he had probably lived in an orphanage setting all his life prior to being adopted. At the time they adopted him, she states that he had behavioral, psychological, and emotional problems. These problems included being hypervigilant, hyperanxious, and hyperkinetic. Zoe also describes her son as having bipolar disorder, psychosis (i.e., delusions of grandeur/fantasy), and Tourette's Syndrome (Tricotillamania). He needed special education and psychological/psychiatric services to help address his problems. The couple used an agency in the Midwestern state where they lived to do their home study and an agency in New England to locate their son. The local home study agency required the couple to do between six to 10 hours of pre-adoption preparation. However, neither agency told them about the possible effects of orphanage living, early abuse, and traumas on a child's development and behavior. Zoe reports that she checked out the placing agency's record "very carefully." She also talked with three or four parents that had used the agency's services. Zoe believes that the placing agency did not provide either accurate or complete information about her son's emotional and other inherited conditions. She states that the agency should have done so and should have given them the name of other parents to talk to who were dealing with a child with similar challenges. Their son needed services for his severe anxiety, ADHD, etc.—"at school, in the community, and at home." However, the agency did not assist them in getting the needed services or in finding an adoptive parents' support group. Zoe stated that she is very dissatisfied with the decision to adopt this child. Before they made that decision, she wishes she had known in depth about FAS/FAE, ADHD, Tourette's Syndrome, and bipolar disorder. Regarding her prior expectations about the child, Zoe stated: "Verbal—not LD (learning disabled)—musical. We would have dealt with ADHD but not mental illness!" Her prior expectations about family life seem reasonable: "Challenging but moments of fun and growth." Zoe's closing comments sum up the situation: "I've interacted with (mostly) moms of kids adopted from Russia/Romania at ages 4-8 [years] who've been in the U.S. 6-8 years—All have problems of one degree or another—AND NO HELP—state [and federal] programs are for domestic adoptees only. We are looking at having to put our son in [a] permanent residential treatment center- and he is not the typical 14 year old mentally ill kid that [is] house[d] [in centers for] our domestic bio/adopted troubled teens."

Concluding Statement

The parents in this chapter describe themselves as either dissatisfied or very dissatisfied with their decision to adopt at least one of their children internationally. It is interesting to note that half of the respondents who adopted two children report that their level of satisfaction differs considerably by child. They were very satisfied with one child and very dissatisfied with the other. In one family, feelings of satisfaction versus dissatisfaction operated like a roller coaster ride. Situational factors like how difficult or frustrating the day was mattered a lot.

The families in this chapter consist of seven couples and three "single" parents. The latter category includes one woman who never married, one who is separated, and one whose husband divorced her after they adopted internationally. The ten respondents in this chapter adopted a total of nineteen children. They speak only about their fourteen troubled children in their questionnaires.

At their adoption, the nineteen children ranged in age from three months to ten years old. The ages at adoption of the fourteen troubled children among them ranged from twenty months to ten years old. The median age of the nineteen children was twenty months old and of the fourteen children, around five years old.

Although four of the adoptees had no apparent problems and one child had minimal problems, 74 percent of the children had many, serious problems. These children had problems in most or all of the health, behavior, and other categories. Seventy-five percent of them had behavioral problems. Three of the respondents had each, unknowingly, adopted two troubled children simultaneously.

Discussion: Issues That Emerge in Chapters 6-8

These parents' words shed light on many of the key issues in the adoption of older children from Eastern Europe. Their experiences in discovering that their children had behavioral, emotional, and psychological problems raise questions about the issues of older domestic adoptees that enter new families after living in abusive and neglectful birth families, experiencing multiple foster care placements, and possible residential care.

In trying to make sense of these parents' experiences, it is important to view them in terms of the variations they reveal first about the child or children they adopted. These variations include age of the child or children at adoption; the child's pre-adoption experiences (neglect, sexual and/or physical abuse, witnessing violence) in his/her birth home and/or in the institutional setting (orphanage or hospital); number, type, seriousness, and duration of any problems—especially behavioral or emotional ones that the child had upon entry in to the adoptive family; length of time the child spent in the orphanage prior to being adopted; and the child's need for post-adoption services.

Five other factors follow. The sixth factor involves how well the agencies these parents used prepared and supported them mattered a lot. These parents got little or no help from their agencies. High quality pre-adoption preparation and knowledgeable, empathetic post-placement services and support are crucial in situations where people adopt children who have long-term behavioral and emotional problems. The seventh factor relates to how honest, knowledgeable, and helpful these parents thought the staff of the home study and/or placing agencies they used were about the child's/children's background, real issues, and likely problems. Eighth is whether or not parents believe that the information they got from their agency or facilitator about their child/children was accurate. Nine involved how complete they believe the information they got was. Parents reported major problems in both accuracy and completeness of information they got before they agreed to adopt their child or children. The tenth factor is parents' ability to obtain needed services and the costs involved with a child with many, severe problems, both financially and emotionally.

Linked to preparation and support is how closely parents' prior expectations matched what they thought their child/children and family life would be like. Did the prior expectations of the satisfied parents in chapter 6 differ noticeably from the expectations of those caught in the middle (chapter 7) and of the dissatisfied parents in chapter 8? The answer is no. The expectations of chapter 8 parents about their children and what family life would be like were about the same as for the parents in chapters 6 and 7. Chapter 8 parents, in general, expected a period of challenge and adjustment after which their child or children would settle into life with his/her new family.

How the parents in chapter 8 differ has less to do prior expectations and more to do with other factors, including their troubled children's many, serious, long-term issues; their lack of preparation to take on a child/children with these extreme needs; the lack of support for parents who adopted a child/children with serious, long-term special needs; and the lack of accessible services to help these children.

Children who have serious behavioral and emotional problems present challenges to the well being of family life and create parenting challenges on a daily basis. The parents and siblings of these children most definitely know that they have not arrived in Paris. The issues many of these adoptive parents raise about adopting older, formerly institutionalized children will be discussed further, along with other related issues, in subsequent chapters.

9

Parents Speak About State and Federal Government Involvement in Regulating Agencies Engaged in Placing International Adoptees with Americans

Although it is very big business indeed, international adoption has been largely unregulated at the federal level. That is, policy and practices with regard to adoptions are set by individual states. Except for federal requirements that pre-adoptive parents must meet and the regulations that define the meaning of "orphan" status, agencies, facilitators, and sending country officials set their own standards, both formal and informal, about which clients they accept and which children they refer to particular clients.

At this writing, the United States has not yet ratified the Hague Convention Treaty on International Adoption. Our tardiness in doing so places us behind other Western nations. Even when the United States signs the Hague Treaty, it remains to be seen how doing so will affect "doing business as usual" in the adoption industry.

Because governments are expected to protect their citizens from harm, I asked respondents a series of questions about what role, if any, the state and the federal governments should play in regards to the handling of international adoptions by licensed agencies that place children with American families. Respondents chose their position from among three possible stances. The governing body should play:

  a. No role;
  b. Speak out against abuses; or
  c. Establish and enforce a policy.

Table 9.1
Variations in Respondents' Support for a Hard-Line Stance for State and Federal Governments to Take on Selected Policy Issues, Reported in Percentages and Ranks[a]

	State		Federal	
Establish and Enforce a policy	%	Rank	%	Rank
Terminate or refuse to renew license	78	1	–	–
Impose Sanctions	72	2	75	1
Require agencies to obtain and disclose all known information before child is offered	60	3.5	68	2
Engage in more careful and regular oversight	60	3.5	–	–
Require all licensed agencies to educate pre- adoptive parents	58	5	61	3
Obtain feedback from adoptive parents about their agencies' handling of their adoptions	56	6	–	–
Establish a central federal agency to oversee international adoptions	-	-	33	4
Pressure officials in sending countries to engage in better oversight of international adoption practices	–	–	31	5

a.   Highest support for a state –level policy =1. Lowest support = 6.
wHighest support for a federal policy = 1. Lowest support = 5.
Respondents were asked items in bold about both the state and federal governments. Respondents were asked items in italics only about state governments and items in bold italics only about the federal government.

Table 9.1 summarizes the respondents' support for establishing and enforcing a particular policy by the state in comparison to the federal government. Support is measured in percentages. Table 9.1 also shows the rank of each statement as determined by the amount of support that respondents expressed. Low ranks indicate more support and high ranks, less support.

What Role Should State Governments Play?

Focusing only on the strongest stance—establishing and enforcing a policy—a majority (from 78 percent to 56 percent) of the respondents supported the following policy actions by state governments. The first column of table 9.1 illustrates the following: 78 percent of respondents said state governments should refuse to renew the license of agencies that have a pattern of unresolved problems; 72 percent said that states should impose sanctions on licensed agencies that have complaint patterns of misrepresentation and non-disclosure of information to pre-adoptive families; 60 percent said that state governments should require licensed agencies which place foreign-born children with American citizens to obtain and disclose all known information about the child/children before they make a referral to a potential family; 60 percent of adopters said that state governments should engage in more careful and regular oversight of agencies' policies and practices in handling international adoptions; 58 percent said that states should require all licensed agencies to educate pre-adoptive parents on the risks of adopting children from particular countries and non-infants from institutional settings; and 56 percent of these respondents said that state governments should obtain feedback about agencies' handling of adoptions from adoptive parents.

What Role Should the Federal Government Play?

Again, if I focus only on the strongest position, establishing and enforcing a policy, respondents' answers showed more variation when it came to the federal governments (Range = 44) than they did when the governing body was the state (Range = 22). The third column of table 9.1 shows parents' responses about establishing and enforcing specific adoption-related policies at the federal level ranged from a high of 75 percent (imposing sanctions) to a low of 31 percent (pressuring officials in sending countries). Close to the bottom was taking a hard-line position about establishing a central federal agency (33 percent).

Second highest support for the federal government establishing and enforcing a policy of requiring licensed agencies to disclose all information about the child/children at the time s/he/they are referred for adoption (68 percent). Third highest support was for requiring licensed agencies to educate pre-adoptive families on risk factors (61 percent).

In addition to being asked about several of the same areas as state government, I also asked respondents what, if any, role the federal government should play in two other areas: Pressuring officials in sending countries to engage in better oversight of the children offered for adoption and what pre-adoptive parents are told about them (31 percent of respondents said the federal government should take a hard-line stance) and establishing a central federal agency to oversee international adoptions (33 percent of respondents supported the federal government's establishing and enforcing a policy).

Comparison of Satisfied and Dissatisfied Respondents' Support for the Hard-Line Policy Stance

Satisfied respondents said they were either very satisfied or satisfied with the decision to adopt their child or children internationally. The "dissatisfied" category includes adopters who categorized themselves as dissatisfied, very dissatisfied, or so so with their decision. I use the percentage difference (or delta value) as the measuring rod for differences. The larger the percentage difference between the two categories of parents, the stronger is the association on a particular variable.

In general, dissatisfied respondents were more likely than satisfied ones to take a hard line position on the policy actions about which I asked. This observation is true for both state and federal policy actions.

State-Level Policies

I asked respondents their position on six policy actions states could take. The percentage differences between satisfied and dissatisfied respondents are shown in table 9.2. The largest percentage differences were about requiring agencies to provide pre-adoption education for prospective adoptive parents

(% Difference = 25), full disclosure of all known information about the child/children at the time of referral (% Difference = 23), better oversight of licensed agencies by state officials (% Difference = 22), and obtaining feedback from adoptive parents about how their agency handled the adoption.

(% Difference = 21%).

Table 9.2
Respondents' Support for a Hard-Line Stance on Specific Policy Issues
at the State Level by Satisfaction-Dissatisfaction With the Decision to Adopt
Their First and/or Second Child Internationally

	Satisfied Respondents		Dissatisfied Respondents		
Establish and Enforce a policy	%	N	%	N	% Difference
Terminate or refuse to renew license	76	63	86	19	10
Impose sanctions	70	58	82	18	12
Require agencies to obtain and disclose all known information before a child is referred	55	47	78	18	23
Engage in more careful oversight	55	46	77	17	22
Require pre-adoption education on risk factors	53	45	78	18	25
Obtain feedback from adoptive parents	52	43	73	16	21

I observed smaller differences between dissatisfied and satisfied respondents on imposing sanctions on agencies with a record of abuses (% Difference = 12) and on not renewing the licenses of sanctioned agencies (% Difference = 10).

Federal-Level Policies

Regarding federal involvement in policy actions, table 9.3 shows that the largest percentage differences between dissatisfied and satisfied respondents involved pressuring sending-country officials to engage in better oversight (% Difference = 27) and requiring licensed agencies to provide pre-adoption education (% Difference = 22). Regardless of whether respondents were satisfied or dissatisfied, the majority in each category supported establishing and enforcing a policy requiring full disclosure of information before a child is referred to a prospective adopter (% Difference = 12), and imposing sanctions on agencies which have a pattern of misrepresentation, and non-disclosure of information (% Difference = 3 for each). However, relatively few respondents were supportive of establishing a central federal agency to oversee international adoptions: The % Difference in each category was only three. Perhaps dealing with the United States Citizenship and Immigration Services (USCIS) was traumatic and frustrating enough to raise concerns about greater federal control of international adoptions.

Table 9.3
**Respondents' Support for a Hard-Line Stance on Specific Policy Issues
at the Federal Level by Satisfaction-Dissatisfaction with
the Decision to Adopt Their First and/or Second Child Internationally**

Establish and Enforce a Policy	Satisfied Respondents		Dissatisfied Respondents		
	%	N	%	N	% Difference
Impose Sanctions	75	(68)	78	(18)	3
Require agencies to obtain and disclose all known information before a child is referred	66	(61)	78	(18)	12
Require pre-adoption education on risk factors	56.5	(52)	78	(18)	21.5
Pressure sending country officials to engage in better oversight of international adoptions	25	(22)	52	(12)	27

Part III

Interventions and Policy Shifts

10

Impacts of Existing Adoption Policies and Practices: When Private Troubles Become Public Issues

The notion of adoptive family well being, the risks to that well being, and the fallout from family crises are considered further in this chapter. Here I link the adoption scenarios I described in chapters 8 (scenario 2) and 9 (scenario 3) to the ideas of troubles and issues.

Troubles Versus Issues

C. Wright Mills coined the term "sociological imagination" as a way to think about and understand the differences, and the connections, between a trouble and an issue. [1] Mills describes a trouble as event or phenomenon that people experience on the personal level. Whereas a trouble is regarded as private, an issue is a phenomenon in the public sphere.

By using the sociological imagination, Mills contends that "we can acquire a new way of thinking about the intersections between biography and history in society."[2] We also can gain insights about how to best address a trouble versus an issue. Specifically, private troubles can be addressed successfully through personal efforts at the individual level. However, the successful resolution or improvement of a public issue requires more than that individual effort. To deal with issues, collective efforts must be oriented toward the way societies and the institutions within societies operate (i.e., the structural level).

For example, consider the events of losing a job or falling into debt. The individual who loses a job or buys things for which s/he cannot pay is clearly experiencing a personal trouble. By extension, his/her family is also experiencing the trouble on a personal level. If we want to get to the root of the personal trouble, we ask: How did the job loss happen? Did the person complete work assignments in a sub-standard fashion?

Did s/he miss important meetings or fail to show up for work regularly or at all? If substandard work or absenteeism were major causes of the job loss, then the person's solution for keeping his next job is largely within his control—all other things being equal.

However, when many people in a town, state, or country lose jobs or cannot find work, unemployment becomes a public issue. The same is true about fiscal irresponsibility and national indebtedness. The major causes are different in these cases.

Economic conditions are usually involved in large-scale unemployment. For example, companies down size, relocate to a different area or part of the country, or go out of business. Therefore, solutions for dealing with mass unemployment must be structural rather than individual. Individual loyalty and hard work may not matter much in such circumstances. What matters more are tax incentives for a company to stay or relocate to a different state or the opportunity to pay workers in other countries less to do, essentially, the same job.

Similarly, when someone has many charges on his or her credit card and cannot pay the bills when they come due, that individual experiences indebtedness and all that goes with it—such as possible loss of a home or transportation to work—very personally. However, when overspending is due to fiscal irresponsibility on the part of an organization, or the managers of a city, or the governing body of a nation, indebtedness has moved to the level of a public issue.

Mills' idea of the sociological imagination is useful not only in helping us to distinguish between a private trouble and a public issue but also in shedding light on the possible intersection of troubles with issues. Although the private trouble and the public issue exist at different levels, they can bear an important relationship to one another. Thus, using the sociological imagination enables us to see personal troubles in a larger socio-cultural context and in a given historical time frame. Through the sociological imagination, we can grasp how social consciousness about phenomena defined as social issues is shaped. We can also identify policies that are (or should be) put in place to ameliorate the issue.

Unfortunately, Americans tend to look for individual explanations for events and to take a "blame the victim" stance in considering possible solutions, or in justifying non-solutions (doing nothing). Using an individualistic perspective is not sufficient to effectively address a public issue. Because the "sociological imagination" stands in marked contrast to the individualistic perspective, it is a useful tool for understanding the current issues and problems of adoption—both domestic and international, and for determining where solutions need to be directed.

Using the Sociological Imagination to Think About Adoption

Adoption is a good example of both a private matter and a public issue. Adoption is a private matter, first, because sizeable numbers of individuals and couples build their families, or attempt to do so, through adoption. Second, adoption is a personal matter because it is a relationship built on loss: The adoptive family's gain of a child occurs through a birth mother's or birth family's loss. Also, many couples only consider adoption when they realize that their dream of having a biological child or children is lost to them because of infertility. Loss and, ultimately one hopes, gain are also experienced profoundly and very personally by the adoptee. Feelings of loss are especially poignant among children adopted at older ages and who have memories of life in another family or another country. Birth parents that cannot raise their children because of financial, emotional, medical, or other problems experience private troubles. Yet, writ large, their problems reveal patterns and become public issues that influence not only their lives and those of their children but also the lives of those who attempt to re-parent these children.

However, adoption is also a public issue. First, this form of kinship is regulated through politics, policies, and practices which are not always in the waiting child/children's or the adoptive family's best interests. Who gets to adopt, the type and age of the child/children available to them is regulated by policies beyond their control. The model that has dominated adoption philosophy and practice presents images of adopters and adoptees. In this model, the adopters are a young, white, married, working-class couple. Once the adoption takes place, the wife, if she worked outside the home prior to the adoption, becomes a stay-at-home mother afterward. The adoptees are healthy, white newborns. This model needs to be updated to reflect the diversity of both interested potential adopters and of the children available for adoption. Second, adoption is a public matter because children whose early experiences compromised their mental health and functioning to a significant degree are at risk for continuing the cycle of abuse and neglect unless they receive appropriate interventions and services at early ages. The "complex baggage" and long term problems, which more than a few children carry with them into unsuspecting and unprepared families, has turned the adoption of many older children and of those who have spent a long time in an orphanage setting abroad into a major public issue. One indicator of the view of Eastern European adoptees as falling into the high risk category is the coverage that troubled adoptions from this part of the world have received in the popular media, both print and televised, since the mid 1990s.[3] Third, adoption is a public issue because discriminatory policies that make adopting domestically more difficult to accomplish push many families into the international adoption market where they may also face discriminatory adoption practices, abuses, and improprieties. For example who chooses the child/children for a particular family? What criteria do they use? How important is money in the process? Are the offered children the ones who have a good chance of functioning successfully in a new family or those with the worst kinds of problems and pre-adoption history? Abuses of fiduciary responsibilities on the part of unscrupulous facilitators and others can, and have, put post-adoptive family well-being at risk.

Important Negative Consequences of Existing Adoption Policies and Practices

The negative consequences of the archaic and discriminatory model described above are considerable and pervasive. The "other side" of adoption, therefore, involves problems both on the private, that is, micro, and on the public, or macro, levels. Policy makers and those engaged in placing children—especially children with behavioral and mental health issues—in adoptive families must recognize that the two levels are inter-related. The families in chapters 7 and 8 and some of those in chapter 6 are living with the effects of policies that did not result in facilitating adoptive family well-being.

Micro Level Consequences: Creating Families in Crisis

There are tremendous personal, emotional, and financial burdens involved in living with, and advocating for, children who have serious unanticipated, long term needs. In the worst position are people who have unknowingly adopted a troubled child and/or siblings that appear(s) to be "normal" on the surface but who actually have many needs and problems that are not obvious to the untrained eye. The children of whom I speak are the "walking wounded." Because they may carry their "wounds" on the inside, others do not see what their parents see.

Adoptive parents sometimes report being "stretched" to take on more children than they planned to parent (that is, to adopt a sibling set of three instead of two children or to agree to a "package deal" where, in order to get one healthy child, they also had to adopt a seriously troubled one). The practice of "stretching" can put an unprepared, uninformed adoptive family in a crisis situation.

Under the best of circumstances, good parenting is hard work. Now enter the realm of parenting, or re-parenting, a child or children who has one, or more, unanticipated long-term, special needs. Dealing with chronic medical/physical problems is difficult, but dealing with several children who have Reactive Attachment Disorder and other problems—including, for example, Fetal Alcohol Exposure, probable sexual abuse, extreme deprivation and neglect—is far more challenging. Children who have serious attachment problems cannot function normally within the intimate structures of family life. As infants, they never developed a trusting relationship with adults. They may have had to rely on themselves to survive. No adult may have ever offered them comfort. They may view parents in general as mean abusers and therefore, are unwilling to give up control to adults in a new family. Such children may act out in angry rages regularly, create daily chaos in the new family, and resist having their hearts "touched" by a loving parent. As many parents of non-infant adoptees have discovered, children who have attachment issues are so challenging to parent that even adopting one of them changes family life dramatically.

The parents of children who have attachment issues experience very high stress levels and typically get very little support either from their adoption agency or from the professional community—for example, from teachers, health professionals, and psychologists who are unfamiliar with attachment problems and their behavioral manifestations. Sometimes marriages break up. If other (birth or earlier adopted) children are in the home, they are also negatively affected on various levels—emotionally, in terms of school performance, etc.

Under the daily strains and stresses, families can literally fall apart. Some fall apart rather quietly through the parents' separation or divorce, through placing the child in a residential treatment facility, or through disruption of the troubled adoptee. Regardless, the fallout for these families is still deep and painful. For others, their crises may be public.

For example, in 1996, an adoptive mother in Colorado was convicted of the murder of her two year-old Russian born son. Her attorney argued that the child was scarred irreparably by his early life in the orphanage.[4] The jury did not accept that argument.[5] The adoptive mother was sentenced to twenty years in prison. Prior to adopting their Russian son, this woman and her husband were the parents of another son whom they adopted domestically and, apparently, whom she had parented successfully.

In December of 2003, a suburban Chicago woman, Irma Pavlis, the adoptive mother of a six-year-old Russian boy only "home" six weeks, was arrested for abuse leading to the child's death.[6] Pavlis and her husband adopted the boy and his five-year-old sister from Russia through an independent facilitator they found on the Internet. No allegations of abuse were leveled against Pavlis regarding the girl. According to Thais Tepper, Co-Founder of the Parents' Network for the Post-Institutionalized Child, at least twelve other murders of Russian-born or Eastern European adoptees were reported in the media through 2003.[7] In a more recent article, Freiss reports the number of deaths of Russian adoptees to America at fourteen.[8]

Some adoptive parents of international adoptees have been charged with cruelty,[9] child abuse,[10] and attempted child selling.[11] Others have been arrested and have had their children, biological and adopted, removed reportedly from their home without any compelling evidence against them.

More than a few such cases have been reported in the media in connection with families who have adopted older children from Russia. In one case that received widespread media attention, an Arizona couple, on their way home from Russia with their two adopted (previously unrelated) four year-old daughters, was arrested on charges of child abuse at Kennedy Airport. Passengers and crew on their flight alleged seeing them abuse the girls in their efforts to control the children's behavior on the flight.[12]

People's lives and reputations can be ruined through allegations of child abuse whether the allegations are substantiated or not. Despite stereotypes to the contrary, adoptive parents are less likely than birth parents to abuse their children.

Added to the emotional burdens are the financial costs of assessments and therapies that cost in the many thousands of dollars and which are generally not covered in health plans. Special needs children who are adopted internationally typically do not qualify for Supplemental Security Income (SSI) and may not qualify for state-supported medical assistance, unless their parents become low income. Their parents may also not qualify for, or cannot find, respite services to give themselves even a short break from the daily rigors of parenting. Sitters are virtually impossible to find for children who are difficult to manage or who are hyperactive. Moreover, since many of the children who are adopted at older ages and from the circumstances described above have problems forming and maintaining relationships with other children, they tend to spend much or all of their free time with their parent(s). Even with the best of intentions and effort, most families cannot provide the continuous level of structure that formerly institutionalized children both crave and require.

What the Research Says

Research on families and adoptees reinforces the importance of understanding the factors that can lead to increased parental stress and the risk of adoption disruptions. Canadian researchers compared a group of Romanian children adopted by Canadian parents with two control groups: Romanian adoptees that had spent less than four months in an institutional setting prior to adoption and Canadian-born non-adoptees.[13] The experimental group of adoptees had spent at least eight months in an orphanage setting before they were adopted. These researchers report that parenting stress can be predicted by variables related to the child and to the adoptive family. In regard to the former, these researchers include the number of behavior problems a child has and the security-ambivalence of attachment to the adoptive parents. In regard to the adoptive family variables, they identify income, mother's age, and number of Romanian children adopted into a family. One conclusion these researchers draw is that the relationship between parenting stress and the child's behavior problems was positive and "particularly strong."[14]

More recent research compares domestic special needs and Romanian adoptees.[15] This research also indicates that an early history of adversity and trauma—including physical and/or sexual abuse, severe neglect, and institutionalization on the part of the child, a prenatal history that places the child at-risk for poor health, developmental delays, and problems in psycho-social functioning all impact negatively on children's behavior at a later age. These researchers found that more behavior problems (of the child) were associated with a decrease in parents' satisfaction with the parent-child relationship.[16]

Other research on special needs domestic adoptees identifies sibling group adoption as an important variable associated with significantly lower family functioning.[17] These researchers developed a seven-variable model that accounted for about of 69 percent of the total variation in family functioning. They discovered that three variables accounted for over 52 percent of the total variation. In order of predictive power, these variables are sibling adoption (25.3 percent), number of child's behavior problems (17.08 percent), and the child's contacts with the law (10.52 percent). The other four variables in the model accounted for less than 16 percent of the remaining total variation: Spouse or partner support (5.36 percent), child's age at adoption (4.27 percent), relative support (3.73 percent), and school support (2.33 percent).

Considering the Alternatives

What do families do when they cannot cope with their child's problems, even after years of therapy and effort? Some consider terminating the placement and moving the child out of the family. Others may consider suing the agency for fraud or wrongful adoption.

Disruption and Dissolution

Disruption is defined as termination of an adoption prior to its legal finalization whereas dissolution is defined as the termination of the adoption after it is finalized.[18] Although domestic adoptions may end either through disruption or dissolution, in general, the term dissolution seems more apt to describe the termination of international adoptions in cases where the adoption decrees are finalized in the child's birth country before even living with the adoptive family.

Children adopted domestically live with their pre-adoptive parent(s) for a period of time, usually six months, before the adoption is finalized in family court. However, in the case of international adoptees, the child's birth country may require that the child/children be legally adopted there before s/he/they is (are) allowed to leave. This requirement has typically been the policy in Russia and in other Eastern European countries. Even with the recent change in Russian adoption policy, which requires parents to typically make two trips to Russia and to spend time with the child or children before they go to court, adoptive parents may not recognize problems in the short space of time they are interacting with the child during limited, pre adoption visits.

During the early part of the 1990s, it was not uncommon for children to be legally adopted in their birth country before even being seen by their adoptive parents and without the adoptive parents stepping foot in court. The adoption may have been completed in the child's birth country before parents could even learn more about the child/children or decide to refuse a placement that seemed like a poor match for them. In fact, a decision to dissolve an adoption may not be made for many months or even years after the child has lived in the adoptive family. Adolescence is usually the critical period for moving a troubled child out of the home either temporarily or permanently.

Disruption statistics on children adopted in the United States indicate that about 10 percent to 15 percent of adoptions involving children three years of age and older terminate prior to legal adoption.[19] Jewett points out that disruption of older child adoptions normally occurs when the child or children have had very damaging early experiences and where families do not anticipate adjustment problems.[20] Barth and Berry add the following variables to the at risk of disruption situation: families "with high expectations for immediate and full integration of the child into the family"; families where bonding does not occur; and families that are "stretched" beyond their expectations and ability to cope with previously undisclosed problems. [21] These researchers and others agree that emotional and behavioral problems of the adoptee are also strong predictors of adoption disruption.[22] Research on domestic adoptees adopted at older ages has shown that aggressive acting out, in contrast to withdrawn behavior, is a key predictor of disruption.[23]

In an in-depth interview study of twelve couples and three single parents of special needs children aged four to seventeen whose adoptions were disrupted, Schmidt, Rosenthal, and Bombeck identified six themes that, in their view, explain (were the causes of) the disruption: [24] themes/variables associated with the child include an inability to form an attachment to the adoptive family and difficulty letting go of the birth family and accepting their loss in this regard. Themes/variables associated with the adoptive parent include expectations of a less difficult child and unresolved infertility issues. Themes/variables associated with problems in pre-adoption information and post-adoption support include gaps in information about the child and his/her history and lack of social worker expertise and support of the parents regarding the problems that parents experienced with the child before his/her removal from the adoptive home and the issues they experienced subsequently. According to these researchers, the two most important themes were the inability of the child to attach to his/her adoptive parents, and the adoptive parents' expectations of a less difficult child. The single most dominant theme was the child's inability to attach. The following quote offers a telling snapshot of what life with these very challenging children was like:

Some children expected structuring of their lives as they had been structured in group settings and could not adjust to greater freedom, to less formal recreation, to making choices, to the interchange and the 'ups and downs' that occur in any family. Having memories of their own destructive, disruptive homes, they protected themselves from expected rejection with manipulation, baiting, lying, teasing, cruelty, withdrawal, arousing anger, and non participation. [25]

In contrast, these researchers identify variables that appear to predict a positive adoption outcome.[26]

The child variables are younger age of the child at placement, absence of behavior problems, and having no prior history of sexual abuse. The agency variable is providing complete background information about the child. Finally, being adopted by the child's foster parent is a predictor of a positive adoption outcome. The literature on special needs domestic adoptions also identifies two other variables that are important to the successful functioning of families that adopt older children: First is the involvement of parents in support groups was regarded as important by parents in reducing the risk of disruption, according to Rosenthal and Groza.[27] Others, writing earlier, also considered post-adoption support as important.[28] The second variable is developing flexibility in decision making.[29]

Statistics on the percentage of disruptions or dissolutions of international adoptees seem to vary, by country, child's age, and early circumstances. In an article in *The Boston Globe*, Joyce Pavao, Director of the Center for Family Connections in Cambridge, Massachusetts, was quoted as saying that international adoptions tend to "fail at rates similar to state placements... particularly when children come from orphanages or war torn countries."[30]

According to Barbara Holtan, former Director of Tressler Lutheran Services and a guest on ABC *Nightline*, adoptive parents of Russian-born children have sought to disrupt these adoptions in numbers previously unseen by the Tressler agency in their prior twenty-five years in operation. Holtan stated that in a 41-month period, Tressler Lutheran Services was approached to "replace" forty-three Eastern European adoptees.[31]

Estimates for the dissolution of Russian adoptees placed at older ages can be as high as one in five. Dissolutions, then, may not be as rare as some people think.[32] Based on anecdotal evidence, it appears that terminations of private agency adoptions center around the issue of unmanageable behavior problems. Serious, undisclosed health problems of the child may also be a factor in some adoption dissolutions.

Of course, an "intact" (non disrupted) adoption is no guarantee that it is a happy, successful one. Some parents, like Wilma and her husband in chapter 9, may hang in with their troubled children, because they don't know what else to do. Others may be embarrassed to acknowledge and talk about their child's problems, especially if they waited years to adopt. Still others may blame themselves for not knowing enough about their child's pre-adoption history—even though the information was not made available to them. Some continue to hope that their child's problems and behavior will "turn around" before too long.

Taking It to the Courts: Wrongful Adoption Suits

Wrongful adoption suits are a relatively new phenomenon in the adoption of domestic children and even more so in regard to international adoptions. However, such suits have become more common as the number of special needs placements has increased. Prior to 1986, disruption was the only remedy open to adoptive parents who claimed that their adoption agency had intentionally withheld, failed to disclose, or were guilty of "reckless and negligent withholding" of crucial information regarding their child's health or family background that might indicate a great likelihood of future problems. In 1986, in a case heard by the Ohio Supreme Court (Burr v. Board of Commissioners), the court ruled that "wrongful adoption was a valid cause of action against adoption agencies and that adoptive parents could recover monetary damages."[33] Since 1986, other states—including Wisconsin, California, Minnesota, and Arizona—have allowed adoptive parents to file wrongful adoption suits. By the early 1990s, dozens of adoptive parents had filed such suits.[34]

Wrongful adoption suits focus on an agency's actions, not just on problems, which a child may later develop.[35] According to the theory on which such suits are based, wrongful adoption suits are considered a valid course of action, because agencies are potential adoptive parents' only source of information about a child's medical and genetic background and are supposed to match a child's/children's needs with a family's preparation and capacity to give the child/children the care they need.[36]

In the case of children with special needs—medical or emotional and psychological—the agency's obligation to do careful matching with a family which has the desire, capacity, preparation, and support to parent such a child or children is absolutely essential. Recent research on children adopted in the United States indicates that failure to disclose seems especially prevalent in cases of physical and sexual abuse. These pre-adoption experiences and others—such as exposure to alcohol in utero [in the uterus] and a history of neglect, are also likely to be omitted from the pre-consent information given to prospective adoptive parents of international adoptees coming from countries where the risk of such background issues is likely to be high.[37]

The success of wrongful adoption suits is another matter. Based on available information about domestic adoption law suits, they are more likely to result in a financial award when an adopted child has a clear cut, documented medical condition, at-risk genetic background, or condition of the birth mother, which puts him or her at high risk and the agency knew about, but did not disclose, the condition or genetic background, to the pre-adoptive parents.[38] Suits which focus around less tangible or harder-to-document problems like emotional, psychological or serious behavioral problems do not seem to generate much jury sympathy.

Moreover, the geographic location of the court in which a wrongful adoption suit is heard may have bearing on the determination of agency liability for fraudulent adoption practices. For example, courts in the southern United States seem to be the least sympathetic in finding for the adoptive parents in such cases.[39]

Paying Attention to the Research

Published research on the risks to post-adoptive family functioning began to appear in the professional social work literature more than two decades ago. Recent research has expanded knowledge of the risk factors to adoptive family well being.

Why, then, hasn't this research been taken seriously and used to improve policies and practices in older-child adoption, both domestic and international? Unfortunately, the philosophy of "business as usual" still seems to prevail in the adoption industry. If most people conducted their actual businesses this way, they would be out of business! Resistance to change in the adoption field appears to be very strong. Despite this resistance, factors that predict the likelihood of successful adoptions and those which are red flags to likely problems should be acknowledged and incorporated into social work practice where they can be used as guidelines to assist and better prepare pre-adoptive families to make informed decisions about the particular child or children referred to them. Pre-adoptive parents need to be absolutely clear about the issues they feel they can (or cannot) manage.

Macro Level Consequences

Macro level consequences include social, financial, and other costs incurred by the state, federal, or local levels for services needed by increasing numbers of "special needs" children. Budgets for special education services will be stretched to the breaking point as more children with somewhat unusual special education needs enter a system unprepared for them. Such needs will go beyond ESL programs and language remediation. They will include teachers having to deal with children who have attention difficulties, possible hyperactivity, oppositional and disruptive behavior, and a host of other problems that impact on their ability to learn in traditional classroom settings. Costs to states for post-adoption services such as respite or CIS (Crisis Intervention Services), and residential care for children released into state custody will also increase. There will be an increased burden on the courts in handling wrongful adoption suits. The domestic child welfare system will be further strained by having to deal with the fallout from disrupted or dissolved international, as well as domestic, adoptions. In addition, caseworkers will spend time and effort involved in finding new families or placements for children in need of them. The will be costs to society in social services when children with severe mental health and behavior issues grow up into dysfunctional teens and adults.

The responsibility of paying for appropriate and expensive assessments, such as neuro-psycho-logical evaluations, assessments for sensory integration and central auditory processing problems, will be passed back and forth between school districts and health care delivery systems with the child and the family caught in the middle. Health care delivery systems will be pressured to increase mental health services and expand their coverage to include specialized and costly non traditional therapies, such as holding therapy. To be most effective, holding therapy needs to be done intensively and extensively. That is, therapists trained in attachment and bonding issues/problems should work with parents and the child intensively for a given period of time. The extensive component involves follow-up with a psychologist, for an unknown length of time.

Massive amounts of money and services will need to be earmarked to aid in the task of rehabilitating children, especially older children, who come to the United States with multiple problems including fetal alcohol exposure, pre-adoption abuse in violent families and/or institutions, neglect, and many months or years of their lives spent in institutions.

If business continues as usual, recent policies that offer states incentives to push the adoptions of older children from the domestic child welfare system will not result in the forever families politicians envision. Families that adopt older children domestically also require open, honest, in-depth preparation, post-adoption support, and access to needed services. Without high-quality, pre-adoptive training and the post-adoptive services and support adoptive families need, the well-being of families that adopt older, troubled children will be at risk—regardless of whether the adoptees are born in the United States or elsewhere. If these federal policies are to produce the desired outcome, the philosophy of "doing business as usual" must change.

When Private Troubles Also Become Public Issues: Concluding Statement

When people adopt an older child or children either through the state welfare system or internationally, they may find that their long awaited child has more serious problems than they expected because of undisclosed or unknown early abuse, severe neglect, and failed or broken attachments. Moreover, families typically get little or no help dealing with the child's special needs once the adoption is completed.

In families where the burdens are too heavy to bear, troubled adoptees may be released, albeit reluctantly, into state custody. If other families cannot be found, even with the promise of state subsidies, these children may be placed in residential care at considerable state expense. When they age out of care, many of these children find themselves on the street. Without multi-level and appropriate interventions in early childhood, children who lack any attachment to positive role models and who have a history of early abuse may develop the characteristics of sociopaths or psychopaths and turn into adolescents and adults who feel no guilt or remorse about hurting others and taking what they want when they want it without regard for the consequences.

Current adoption policies and politics have far reaching and long term consequences for children in need of stable families in this country and for people seeking to adopt waiting children. Because the private troubles of family dysfunction are also public issues, adoption policies need to be re-examined and improved. The beneficiaries of needed changes will be many.

Notes

1. C. W. Mills, 1959. *The Sociological Imagination.* New York: Grove Press.
2. Ibid, p. 7.
3. King, P. and K. Hamilton. 1997. "Bringing Kids All the Way Home." *Newsweek.* (June 16), pp. 60 65. Deane, B. 1997. "International Adoptions: Can Love Beat the Odds?" Woman's Day. (April 22), pp. 95 98. Horn, M. 1997. "A Dead Child, a Troubling Defense." *U.S. News and World Report* (July 14), pp. 24 26, 28.
4. K.D. Fishman. 1992. "Problem Adoptions," *The Atlantic Monthly* (September), pp. 37 39, 42, 45 46, 49 50, 52, 55 56, 59 61, 64, 66, 68 69; C. Lash 2000a. "Corruption, Lack of Regulations Have Resulted in Troubled Orphans: More U.S. Adoptions of Russians Fail." *Post Gazette.* (August 13), online; C. Lash 2000b. "The Boy They Couldn't Raise." *Post Gazette.* (August 13), online; C. Lash. 2000c. "Overwhelmed Families Dissolve Adoptions: More American Parents Find they Can't Cope With 'Troubled' Children." *The Post Gazette* (August 14), online; CBS News *48 Hours* 2000.
5. M. Romano. 1996. "Mother Arrested in Death of Child." Rocky Mountain News. (February 13); Horn 1997, Ibid.
6. USA Today 12/23/03: 3A; E. Peterson. 2003. "Adoptive Mother's Bond at 3 Million." *Daily Herald.* (December 23); R. Working and A. Madhani. 2003. "Parents Often Not Ready for Needy Foreign Kids." *The Chicago Tribune* (December 28), online copy; R. Working, R. 2004. "Adoptee Deaths Rare, Experts Say; 12 Russian Cases Troubling, Puzzling." *The Chicago Tribune* (May 21), online copy (5/24/04); R. Working and Alex Rodriguez. 2004. "Rescue of Boy Ends in Tragedy." *The Chicago Tribune* (May 21), online copy (5/24/04).
7. See Working and Madhani, ibid.
8. See Friess, Special to *USA Today* 9/13/05.
9. K. Prendergast. 2001. "Couple Accused of Cruelty to Adopted Teenager." *Media News Group, Inc.* (July 23).
10. K.Q. Seelye. "Couple Accused of Beating Daughters Tell of Adoption Ordeal." *The New York Times.* (Sunday, November 2), Section 1, p. 37.
11. S. Fragin. 2000. "Did She Try to Sell Her Child?" *Redbook* (May), www.redbookmag.com.
12. Horn 1997, Ibid.
13. Mainemer and others , 1998, Ibid.
14. Ibid, p. 164.
15. V. Groza and S. D. Ryan. 2002. "Pre-Adoption Stress and Its Association With Child Behavior in Domestic Special Needs and International Adoptions." *Psychoneuroendocrinology,* Vol. 27, No. 2), pp. 181-197.
16. Ibid, p. 195.
17. P. Leung and S. Erich. 2002. "Family Functioning of Adoptive Children With Special Needs: Implications of Familial Supports and Child Characteristics." *Children and Youth Services Review.* Vol. 24, No. 11, pp. 799-816.
18. J.A. Rosenthal and V. Groze. 1990. "Special Needs Adoption: Study of Intact Families." *Social Service Review.* (September), pp. 475 505.
19. J.A. Rosenthal, D. Schmidt, and J. Conner. 1988. "Predictors of Special Needs Adoption Disruption: An Exploratory Study." *Children and Youth Services.* Vol. 10, pp. 101 117;
20. C.L. Jewett. 1978. *Adopting the Older Child.* Boston: The Harvard Common Press.
21. R.P. Barth and M. Berry. 1988. *Adoption and Disruption: Risks, Rates, and Responses.* New York: Aldine DeGruyter, p.55.

22.   Sack, W. H. and D. D. Dale. 1982. "Abuse and Deprivation in Failing Adoptions." *Child Abuse and Neglect*. Vol. 6, pp. 443 451; W.J. Reid., R. M. Kagan, A. Kaminsky, and K. Helmer. 1987. "Adoptions of Older Institutionalized Youth." *Social Casework*. Vol. 68, pp. 140 149; Rosenthal, Schmidt, and Conner 1988, Ibid.

23.   Sack and Dale 1982. Partridge, S., H. Hornby, and T. McDonald. 1986. *Legacies of Loss, Visions of Gain: An Inside Look at Adoption Disruption*. Portland: University of Southern Maine; Barth and Berry, Ibid, 1988; Reid, Kagan, Kaminsky and Helmer, Ibid, 1987.

24.   D. Schmidt, M, J. A. Rosenthal, and B. Bombeck. 1988. "Parents' Views of Adoption Disruption." *Children and Youth Services Review*. Vol. 10, pp. 119 130.

25.   Ibid, 1988, p. 123.

26.   Ibid.

27.   Ibid, 1990.

28.   B. Tremitiere. 1979. "Adoption of Children with Special Needs—the Client Centered Approach." *Child Welfare*. Vol. 58, pp. 681 685. Elbow, M. and M. Knight. 1987. "Adoption Disruptions: Losses, Transitions, and Tasks." *Social Casework*. Vol. 68, pp. 546 552; Reid, Kagan, Kaminsky and Helmer. Ibid, 1987; K. A. Nelson. 1985. *On the Frontier of Adoption: A Study of Special Needs Adoptive Parents*. New York: Child Welfare League of America.

29.   R.M. Kagan and W. J. Reid. 1986. "Critical Factors in the Adoption of Emotionally Disturbed Youths." *Child Welfare*. Vol. 65, pp. 63 73; Rosenthal, Schmidt, and Conner. Ibid, 1988; and Sack and Dale, Ibid, 1982.

30.   J. Hart. 1997. "For Adoptive Families, Love Is Not Always Enough." *The Boston Globe* (May 14), Metro/Region, p. A1.

31.   This Nightline Episode aired on July 22, 1997.

32.   S. Saul. 1997a. "Broken Dreams/In Some Foreign Adoptions, Hope Fades To Hard Reality." *News Day*. (January 2), p. A05. S Saul. 1997b. "Agony Not Joy/Greatly Torn, Some Give Up Adoptees They Can't Handle." *News Day*. (January 3), p. A06; S. Saul. 1997c. "Couples Wait With Empty Cradles As Adoptions Stall, Agencies Taken to Court." *News Day*. (January 5), A08.

33.   M. De Woody. 1993. "Adoption Disclosure of Medical and Social History: A Review of the Law." *Child Welfare*. Vol. LXXII, No. 3 (May June), pp. 195 218.

34.   R. Cordes. 1993. "Parents Kept in the Dark Find Ray of Hope in Wrongful Adoption Suits." *Trial*. Vol.29, (November), pp. 12 14.

35.   J. Lewis. 1992. "Wrongful Adoption: Agencies Mislead Prospective Parents." *Trial*. Vol. 28, pp.75 78.

36.   Ibid.

37.   According to Lewis, Ibid.

38.   See De Woody, Ibid, 1993.

39.   According to the author's personal correspondence with an attorney in the state of Georgia, for example, the first decision from a Georgia court addressing fraudulent adoption practices (Eleventh Circuit Court of Appeals) appears to have been made in 1996. See Benfield, re Cesnik v. Englewood Baptist Church, private correspondence, July 5, 1996.

11

Mapping Changes Needed
in Adoption Policy and Practice

In order to achieve important, structural, and long-term changes in adoption policies and practices, so-called "personal" problems must become politicized as "public" issues. That is, what appear to be a small number of adoptive families with problems must be recognized as only the "tip of the iceberg." In this chapter, I provide a rationale for why interventions and policy shifts are necessary and where changes must focus. I discuss the basic assumptions and activities of two models for handling adoptions. This chapter links material I discussed in chapters 1 and 2 with the solutions and strategies that follow in chapter 12.

The Traditional Model for Handing Adoptions
in the United States

The traditional model operates around the processes of supply and demand and involves three actions. On the supply side are babies and young infants who need permanent families. Numbers of babies may vary depending on social, economic, political, and cultural conditions. On the demand side are potential adopters who want to parent a newborn or young infant. In the traditional model potential, adopters are young, married, childless, and the same race as the prospective child. In terms of social class, prospective adopters who adopt through child welfare (public) agencies are expected to be working or lower-middle class. The prospective father works outside the home. The prospective mother may or may not be employed. If she is, the expectation is that she will quit her job and be a full-time mother once the child is in the home.

The traditional model for handling adoptions consists of three actions. In Action I, the potential adopter makes contact with a social worker or home finder in the adoption agency or adoption unit of the child welfare system. In Action II, gatekeepers screen potential adopters, using traditional criteria and a "front-load" emphasis. That is, the home study focuses on qualifying potential adopters as "fit" to parent a newborn or infant. There is little or no pre-adoption preparation for the new parents. In Action III, the social worker or home finder places babies with adopters s/he defines as suitable. There are short-term follow-ups until the adoption is finalized. There are no post-placement services of support offered or discussed for the child or the adoptive parents.

A Rationale for Changes in the Traditional Model

The rationale for why interventions and policy shifts are needed hinges on three central issues. First, the traditional model of adopters and adoptees that dominates adoption practice and, at least implicit policy, is too limited. The pool of potential adoptees and adopters has changed dramatically. Second, appropriate pre-adoption preparation is essential. The policy and practice of placing non-infants and/or siblings with a history of pre-adoption traumas into unprepared families puts more than a few adoptive families at risk of adoption failure. Third, access to appropriate post-placement services is also essential for children with pre-adoption histories of neglect, abandonment, and abuse. Unfortunately, not enough of the right kinds of services are available to, and obtainable by, post-adoptive families that need them.

Where Changes Must Focus

Revamping Adoption Policy and Practices by Creating a New Adoptee/Adopter Model.

The working model built on infant adoption by a childless, young, heterosexual couple of the same race, ethnicity, and similar social-class background needs to be expanded. The revised model must include adoptions of non-infant children and of sibling groups whose members have suffered early trauma and loss, whether domestically or abroad. The revised model also needs to reflect diverse types of potential adopters and of family structures. In addition, the model needs to be placed in a socio-cultural context. Community resources such families are likely to need and where and how these resources can be accessed are an important component of the revised model.

Restructuring the Adoption Process

Policy and practice changes must insure that the adoption process, both domestic and international, becomes less arbitrary and less discriminatory regarding who gets to adopt and what kind of child/children s/he/they are offered. The process itself must become more open and more egalitarian. As it stands now, the adoption process has significant power inequities. Gatekeepers who have access to a large pool of potential adoptees can qualify, or deny access, to specific adopters. They hold most of the power. If asked, most prospective adopters would probably state that they have little, or no, power in the adoption referral and placement processes. The personal and financial lives of prospective adopters are scrutinized in depth. Their home is surveyed not only as to its condition, but also regarding the number of bedrooms and bathrooms it contains. The screening process is focused on the would-be adopters. If they are deemed "fit to adopt," sooner (or later) they may get a referral of a particular child or children. They may state a preference for a child of a specific gender, general age, and/or race. Often, however, they are not told how particular children are selected for prospective parents. They may receive a picture of a child and a brief medical statement as to his/her physical health. Health conditions may be identified. In adoptions from Eastern Europe, for example, some conditions may be generic to adoptees slated for international adoptions. These conditions may or may not be accurate for the referred child. Other important conditions, like FAS/FAE, PTSD, etc. may be omitted entirely. They pay most of the costs of (international) adoption up front, file their papers with the U.S. government, then wait to be summoned to travel to meet their prospective child or children. Once in the child's birth country, even if things do not appear "right," few families feel comfortable enough to raise questions or to complain about irregularities.

Increasing Accountability to Clients

Placing agencies or facilitators must be more accountable to prospective adopters up front. They should aim to maximize opportunities for success from the outset through careful screening of adopters (but not based on the presence or absence of traditional characteristics) and by doing high-quality assessments of potential adoptees' backgrounds, issues, and needs before they refer him/her/them to a specific adoptive parent or family. Home study agencies or social workers must do better preparation in the pre-adoption phase.

Moving from a Reactive to a Proactive Stance

In a reactive stance to a fire, for example, we race around trying to put it out. We may put the fire out "successfully," but the outcome in terms of loss of possessions and life may still be disastrous. In a proactive stance, we develop precautionary measures that reduce the likelihood that a fire will ignite in the first place or, if it does, that it can be put out with a minimum of risk and loss. Both adoption agencies/facilitators and governments, both sending and receiving, must move toward informed action when it matters most.

Identifying and Promoting a New Role for Social Workers:

There needs to be a major philosophical shift in social work practice. This shift must focus less on gatekeeping and more on partnering with families both before and, if needed, after the adoption takes place.

A Different Model for Handling Adoptions of Older, Special Needs Children

The supply of potential adoptees includes children in the domestic child welfare systems, available through private agencies operating domestically, and both infants and older children born in other countries. The children available domestically may not be infants, may include siblings who need to be placed together, may be minority or racially mixed, and may have long-term special needs. Regarding children available for out-of country adoption, there is a sizeable pool of adoptees under age one, or between one and two years old available for adoption in some sending countries. There are sizeable numbers of older children, sibling groups, and children with long-term issues available from Eastern European countries. Racial and/or cultural differences are likely between adoptees born abroad and their adoptive parents.

On the demand side, potential adopters may or may not be married, are often highly educated (college degree and beyond) and middle to upper-middle-class in regard to socio-economic status, often white, age forty or older when they apply to adopt, include racially-mixed couples, and homosexuals as well as heterosexuals. This model consists of eight phases or actions, most of which occur during the pre-adoption stage.

The Pre-Adoption Stage

Action I involves the potential adopter making contact with an adoption agency or facilitator. Sometimes, prospective adopters surf the

Net for prospective agencies and children. Others may get information about specific agencies by attending an adoption conference or through a friend.

Actions II –VI involves the home study agency or social worker in four kinds of activities. First, they qualify the potential adopter as an acceptable adoptive parent. Second, they match the child's/children's need to potential parents' strengths and resources (financial, emotional, social, etc.). Third, from the placing agency's in-country facilitator or other reliable sources, they secure detailed information about the referred child's pre-adoption history and health—including physical, behavioral, and emotional health. Fourth, the Home Study agency trains potential adopters on the issues and risks of adopting a child or children with the referred child's issues and needs. Fifth, they secure pre-adopters' informed consent before proceeding with the adoption.

If the goal of adoption is really centered on the "best interests" of the child/children, then failing to prepare pre-adopters adequately works against that goal. The level and quality of pre-adoption preparation needs to be enhanced because the risk to the success of non-traditional adoptions (that is, older-children and siblings, or multiples, placed in the same family at the same time), is much higher than for traditional adoptions (that is, a single newborn or young infant adopted by a young couple).

The Adoption Stage

In Action VII, the child/children is/are placed with the new parent(s).

The Post-Adoption Stage

Action VIII focuses on follow-up visits by the home study agency and information about services (i.e., medical, educational, therapeutic, respite, etc.) and support (i.e., emotional, social, financial, etc.) available in the larger community.

Couples who adopt today may not be childless. They may already have birth children or a child adopted in infancy (by at least one of the parents) already in their home. Their expectations about parenting an older, adopted child may be based on their experiences with the child or children they parented from birth (let's call this the "normal" child model, for want of a better term). Childless pre-adopters may use their own childhood experiences and the child-rearing practices of their family as their working model for how they will raise their child/children. However, as experts like Keck and Kupecky[1] point out, their experiences and expectations may not match the older-adopted child's/ children's reality. It is not uncommon for these parents to find that the child-rearing techniques that worked before fail miserably for children coming from traumatized pre-adoptive backgrounds. What happens then is that previously well-functioning families find themselves in a crisis situation.

Families who adopt children who have behavioral and emotional issues that people outside the family do not see (because the child behaves very differently with them) or do not understand are often blamed for their children's problems. To understand families in crisis, it is necessary to understand the intersection between the private lives of families and the public domains that intersect with their lives. By public domains, I mean the neighborhood, school, doctors' offices, even extended family members and "friends."

Needed Services Must be Available and Affordable

Family crises can be avoided or reduced in severity by being proactive. Success in obtaining services assumes that the needed services are appropriate (for their child's real problems), available (in or close to the community in which they live), and affordable (covered, at least in part, by health insurance or another available plan). When families in crisis cannot obtain the services they need in a timely fashion, family functioning continues to spiral downward.

Developing Greater Positive Community Involvement is Essential

The community plays an important role in the success or failure of older-child adoptions. In one of the last issues of Rosie,[2] an article appeared described an interesting experiment in foster and adoptive family living. A nurturing community was created where adoptive parents and their children, pre-adopters, foster parents and their foster children lived. Service providers were in close proximity. The community was small enough for re-create the best features of the gemeinschaft.

The benefits of Model II in working toward the "best interests" of children and of the people/families who adopt them are clear. Can Action VII of this model work in already-existing communities? I believe that it can. To work, such communities need a "critical mass" of empathetic resources. The resources are both human and financial. In regard to the latter, money needs to go where it is most needed—into post-adoption support (including respite) and services—especially specialized mental health and special education services.

Who has the responsibility of supporting children and their families, however formed? What role(s) should states play in supporting the "best interests of child and their families?" Besides families that are committed to adoption, alliances of groups and entities at the micro and macro levels are necessary. Enter the politics (alliance) of members of the "new triad" comprised of adoptive families; agencies and the service providers linked to them; and governments (at the federal, state, and local levels), foundations, and other funding sources.

Many writers use the "village/community model" as the structure through which positive change to occur. In her book entitled *Nobody's Children*,[3] Attorney and adoptive parent Elizabeth Bartholet wrote about the plight of children in the U. S. foster care system that are in need of permanent families and what she believes can be done to make this a reality. I agree that we all need to be concerned about children that need and want "forever families." Our concern must be local, national, and global—more so in some cases than in others, for example, orphans, runaways, dysfunctional birth parents, abandoned children. Bartholet's premise should be extended to children born in other countries whose birth parents have the same kinds of problems—poverty, alcoholism, drug addiction, for example, as do the biological parents of many children in the U. S. foster care.

Concluding Statement

Adhering to rigid policies and practices that need to be revised, which harms rather than helps both the children placed in adoptive families at older ages and the people who adopt them, is both unrealistic and unethical. Maintaining the "status quo" can be compared to a "finger-in-the-dyke" approach to reality of adoption in the twenty-first century. As in the story of the boy and the dyke, the "finger" will not hold back the momentum of the floodwaters waiting to break through and overwhelm those in its path.

Notes

1. Keck, G. C., R. M. Kopecky and L. G. Mansfield. 2002. *Parenting the Hurt Child: Helping Adoptive Families Heal and Grow*. Colorado Springs, Colo: Pinion Press.
2. Shapiro, M. 2001. Faith, Love, Hope. *Rosie Magazine*, 128, 7 (May) p. 150-60.
3. Bartholet, E. 1999. *Nobody's Children: Abuse and Neglect, the Foster Care Drift, and the Adoption Alternative*. Boston: Beacon Press.

12

Solutions and Strategies that Are Linked to Clients' Rights and Agencies' Responsibilities

Adoption of children who need families—whether domestic or international—is sound social policy. However, adoption policies that truly operate in a child's best interests require careful grounding in relevant research. All three members of the traditional adoptive triad: birth parents, children in need of a family, and the adoptive parents, have rights.

In this chapter I focus on the rights of children in need of adoption and of the people who adopt them. I will also address the responsibilities of home study and placing agencies to their clients—in this case, both to the child and to the family that adopts him or her. In doing so, I will integrate clients' rights and agencies' responsibilities with important solutions and strategies. Finally, I will discuss my recommendations for the role that governments can play in improving policies and practices in international adoption.

The Rights of Prospective Adoptees

Children of any age for whom adoption is deemed to be the best solution should be placed with adoptive parents in an expeditious manner. As attorney and adoptive parent Elizabeth Bartholet points out: "Delay in adoptive placement has been regularly proven to be the single most important factor affecting adoptive adjustment."[1] Therefore, it is important that children available for adoption not be viewed as commodities to be marketed to the highest bidder or as the property of a birth family or of a country. It is in the best interests of the potential adoptee that, regardless, of age, s/he be viewed as having the rights of a person.

These rights include the following: First, children who are old enough (for example, as early as age three) to understand that they will be placed in an adoptive family and will not be reunited with their birth parent(s) should be consulted about this decision. Some children may really want to be part of a family. Others may really only want a safe place to live until they can be independent. The latter may not desire, or be able, to function adequately within the intimacy and expectations of life in a family on a full-time basis. The conclusion drawn by some is that an adoptive family might not be the optimal placement for all (i.e., older, severely traumatized) children who cannot live with their biological parents.[2] In such cases, other options like long-term, therapeutic foster care should be considered. Community resources need to be developed where children can get the support they need at least until they reach age twenty-one.

Second, children who are adopted from institutions, at ages beyond infancy, have the right to the best chances of a successful adoption outcome. Success includes being prepared for life in a family different from the one they may have known in their early years. To increase the chances of adoption success for non-infants, interventions that socialize children into family living should be in place before older children are adopted either domestically or internationally. Third, once adopted, children should have easy access to a range of post-placement services geared toward helping him/her deal with "adjustment" problems that continue for longer than six months. Issues and problems that linger are likely to be much more complex and deep-seated than adjustment issues.

The Rights of Prospective Adoptive Parents

Prospective adopters have the right to be treated with respect and have their strengths and limitations taken seriously as potential adopters of a particular child or children. As people who have been pre-approved to adopt—that is, to parent, they should have the right to a good faith effort by their placing agency, facilitator, and/or the orphanage director to do the best possible job on their behalf. Doing the best possible job includes learning and passing on to pre-adopters everything known about the child, his/her background, and circumstances of placement in state or orphanage care in advance of the pre-adoptive parent(s) accepting the referral of a child or children. Providing full and accurate information to prospective adoptive parents is vital to the success of both domestic and international adoptions. Full disclosure of information is especially important for the success of older-child adoptions, especially when a child has serious medical, psychological, behavioral, and/or emotional problems or comes from a family with a history of serious problems including, for example, alcoholism, drug addiction, mental illness, or retardation.

Second, pre-adoptive parents should have the right to know if a child was removed from a birth family because of abuse and/or neglect or was voluntarily placed for adoption due to economic or other reasons. Third, if one, or both, birth parent(s) is/are known to be deceased and information exists about how they died, this information should be shared in the pre-adoptive stage, before prospective adopters agree to accept a particular child. Fourth, prospective adopters should also be informed in depth about the known effects of orphanage living on children's development, behavior, and ability to attach to them.

The right to informed consent is especially important in international adoptions. In this type of adoption, prospective adoptive parents often accept a child or children based only on minimal information: a picture, a sketchy written report, and a facilitator's statements or assurances about a child whom adoptive parents may meet for the first time only when the adoption takes place in the sending country.

Although very young children and those from non-abusive and non-institutional backgrounds may adapt to family life and attach to adoptive parents relatively easily, this outcome is neither easily accomplished nor guaranteed for older, previously maltreated, and formerly institutionalized children, or for children who have experienced multiple moves in the foster care system before being adopted. Therefore, the accuracy and completeness of the information made available to prospective adoptive parents in advance of their accepting a child or children are vital to the child's/children's future well being and to the right to informed consent and adequate preparation of the adoptive parent(s) to take on the challenge of parenting, or re-parenting, an adopted child or children.

The Responsibilities of Agencies to Pre-Adoptive Parents With Whom They Place Non-Infants and Special Needs Children

The discussion that follows assumes that the agency that does the home study agency may not be the agency that locates and places the child/children. In cases where the same agency does both the home study and arranges the placement, the agency's responsibilities should be easier to manage and to track.

Agencies or licensed social workers that do home studies have an obligation to be knowledgeable about the issues involved in international adoption, especially of older children, and about the risk factors and other concerns for children adopted from certain countries. They also have a responsibility to prepare pre-adoptive couples and individuals adequately, realistically, and to alert clients to key issues and areas of possible concern regarding the child/children and the country from which they plan to adopt. They have a responsibility to link prospective adopters with other families who have adopted a child or children with similar issues or problems before these clients adopt. They should offer or have links to a variety of services that the child and/or family might need after adopting. Since home study agencies are always located in the state where the clients live, they should expect to be involved with the family on an as-needed basis for more than six months.

When placing agencies are not the ones that do a pre-adoptive couple's or individual's home study, the placing agency needs to work "hand in glove" with the home study agency to be sure that all known information about the children or children being offered is passed on both to the prospective adopters and their home study social worker for review and discussion. This information should include the child's physical, mental, and emotional health, and behavior in the orphanage, length of time spent in the orphanage and/or other settings such as hospitals, medications and treatments the child received while in the institutional setting(s), the child's family background and known risk factors like alcoholism and/or drug addiction, whether s/he suffered physical or sexual abuse, other trauma, or parental neglect. If a child has known or suspected special needs, the home study social worker should discuss with the clients the availability, or lack of availability, of services likely to be needed and how they might be arranged. The latter should include discussion of projected costs and sources of likely payment, including out of pocket costs.

The literature on older-child domestic adoption indicates that some agencies that place children with special needs have not been doing a good job of informing and preparing parents, and supporting these high-risk adoptions. As parental dissatisfaction and the filing of wrongful adoption suits in cases of domestic adoptions show, the problems that adoptive parents have encountered in the way special needs placements have been handled are not unique to international adoption agencies.[3]

In a survey of ninety-one families who had adopted domestically in the state of California, Barth and Berry found that 20 percent of the families said that their agency did not do anything to help them learn more about adoption.[4] In a study of 171 families who had adopted special needs children domestically, Nelson reported that six in ten families said that their agency did not prepare them adequately for the adoption.[5] This researcher identified the two best predictors of an adoption's "success." These predictors are the child's ability to attach to his/her adoptive parents and parents' satisfaction with agency preparation. In both of the studies, parents who did not feel that the agency did a good job of preparing them most often cited "inaccurate or insufficient information about the child, including his past experiences and his current functioning."[6]

Parents who feel that there is a significant mismatch between what they expected from adopting, or from the child, and what actually happened are at high risk for disruption, especially when the unanticipated problems include the child's failure to attach to his/her new parents and his/her continual behavior problems. The two problem areas are often related because children who do not attach continually test, thwart parental authority/control, act defiant—even at a very young age—argue, throw frequent tantrums, and refuse to respond to parental discipline. According to McKelvey and Stevens, to increase the chances of a successful adoption "... experts agree that adoptive parents must be handpicked to fit the child's needs, know the risks from the very beginning and have help preparing for the challenge."[7]

Unfortunately, it appears that adoptive parents are too often not provided with either accurate or complete information about the child they agree to adopt and the circumstances of his/her background before they make that decision and sometimes even afterward when they are struggling with serious, unanticipated problems. Once the adoption is completed, the file may be sealed and obtaining important information, especially from a foreign bureaucracy thousands of miles away, may be impossible.

What Placing Agencies Can Do to Make Adoptions of Older, Special Needs Children Work Better

In this section, I identify and discuss nine ways in which placing agencies can increase the likelihood of successful adoptions. My first recommendation is that placing agencies obtain all information known about an identified child before the agency refers the child for adoption. The placing agency should present all information about the child and his/her/their birth parents to prospective parents in writing before the latter make a final decision to adopt the child/ children. Placing agencies should send prospective adopters the information before they send any pictures of the child/children to the prospective adopter(s).

Agencies and facilitators that place children from orphanage settings, especially in Russia and other Eastern European countries, must work hard[er] if they are to work in the best interests of the children and the families who adopt them. Specifically, agencies should engage in five important actions: in regard to the first action, agencies should obtain all available information on the child/children before they are offered for adoption. No information should be condensed or omitted. Sources outside the orphanage should be tapped as necessary to provide as complete a history as possible. Included should be birth information, known biological family information, physical and emotional health of the child, any behavioral or other issues the child has, details about the child's life, routine, and interaction with both children and adults in the orphanage. They should also verify, to the extent possible, the accuracy of the information they pass on to waiting families. Finally, agencies should improve ways to evaluate and successfully place for the long run at-risk older children and sibling groups.

If agencies really listen to parents expectations, obtain all the information known about the child/children, and present this information in an open and honest way before people agree to adopt, then parents feel that they have given their informed consent to the adoption and are more likely to "tough it out," if problems which they anticipated do arise. Sending prospective adopters a picture or videotape of the child before, or even along with, the information places vulnerable prospective adopters at a serious disadvantage. People look first at the picture and "fall in love" with the child as they imagine him/her to be, rather than how the child may really be, "baggage" and all.

In regard to the second action, once prospective adopters have identified a sending country from which they hope to adopt, the placing agency should provide to the prospective adopters, in writing, an English translation of that sending country's international adoption policy. The placing agency should also identify all known risk factors for children available for external adoption from that country. Prospective adopters need to know the extent and seriousness of specific risk factors to which the child they may adopt is potentially exposed.

Third, before a child is offered to a prospective family for adoption, placing agencies should evaluate the child for serious, long-term medical, emotional, behavioral and other problems. Because children adopted internationally, especially at older ages, in siblings groups, or simultaneous (unrelated) multiples from deprived backgrounds comprise a segment of adoptees who are in the high-risk pool for physical, behavioral, emotional, and/or other problems. Therefore, better (more accurate and more complete) evaluations must be done before children are offered for adoption. These evaluations must be done by western-trained physicians who use terminology with which western pediatricians and parents are familiar. Diagnostic procedures should include an assessment of the child's physical, mental, and emotional health and development. Areas of concern should be identified. Likely chronic or long-term problems and issues must be pointed out along with recommendations for treatment. The likely consequences of this recommendation are reduced risk of dissolution and lowered stress in adoptive families.

Fourth, adoption agencies should match parents' expectations and abilities/strengths with the child's needs. Both home study and placing agencies listen to what prospective parents say they can and cannot manage/accept. Agencies must be open and honest about the child's actual and likely needs and issues as well as about the child's early history and all information known about birth parents.

Fifth, placing agencies should ensure that pre-adoptive parents spend a sufficient amount of time getting to know the child and his/her daily routine, likes and dislikes, and typical behavior before the adoption is finalized in the sending country. Both the prospective parents and the child should be given time to get comfortable with each other and to start the attachment process while the child is still in familiar surroundings. A few hours or even several days may not be enough time. Although parents may be anxious to get their child/children home, it is in their best interests and that of the child to get as much experience with, and information about, the child from the people who know him/her best before they leave. Once they leave, it will be too late to learn more. After the adoption, the child's original records will very likely be sealed.

Sixth, home study agencies should prepare prospective adopters realistically in the pre-adoption phase. In situations where prospective adopters use a different placing and home study agency/social worker, who should prepare prospective adopters for the issues and needs which their child or children may have? The dilemma arises especially when people use an out-of-state agency to locate their child/children but an in-state agency or social worker to do their home study. Is adequate pre-adoption preparation the responsibility of the home study agency or the placing agency? For families in such circumstances, I take the position that adequate pre-adoption preparation should be primarily the responsibility of the home-study agency. This is the agency that should have the "best interests" of both the prospective parents and their child/children at heart. They are not the ones "marketing" the child. The home-study agency should work, however, in conjunction with the placing agency or facilitator. The latter agency or facilitator should operate in good faith and be proactive in getting and presenting to the prospective parents all of the information known about the child, his/her early life experiences, etc.

Getting the consent of a prospective parent to adopt a particular child or children without adequately preparing him/her/them to parent a child or children who may have long-term special needs is not enough. The majority of adoptive parents who participated in my study recognized that international adoption may involve risks for which prospective adopters need to be well prepared before they adopt and well-supported in the post-adoption years through access to appropriate services.

Thus, agencies need to go beyond qualifying would-be adopters as potentially suitable parents [front-end efforts]. They also need to "arm" prospective adopters with information about where and how to get and to pay for the services their child might need: how to locate a support group, obtain respite, deal with obtaining special education services, and so on [back-end efforts]. It does take more than a family struggling alone to raise special needs children and to help them to become self-sufficient adults to the fullest extent possible.

Seventh, both placing and home study agencies should encourage prospective parents to adopt, at a single time, only the number of children that these individuals realistically think they can parent well. Ames and her colleagues recommend that "Pre-adoption preparation should generally include advice to adopt only one child at a time" and that parents who adopt children from institutions be given specialized preparation.[8] These researchers, and other medical doctors skilled in assessing adoptees born abroad, also recommend that children adopted from orphanages be considered, at least initially, as having special needs. People who adopt special needs children must be ready to commit to a higher level of care and advocacy for them as compared to those who parent children who do not have special needs. According to Ames and the other members of her research team, the results of their investigations of Romanian adoptees to Canada suggest that the best predictor of later problems is the goodness of fit or match between the child's needs and the family's resources. Family resources include time, energy, money, the willingness to seek out and acquire relevant knowledge and expert help, access to services, and likely support from family and friends.[9]

This may mean that the agency encourages prospective adopters to adopt one child at a time. Pre-adoptive parents should take this recommendation seriously unless there are compelling reasons for agreeing to adopt more than one child simultaneously. Compelling reasons might include the need to adopt strongly-bonded siblings together; the financial issues, and added emotional costs to the adopters and the children, of adopting siblings separately; the ages of the prospective adoptive parents; and the health risks to one or more of the children if they do not receive appropriate, specialized medical treatment in the U.S. expeditiously. No prospective adopter should be intimidated or "stretched" into taking on more children than she/he/they can handle.

Raising a special needs child or children is very draining, especially when the children bring serious behavioral and psychological problems into the family, in addition to their other needs. It is also inside the family that the problems are usually intensified, despite the monumental efforts parents are making on a daily basis. So much energy goes into managing day-to-day living that there may not be much [or any] of the anticipated joy and fulfillment they thought life with children would bring after a "brief" period of adjustment.

Attachment takes time to build on both sides. But parents who are struggling to deal with the numerous needs of "high-maintenance" or "challenging" children will not have much energy left to work on building attachments. They may also not have much energy left to take care of their own needs and their adult relationships. "Putting out fires" may be all they seem to be doing.[10]

Ames and her colleagues also recommend that prospective adopters should adopt the youngest child possible.[11] This recommendation can be interpreted as suggesting that, all other things being equal, a younger child will generally have spent less time in an abusive and/or deprived environment, experienced fewer changes in caretakers, and, therefore, has a greater likelihood of attaching successfully to his/her adoptive parents.

Eighth, home study agencies should be able to provide or arrange post-placement support and/or services to adoptive parents and adoptees in need of support and/or services. Arranging, or helping families that need it find, post-adoption support, should also be the responsibility of the home study agency. Neither the home study nor the placing agency should assume that their responsibilities to the adoptive parents and the children are over once they have obtained their fees and the parents get their child/children.

The obligations of agency to the family should continue after the adoption takes place. In cases where prospective adopters used a different placing agency from the one which did their home study, the home study agency should "build" into their fiduciary responsibilities post-placement support. The money for such support can come from the state, private foundations (like the Casey Foundation, The Dave Thomas Foundation), or adding a nominal fee to the cost of home studies to build a pool of "seed money" to support families in need of post-adoption services.[12] Linking parents to local or to on-line support groups should also be part of the post-adoption service. Agencies should organize workshops and conferences of relevant topics and invite families to attend. The bottom line is that the link between the local agency and the family should be as long-term as families want or need. Parents should not be judged negatively if their children came to them with problems which they can't "fix" on their own.

What Facilitators, Placing Agencies, and Their Staff in Sending Countries Can Do to Make the Adoptee's Transition to His/Her New Family Smoother

The concept of mutuality or reciprocity underlies good relationships. For someone to get along well with another person, the two people should be compatible and choose each other. We get to pick our friends based on this idea, why not our families in the case of older adoptees. Instead of a birth mother or an adoption facilitator picking a family for a child, why not empowers the older child to be partner in the selection process? This is really not a new idea. However, it is a fundamentally important idea. In placing international adoptees, placing agencies should do the following: first, encourage officials or orphanage directors with whom they work in sending countries to release for adoption children who have the best chances to succeed in families rather than those whose chances of successful adjustment and attachment are low to unlikely. I do not wish to be construed as elitist because I am not. I do, however, take the position that older children who need, want, and can make it in families are the ones who should be targeted for speedy adoption. In the case of younger children, the child's issues and problems, including information about family background, should be used to help deter his/her likelihood for successfully fitting into a new family.

Policies or staff that target children who have many and or serious emotional, psychological, behavioral, or other problems for adoption are putting those children at risk for failure and the families that adopt them at risk for becoming dysfunctional and overwhelmed. Neither the best interests of the child or his/her adoptive family are served in this case.

Second, agencies should allow older children born outside the United States to give their consent to being adopted outside their birth country.

In this regard, children have rights that should be respected. They have a right to consent to being adopted by people outside their homeland. Some older children may not want to leave their birth country even if the "tradeoff" is an opportunity to get a new family. They may believe (or may have been told) that their biological parent(s) will be back to get them someday. Or, they may believe that this parent needs them and that they (the child) shouldn't leave their birth country. Perhaps they have siblings in another orphanage or have formed attachments to other children in their orphanage. The prospect of losing these ties may be overwhelming.

Third, agencies should offer an older child the opportunity to say yes or no about being adopted by a particular family. The child may have "pictured" the family that she or he wants. Perhaps the child hopes for an older brother or sister, loves animals, or wants to live on a farm. Just as with locating a child for a family, placing agencies should make an effort to locate a family with whom the child can feel at home. Finding a family with which she or he can connect is a step in the right direction. Even in situations where the exact match to a child's wished-for family cannot be found, a child whose wishes are taken into account will feel respected and part of the decision making process. She or he "becomes" part of that new family by choice.

Fourth, placing agencies should assist in preparing previously institutionalized children older than seventeen months to enter their new families. Children "with a prior history" of abuse, neglect, family violence, and so on must be prepared to enter and function in their new family. The family should also be supported through therapeutic and other services afterward.

For children coming from orphanages in sending countries to families in the United States, this means moving the child into a short-term foster arrangement in the sending country—for a period of at least three months, before she or he is adopted. During this transition stage, the child would observe and be involved in interaction with the foster parents and their children. The foster parents and social service staff in the sending country would also be preparing the child for their permanent placement.

Older children need to be "introduced" to their permanent family during this period. Because of the distance involved, the introduction may be through pictures, letters, and possibly, through some phone calls.

In as much as they are able, children placed beyond infancy should be allowed and encouraged to "accept" the new family as theirs. They should be told clearly that the parents who are coming to take them home are not the ones to whom they were born, as many children are confused and angry at "mama" and "papa" for putting them in an orphanage or abandoning them.

Children also should not be told unrealistic things about what their life in America will be like, as often seems to be the case before they leave the orphanage for America. For example, orphanage staff has been known to say things like: "Your new parents are rich"; and "They will buy you everything you want."

"You will have fun all the time." The staff may be well-intentioned. However, building up false expectations only creates disappointment and anger in children and causes problems in families where children's expectations are not fulfilled.

Practices that Work Replacing Ones that Do Not Work For Children

The emphasis in this section is on children adopted beyond infancy. Children who are well prepared to enter a family and who understand what life in a "normal" family is like will be less stressed than those who are operating on a fantasy model or who have negative view of all parents as likely to be "mean" or abusive. Children who lived in dysfunctional, violent families before they entered the orphanage or who lived in an orphanage for their whole life are at greater risk for adjustment problems in their new family than are children who have been able to develop positive relationships with adults and who are looking for such relationships with their new parents.

For Pre-Adoptive Parents

Others have established that children who have experienced neglect, abuse, and trauma in their early lives embody the essential meaning of "special needs" children.[13] Add to these the experience of spending months or even years in an institution (orphanage or hospital) where they probably received little stimulation and enjoyed little or no interaction with staff other than receiving caretaking for their basic needs. Children who have these kinds of pre-adoption experiences comprise a segment of the potential adoptive population who are at high risk for physical, behavioral, emotional, and/or other problems.

It follows, then, that adoptive parents who know what to expect once a child with these risk factors becomes part of his/her new family and are as well prepared as possible to meet the child's needs and deal with his/her issues and potential problems are less likely to be stressed out than are parents who do not know what to expect or who have adopted a child or children with many more issues than they can handle. Good matching of the child's needs with parents' abilities to meet those needs is essential. Realistic pre-adoption preparation is also essential as is getting all known information about the child/children in advance of making the decision to adopt him/her/them. Access to resources and support services are also important stress reducers.

What does not work is have facilitators or agency staff sugarcoat or minimize facts or leave out information about the child's physical health, emotional issues, behavior, etc. What also does not work for people who adopt troubled children is "selling" parents a fantasy of what life will be like in the future, saying that the prospective parents are strong enough to handle anything, or that [their] love will conquer all. Parents who are prepared for the "worst case scenario" but find that their child is in much better shape than they expected will be very pleasantly surprised and far less stressed than those parents who expected their so-called "healthy" child/children to settle into the family after a reasonable period of time, but who discover that his/her problems are much more serious and long-term than they were told or expected.

Unless a pre-adoptive parent is specifically looking for a special needs child, he or she expects that the child s/he adopts is healthy. Such parents hope to have a "normal family life", but the likelihood of this being true for people who adopt children with emotional and behavioral problems is slim. Raising children is very hard work and raising children with problems is even harder.

What also does not work is a "kill the messenger" mentality: denying that the child had problems, because they are not readily visible to the stranger or untrained eye and/or blaming the adoptive parents for their child's/children's problems or for not being able to fix their problems.

For Post-Adoptive Parents

In the post-adoptive phase, parents of troubled children need services and support. They may need various kinds of support and services for years. Typically, these parents have gone to numerous health care and other providers before they find one or two who really seem to understand, and may be able to help, their child.

Adopters of special-needs children become quite good at distinguishing friends from foes. These parents may lose friends and even relationships they used to have with family members because these adults "just don't get it." True friends help or, at least, offer some form of support.

Foes criticize, blame, dismiss, and avoid people coping with challenging children.

What Roles Should Governments Play?

Clearly, governments should be proactive as much as possible. Decisions are being made that affect people's lives for the long run. Thus, governments should safeguard the well being of its citizens by anticipating potential problems. They need to have structures in place to deal with adoption problems efficiently and humanely. As you saw earlier, some adoptive parents believe that governments should involve themselves as little as possible in regulating international adoption. They fear that red tape will increase and access to adoptable children will decrease or be delayed. Others think that government interventions in the United States should be more at the state than at the federal level since the former have traditionally regulated domestic adoptions. Still others consider the pros and cons of government involvement in regulating agencies and facilitators that place children as a "safety net." Both adoptees and adopters need protection from unscrupulous facilitators and placing agencies. However, better protection will probably come with its own costs or negative effects. Pressure groups may sway decision makers into making it more difficult for citizens of a given country to adopt internationally rather than making the process more open and equitable. What the net result will be as government becomes more involved remains to be seen.

I take the position that both the state and the federal governments need to engage in better regulation and oversight of adoption agencies' policies and handling of international adoptions. These are the areas where government involvement can make a positive difference.

Recommendations for Actions by State Governments

State governments, in particular, need to require that all persons (that is, facilitators) and agencies that locate, refer, and/or place either domestic or international children for adoption be licensed, not only in the state in which they are located (that is, have a business address) but also in all states in which they conduct business (that is, actually place children). It is becoming more and more common for potential adopters in one state to work with a facilitator or a placing agency located in another state or another region of the country. In such cases, the adopters may not meet in person with any of the people who are locating and referring a child or children to them for adoption. Business is conducted through telephone calls, letters, and direct bank transfers of money. Requiring facilitators and agencies to be licensed not only in the state where they are located, but also in every state where they do business will aid in protecting people from signing on with unscrupulous or incompetent out-of-state facilitators or placing agencies.

State governments also need to engage in rigorous, regular monitoring of the practices of all adoption facilitators and adoption agencies licensed in the state. State licensing agencies currently do very little to oversee agencies engaged in international adoptions once they are licensed. Oversight functions need to be separated from, but related to, licensing and license renewal. Moreover, the practices of international adoption agencies need to be monitored continually. One way is through random phone calls to agency clients who are in various stages of the adoption process and after placement (at three months, six months, one year, eighteen months, two years).

State governments should require all licensed (domestic or international) adoption agencies to engage in the following five actions: first, provide a written guarantee that they have exhausted all reasonable, available channels (hospital records, social services, etc,) in searching for information on the child they offer and that the information they, or their foreign representatives, have presented to prospective parents is complete and bona fide.

Second, post bonds for full satisfaction of performance. The bond will be held for at least six months after the child/children has/have been in the adoptive home. If a family finds that it needs to disrupt an adoption (after the six-month bond period has ended), the agency should agree to find an alternate placement for the child (with a guarantee of full disclosure to the new parents of the child's problems). The agency should, in such cases, bear the cost of all fees to secure an appropriate new placement.

Third, pay stiff penalties for deception/fraud if they are found to have engaged in misrepresentation, concealing information, or for engaging in any other wrongdoing. Such penalties could include the agency's obligation to pay for therapies or treatment for a child's/ children's undisclosed medical, psychological, emotional, or behavioral problems. The amount of the agency's financial obligation could be up to the full cost of the adoption fee—including a payback of all monies paid directly to the agency, its affiliates, or facilitators by the adopting parent(s) unless the adopting person(s) choose(s) to accept an alternate child who is available through the same agency and this decision results in a satisfactory placement. A second penalty could be the loss of license for a pattern of such abuses (legitimate complaints).

Fourth, agencies should provide/arrange for post adoption services at a reasonable fee level. These services would include more than one or two visits by a social worker or to a therapist. The services would be oriented toward assisting families in making adjustments, identifying problems, and securing outside/additional services.

Fifth, agencies should post a full public statement of finances yearly. This statement would include an accounting of how all monies are spent (staff salaries, fees, gifts, or equipment to foreign personnel, officials, orphanages, etc).

Sixth, state governments should limit portion of fee to be paid in advance of the actual adoption [based on the date of court legalization] to 50 percent of the fee. The remaining 50 percent will be paid to the agency within ninety days if the adoptive parents agree that the adoption is successful.

Seventh, states should standardize fee structures across agencies for adoptions within a given country. Fees would change only if the foreign country raised its overseas fee or some component of it.

Eighth, states should require that agencies freeze or limit on fee increases while a pre adoptive couple or person has been registered with the agency and is waiting to adopt (for at least a twelve month period). The only legitimate reason for a change in fees during this period would be an increase required by the sending country levied on all people who are adopting there. The agency should make every effort to process waiting parents' adoptions before fee increases take effect and to notify other clients promptly of the fee changes. Clients who have not yet had a child assigned to them should have the option to choose a different country with no more than a minimal financial penalty.

Ninth, states should make available a "disaster" fund at the state level—paid for by a tax on private adoption agencies engaged in international adoption placements and through a percentage of the fees collected by the B.C.I.S. for processing clearances, exit visas and other fees involved in international adoptions. The purpose of this fund is to assist families with extraordinary problems/expenses of their adopted children, especially in cases where the placing agency or facilitator they used has gone out of business.

Tenth, states should offer post-adoption resources for people who adopt troubled children. Such resources should include, for example, respite services, state-subsidized insurance for adoptees to supplement adoptive parents' private health coverage. State-subsidized coverage is especially important for children who have long-term mental health and behavioral problems. A second resource for seriously troubled adoptees would be to get appropriate treatment, including out-of-home placement, without the parent(s) being required to give up his/her/their parental rights, even temporarily. Eleventh, states should locate and work with private agencies, in and outside their state, to facilitate the re-adoption of children who must be removed from their first adoptive family.

Finally, states should institute an independent, bi partisan "watch dog" group, composed primarily of adoptive parents and others who have no financial stake in adoption, to monitor state regulations and agency performance.

Recommendations for Actions by the Federal Government

The federal government needs to create a central registry of agencies and facilitators placing children with American families. I agree with the Hague idea of developing a central registry of all licensed adoption agencies operating in the United States. This registry would serve a variety of functions, such as collect and make available to interested parties the track record of agencies engaged in international adoption; collect and maintain up-to-date, detailed statistics on children adopted both domestically and internationally, as well as on adopted children living in residential placements and identified as either returning back home or not expected to return home, and on disrupted/dissolved adoptions.

The central registry would also provide vital information about an agency's history, staff, policies, number and types (newborns, older, special needs, etc.) of children placed annually and from what countries, fee structure, and conduct an annual overall performance rating for each facilitator and agency regarding client satisfaction with the agencies' policies and practices.

The federal government needs to revisit the purpose of the tax incentives it offers Americans to adopt. Should tax credits be available to all taxpayers who adopt? Or, should incentives only be geared toward helping singles and couples who adopt special needs children only, either domestically or internationally? Why not introduce a retroactive tax credit for people whose children are really special needs, although they were not identified as having special needs when the parent(s) adopted him/her/them and the tax credit deduction came into effect after the adoption was finalized. Incentives would be offered per special needs adoptee as long as the child is under twenty-one at the time the parents apply for the credit.

Recommendations for Actions by the State and Federal Governments

Both the state and the federal governments should engage in better "front-load" protection efforts for adopters and adoptees. These efforts should include, first, requiring all agencies that place children with American citizens to make full disclosure of the child's/children's actual health problems, background issues/family history in advance of consent to adopt [i.e., obtain true informed consent]. I agree with Johnson, Edwards, and Puwak (1993) who encourage international adoption agencies to do clinical assessments and more rigorous health examinations of children before they refer the child/children for adoption. Well-done assessments are clearly a good way to identify learning delays and other problems that already exist. However, I take the position that agencies and facilitators engaged in the business of adoption should be required by law to do these assessments and examinations, rather than just encouraged to do them.

Second, governments at both the state and the federal levels should negotiate disincentives for officials in sending countries to process adoptions "in country" before the adoptive parents actually meet, and interact, with the child. Although Russia has moved toward discontinuing the practice of processing adoptions before adopters even meet the child/children, this practice should be declared illegal everywhere. Adoptions should not be processed or considered legal until the adopting parent(s) see the child/children in person and interact(s) with him/her/ them intensively for a "reasonable" period of time. The amount and quality of contact that is defined as "reasonable" should be flexible enough to cover a range of situations. For example, interacting with an infant is very different than trying to get to know a toddler or an older child. Also, the pre-adoption histories of some children available for adoption make the length and quality of pre-adoption interaction with a prospective adoptive parent(s) of paramount importance.

Third, both levels of government should be involved in trouble-shooting major adoption problems, especially adoptive parents' claims of serious improprieties or wrongful adoption. After an independent assessment claims and evidence against an agency, governments should prohibit the principals (owners or Board of Directors) of any agency that has gone out of business to avoid lawsuits and without completing all adoptions for which they were paid from operating as an adoption agency under another name or in a different state. No one who has been an owner, served as a top administrator (Director, Associate Director, CEO, or board member unless the latter was on a volunteer basis and involved no financial remuneration by, or financial interest in, the agency) of an agency which closed under the circumstances identified above should be allowed to own, have a financial interest in, or take a salaried position in another (newly licensed or existing) adoption agency. Some issues are immediately apparent. Others are not.

States should offer mechanisms such as arbitration to resolve disputes between adoptive parents and placing agencies/facilitators in an expeditious and satisfactory (to the adoptive family) way. Adoptive parents should not have to rely only on an agency specific grievance process with no "bite" in it or on the costly and lengthy process of taking an agency to court in a wrongful adoption suit.

Finally, both the federal and state governments should fund longitudinal research on the outcomes of older-child and sibling-group adoptions in comparison to infant adoptions. At the federal level, this research can be supported through National Institute of Mental Health (NIMH) or another federally funded agency. Longitudinal studies must investigate the long term effects of early deprivation and institutional care on children's development, their prospects for a normal life, and their ability to function in a family. This research should be application-oriented in that it develops an enhanced list of predictors of adoption success and failure to be used in training personnel who place older children and service providers who support adoptive families in crisis.

Notes

1. E. Bartholet, 1994. "What's Wrong With Adoption Law," *Trial* (February), pp. 19 23.
2. E. Cole. 1985. "Permanency Planning—A Better Definition." *Permanency Report* (Summer), p. 4; Jewett 1978, Ibid.
3. McKelvey, C. A. and J. Stevens. 1994. *Adoption Crisis: The Truth Behind Adoption and Foster Care.* Golden, CO: Fulcrum Publishing; DeWoody 1993, Ibid; Cordes 1993, Ibid; Lewis 1992 Ibid; L. Belkin, 1988a. "Adoptive Parents Ask States for Help with Abused Young." *The New York Times* (Monday, August 22); L. Belkin 1988b. "Adoptive Parents Lose Court Case." *The New York Times* (Sunday, November 13).
4. Barth and Berry 1988, Ibid.
5. Nelson 1985, Ibid.
6. M. Berry, 1990. "Preparing and Supporting Special Needs Adoptive Families: A Review of the Literature." *Child and Adolescent Social Work.* Vol. 7, No. 5 (October), pp. 403 418.
7. McKelvey and Stevens, Ibid, 1995, p. 49.
8. Ames and others, Ibid, 2000, p. 36.
9. Ibid, 2000, pp. 37-38.
10. Credit this phrase goes to Helmut Reinhardt.
11. Ames and others, Ibid, 2000, p. 33.
12. Cited from a Report of a Conference on Post-Adoption Services, December 7-8, 1995. This conference was sponsored by Casey Family Services. Specific reference is to statements made in Workshop XI: Joyce Maguire Pavao, Presenter.
13. See Johnson, Ibid, 1997 and Ames and others, Ibid, 2000.

Part IV

Producing Positive Changes
for the Long Run

13

Bringing about Changes that Are in the Best Interest of Adoptees and Their Adoptive Families

Adoption has finally come "out of the closet." This type of family formation has changed from being a once-secret kinship to a celebrated event. For the first time in its history, the most recent census of the U. S. population included information about adoption as a demographic characteristic.[1]

With President Clinton's legislation of 1997, adoption assumed a preeminent place to foster care as the former is viewed as providing stability and permanence and the latter, temporary care. According to Modell, a surprising element in the Clinton legislation is that adoption also assumed preeminence over reunification as a goal for children in need of a stable and loving home.[2]

Attitudes and Views about Adoption, Adopted Children and Adoptive Parents

How much have attitudes and views about adoption, adoptive children and adoptive parents changed? Although Benet states that adoption was accepted more readily in the United States than it was in Europe, where the hereditary notion of status was strong, it seems she believed that adoption was only marginally accepted in the U. S. The following quotation captures the flavor of Benet's conclusion: Adoption is

> ...viewed as second best, as something that is not 'supposed' to happen. It is, in most people's minds, an indication that the child's original parents failed to care for him, and that his adoptive parents failed to have their own children.[3]

The primacy of the blood tie appears to underlie the negative attitudes or notions which adoptive parents often feel others have about them and their adopted children. Cohen reports that the primacy given to the blood tie was obvious in the social work literature of the past.[4] It was assumed that the blood tie was essential for good parenting.

Although Benet wrote about adoption about thirty years ago and Cohen about twenty-five years ago, it seems that not much has changed in regard to societal and clinician attitudes toward adoption, adopted children, and adoptive parents. While surveys of non-adopters show support for adoption, Americans appear to be, at best, ambivalent toward adoption. At worst, they stigmatize both the adoptive parents and the children they adopt as different, somehow less, not a "real" family.

Writing more recently, Bartholet points out that these notions continue to parallel clinician's views of adoptive families and those embedded in adoption law.[5] Adoptive families are viewed as second best to families based on blood ties. The law still emphasizes nature over nurture and the rights of biological parents over those of children.[6] Biological parents are viewed as entitled to their children, adoptive parents are not.

The second class status of adoption also permeates conversations. How often do adoptive parents hear questions like the following, in casual conversation, when someone first meets their child/children: "What happened to his/her/their real parents?" "What do you know about his/her real parents?" "Where did you get him/her?" (if a child does not resemble his/her adoptive parents) "How can you love someone else's child?" "Is that your grandchild?" (if the adoptive parent(s) look(s) older) and "It was so good of you to take that child/those children in."

People are also ambivalent about adoptees. Many people seem to feel sorry for adopted children, perhaps because they view such children as having been "given away" or "discarded" by their birth families. Sometimes this feeling prompts some to be overly generous to adopted children, especially children from previously impoverished circumstances. Relatives and even strangers want to shower the children with gifts or toys, or make excuses for an older adoptee's "odd" behavior saying something like: "Well, what can you expect? He's adopted" or "Give him time, he'll come around."

Likewise, people may view adoptive parents in unrealistic and ambivalent terms—some positive, others, negative. Adoptive parents are viewed as "saints" for taking on a child/children no one else wanted; as "expecting too much" or guilty of child abuse if adoptive parents talk about problems they are encountering with their adopted child/children. As stated earlier, adoptive parents are sometimes blamed if/when their child has problems, which are not quickly or easily "fixed" or if the parents are frustrated that the child has successfully manipulated the clinician they assumed would be able to help their child.

In an interesting study of childlessness among Canadians, Miall examines infertility, whether voluntary or involuntary, as a form of "deviant" or non normative behavior: being childless can result in the assignment of stigma, or a sign of disgrace.[7] Based on a survey of a snowball sample of seventy-one infertile women who had either already adopted or who expected to adopt, Miall identified three key differences her respondents perceived about the community's attitudes toward adoption and adoptive parents.[8] First, she points out that the biological tie is regarded as essential for bonding with a child. Second, respondents perceived the community's attitude toward adopted children as being second rate or inferior to biological children because of the adoptee's unknown, and suspect, genetic background. Third, respondents also perceived the community's attitude toward adopters as not the child's real parents, because there is no blood tie between them.

The continued existence of biased views and attitudes towards adoption, adoptees, and adopters results in an inhospitable, even hostile, social context for adoptive families. This climate is especially problematic when adoptive families are trying to deal with emotional or behavioral problems their child/children have. Too often, professionals who should be there to help—therapists, medical personnel, and teachers—are not familiar with the problems experienced by children who were adopted at an older age and/or from an orphanage setting or are easily taken in by the charm of attachment disordered children into thinking that 1. they have no problems, 2. their children's problems can be or are solved (through traditional therapies), or 3. the adoptive parents are the problem. Many people, including the professionals who come into contact with children adopted at older (non newborn/infant) ages, assume incorrectly that "good food, a lot of love, and a few trips to the mall" are enough to turn formerly-abused, neglected children around.[9]

Support Groups and Beyond

Adoptive parents' support groups can serve at least three important functions: providing information, providing a perspective on issues, and raising consciousness. People who join a support group realize that their concerns, problems, or issues are not unique to them. Members begin to understand on a fundamental level that they are not alone.

Social change often comes about through involvement in support groups and consciousness raising. How? We need to recognize the connection between the "personal" and the "political." A battle cry of the 1960s was that the personal is political and, thus, can become the basis for social action. Adoption fits well into both categories because adoption is a personal event that is influenced by political forces and other forces beyond the control of the individuals involved.

The ground swell of adoption-related movements have, so far, included two of the three members of the triad, birth parents and adult adoptees. In the 1970s, adoptees' and birth parents' movements began to gather momentum.[10] Adoptees petitioned for unsealing their birth records and some birth parents for about what had happened to the child or children they gave up for adoption.

Now is the time for a movement of adoptive parents' rights and issues of concern to them. With the changes in the type and circumstances of many children available for adoption from the domestic child welfare system and the large numbers of children being adopted beyond infancy from orphanages and other institutional settings in Russia and other Eastern European countries, for example, adoptive parents need to have more visibility and a more influential voice.

Such a movement is late in coming for a variety of reasons: the traditional model of infant adoption did not seem to require it. The fact that many adoptive parents of infants wanted to be viewed "as if begotten" families did not encourage it. The desire for adoption to be a private, family matter did not support it. Another factor that has forestalled a social movement of adoptive parents is fear—fear that they will be labeled as "bad parents" if they discuss their children's problems with others who may not understand where they are coming from. Also, life in the day-to-day may be such a struggle that some parents do not have the time or energy to get involved in advocacy efforts, which go beyond meeting their families' immediate needs. Yet, these parents are concerned about their children's futures as the children move into adolescence and young adulthood. At the same time, many of the parents who adopted when they were in their forties or fifties are facing their own aging and mortality.

The likelihood of adoption remaining private for long has changed for people who have adopted older children who need services, because of their troubled pasts. Adoption is also not a private matter for people whose children do not share their adoptive parent(s) physical, racial, or ethnic characteristics.

Not all adoptive parents will see the need for the emergence of an adoptive parents' movement, and that is okay. At the core of all successful movements is a group of committed activists and advocates who work in the trenches. But movements also require the support of others to be successful. They need top form coalitions with well-established groups like the North American Council on Adoptable Children (NACAC) in this case.

Parents of internationally adopted children are already working at the grass-roots level to provide information and support to people who have adopted special needs children and to those interested in adopting. Some operate through websites, newsletters, email contact, or direct meetings.

What is different about the parents of internationally adopted children is that they tend to be well-educated people who are likely to talk about their children's needs and issues. They are not likely to be easily intimidated by "the system" or driven away. As such, their tenacity can be a model to parents who adopt special needs children domestically.

Part of any social movement is resocializing members and others to see the "true believers"[11] and their objectives in positive terms. Adoptive parents and the (especially older) children they adopt are often viewed in stereotypical, unrealistic ways which have both positive and negative dimension/components. For example, adoptive parents may be viewed as saints and humanitarians or as defective because they can't produce biological children or as suspect by those who believe that one can only love a biological child. Adoptees are sometimes viewed as lucky children who must be grateful that they now have a good home, as "poor orphans" who should still be pitied or as "bad seeds" about whom time will tell.

In my opinion, a better way to view adoptive parents of special needs children is as committed, determined people who love their children and who will do everything in their power to provide the life and services their children need. But in some cases, the needs of children overwhelm the family and other placements need to be arranged, either temporarily or long term. Parents in such circumstances need to be supported, not criticized. And placements for children in need of them should be not only easier to arrange, but also more effective in helping the children to function better in families and to establish healthy, personal relationships with others. Real parents speaking about real issues and continuing, longitudinal research on adoptees are two key ways through which stereotypical views can be put into proper perspective.

The social dimensions of the hidden side of adoption, the private issues that some families have to deal with all the time, are considerable. These issues will place monumental financial, psychological, and emotional burdens on growing numbers of families. "As these troubled adoptees get older, they will become ticking time bombs for the nation." Dealing with these issues will have a significant impact on societal resources in the areas of education, health care and human services at the state level. Massive amounts of money and services will need to be earmarked to aid in the task of rehabilitation. Without appropriate interventions early on, the social costs will be even higher.

The Power of an Adoptive Parents' Movement

Although an adoptive parents' movement may not be enough, in and of itself, to bring about major or structural changes, bringing issues to the attention of policy makers and to other powerful advocates for improving adoption is an important first step. Collaboration with powerful, committed individuals and groups to press for change is the second. Policy makers need to be familiar with both the latest wave of adoption research and the experiences and recommendations of real families who have adopted challenging children. Putting a face on the issues and statistics is the context within which effective policies can be formulated. Without the perspective of high-quality research and honest parents willing to talk about their children's needs, policy makers are less likely to work toward changes that are in the best interests of adoptees who are challenged by special needs and of the very special people who adopt, and stick by, them for the long haul. Such continuing research needs to be supported through grants from government and private foundations. Of course, there is also a need for research on how amenable to modifying policies those in a position to do so are as well for assessing of the effectiveness of policy changes, which are enacted.

Notes

1. Reference: *USA Today* article, 8/24-26, 2003.
2. J.S. Modell, 2002. *A Sealed and Secret Kinship: The Culture of Policies and Practices in American Adoption.* New York: Berghahn Books.
3. M.K. Benet, 1976. *The Politics of Adoption.* New York: The Free Press. p.17.
4. D. Cohen, 1978-79. "Adoption." In *Readings in Marriage and the Family.* Guilford, CT: Dushkin Publishing, pp. 116-119. Metro/Region, p. 1.
5. E. Bartholet, 1994. "What's Wrong With Adoption Law," *Trial* (February), pp. 19-23. Ibid, 1993.
6. Ibid, 1994.
7. C.E. Miall, 1987. "The Stigma of Adoptive Parent Status: Perceptions of Community Attitudes Toward Adoption and the Experience of Informal Social Sanctioning." *Family Relations.* Vol. 36 (January), pp. 34-39.
8. Ibid.
9. Conversation with Thais Tepper, Co-Founder, The Parents Network for the Post Institutionalized Child, December, 1995.
10. Modell, Ibid.
11. E. Hoffer, 1942. *True Believer.* Scranton: Harper Collins Publisher, 1942.

Epilogue:
Out of the Past and into the Future

Adoption may be defined in different ways—as a personal event, a secret to be hidden, a "fictive connection" through which strangers become relatives, a social contract between several parties (birth parents, adoption agency or child welfare services, and adoptive parents), a social problem (for a woman who cannot parent her child and for a society which must deal with the consequences), or as a solution to a social problem for children in need of families. However one defines adoption, this way to build and add to families is here to stay.

The family is the cornerstone of society. As a social institution, however, the family is embedded in the larger structures of society. Changes in one area of society—such as in adoption policies and practices, within and between countries—impact on families both directly and indirectly. For example, adoption policies affect which children are available for adoption domestically or internationally, who gets to adopt children with particular characteristics, how long the process will take, how likely the adoption is to be successful, and what, if any, services are available after the adoption takes place. Adoption practice often assumes that the agency's or the social worker's job ends with the adoption. People that have adopted essentially healthy children may not question the "rightness" of this assumption. Some, in fact, will embrace it, as they wish to be viewed as "real" families. Others who experience life's twists and turns recognize the need for supporting families achieved in different ways because, whether created through blood ties, blending, or adoption, we cannot allow this cornerstone of society to bear so much weight that it crumbles under the pressure. Just and compassionate policies and practices can make a tremendous difference in family functioning and the well-being of all members.

This book examines the reality of sibling-group and older-child adoptions. The implications for adoption policies and practices discussed in this book are grounded in research about the adoption experiences of real families. Their experiences and the implications they suggest speak to what it takes to optimize family functioning when people adopt children that have pre-adoption issues and post-adoption needs.

I have focused my attention and research on adopting from Eastern Europe, and Russia in particular for two reasons: first, because Russia is the major contributor of Eastern European adoptees to the United States and to the world and, second, because adoptions from that part of the world are my area of professional expertise. In comparison to children adopted from China, Central America, and Korea, adoptees to the U. S. from Russia and other Eastern European countries are likely to join their new families at ages beyond infancy. In this regard, Eastern European adoptees are similar to children adopted from the U. S. child welfare system. They are also similar to domestic adoptees from the child welfare system because children adopted beyond infancy and who come from deprived early environments are more likely to have pre-adoption experiences associated with birth-family dysfunction. These experiences may include physical and/or sexual abuse, neglect, abandonment, witnessing domestic violence, and exposure to alcohol or drugs in utero.

However, physical, mental, and environmental health risks to adoptees born in Eastern Europe may be more severe. According to statistics, cited in chapter 3, the health of women and children in Russia has deteriorated. So, the potential for problems is worse now than when the families in my study adopted.

The large majority of the parents I studied adopted during the 1990s. Even so, only eight percent of these parents stated that the child/children they adopted had no problems upon entering their family. Four out of five of the parents reported that their adopted child/children had at least one problem at the time of his/her adoption. Physical health problems were present in over sixty percent of the children. The next two most frequent problems mentioned were behavioral (49 percent) and emotional (46 percent). Psychological (31 percent) and other (24 percent) problems ranked third and fourth. Examples of problems in the "other" category included developmental delays, speech, and learning challenges. Perhaps most important is that the children who had problems tended to have them in more than one category. A majority (54 percent) of the adoptees had problems in two (16 percent) or at least three (38 percent) areas.

A recent article by Associated Press national writer David Crary carried the title "Adoptions of Foreign Children Decline Sharply.[1]" Referring to the 2006 total figure from the U. S. State Department, Crary points out that declines were reported in countries which have been major sources for international adoptions by Americans in previous years. Among the Eastern European countries for which 2006 statistics are available, declines were shown in the number of Russian children adopted by Americans (from 4,652 in 2005 to a reported 3,706 in 2006). This change reflects a 20 percent decline in just one year. Declines were also reported in the number of children adopted from the Ukraine and Kazakhstan.

By my calculations, 381 fewer Ukrainian orphans, a decline of 45.3 percent, were adopted by Americans in 2006 (N=460) than in 2005 Similarly, 168 fewer Kazak children, a decline of about 22 percent, were adopted by Americans in 2006 (N = 587) than in 2005 (N = 755).

The question arises as to whether we are witnessing the beginning of a new trend in international adoptions by Americans, reflecting changes in both popular sending countries and in numbers of children Americans adopt internationally overall. The answer to that question remains in the future. At this writing, it appears that changing rules about who can adopt have made adoptions from some sending countries more difficult or impossible for people with certain social or other characteristics such as age, marital status, and mental health issues. Romania is currently limiting foreign adoptions to relatives of Romanian orphans available for adoption. In 2005, according to U. S. government records, no Americans adopted Romanian orphans. The United States is expected to ratify the Hague Convention on Intercountry Adoptions later this year. The effects of that change on trends in international adoption also remain unknown.

However, as long as the social and cultural forces that created the need for orphans from Eastern Europe to be placed with families outside their birth countries continues to be strong, Americans and others world-wide will be interested in adopting them. Adopting internationally has, and will continue to have, implications for the domestic adoptions of special needs children. The trend toward adopting older children and two or more children simultaneously from Eastern Europe or other countries will also mean that their adoptive families need to be well-informed about the child's needs in advance of accepting the referral, well-prepared to manage those needs, have access to appropriate services, and be well-supported for as long as necessary after the adoption takes place and the children are in the home.

Unfortunately, significant change takes time. No one can know in advance how long change will take until that change is evident as a trend rather than as an anomaly or a short-term gesture. When one listens to parents' conversations in support groups about their adoption experiences, there is no evidence to suggest that the "business as usual" model that views children as commodities and adoptive parents as lucky to adopt even a troubled child has undergone any noticeable change. Why should we expect the forces of important changes to come from agencies? Certainly, private agencies have much to gain and little to lose by doing more rather than less to increase the chances of enhancing adoptive family well-being. So, if not from within, then the pressure for positive change must come from adoptive families and those committed to enhancing family well-being through changing out-of-sync adoption policies and practices that put the well-being of families and their special needs adopted children at risk.

Notes

1.   Crary, David 2007. (January 6). Foreign Adoptions in U. S. Drop in 2006. http://news.yahoo.com/s/ap/2007106/ap_on_re_us/foreign_adoptions&printer=1   and condensed version of same, entitled "Adoptions of Foreign Children by Americans Decline Sharply," 2007 (January 7), *The Providence Journal*, Nation, p. A6.
2.   The 2006 statistics for the Ukraine and Kazakhstan were obtained form the following site: http://travel.state.gov. The totals for these countries for 2005 came from the U. S. C. I. S., Table 12. Immigrant Orphans Adopted by U. S. Citizens by Gender, Age, and Region and Country of Birth: Fiscal Year 2005.

Postscript
A Survey Approach:
How? Why? Who?

As is common in studies of attitudes, opinions, experiences, and behavior, my study is based on surveying adoptive parents. However, my research differs from work of some others who have studied international adoption recently in at least four important ways: first, I focus primarily on non-infant adoptees from Russia as well as from other Eastern European countries. Second, my work tends to be broader in focus than a single topic or issue. Also, some of the topics I cover are also different. For example, I investigate the process of international adoption, obtain and report on parents' views of the agencies with which they dealt in adopting their child or children, ask parents about their position on important policy issues, and make recommendations for needed changes at the macro and micro levels. Third, I combine quantitative and qualitative data to provide a fuller picture of the issues and circumstances about international adoption that emerge. Fourth, I began this project with the intent to follow up on as many of these adoptive families as possible over time. Data from two additional waves of surveys are in the early stages of analysis.

The data included in this book come from my questionnaire survey (phase I). That questionnaire consisted of forty-four open- and closed-ended questions and statements, some with contingency questions. I organized the questions into five sections: information about the children; questions about the agency/facilitator respondents used; respondents' adoption experiences; their views about the involvement of the state and federal government in regulating international adoption; and background questions about the respondents. See appendix A for more details. Depending on the number of children a respondent had adopted, the questionnaire took between twenty minutes (for those with one adopted child) to about forty minutes (for those who adopted three or more children) to complete.

I sent each adoptive parent who agreed to participate in the study a personally addressed and individually signed letter. The packet they received also contained a self-addressed, pre-stamped envelope to ease in the return of the completed questionnaire.

How I Obtained Respondents

I designed my research around a snowball sampling approach. Gathering a snowball sample is, itself, a process. The researcher begins by identifying potential respondents to participate in his or her study. He or she then asks participants for the names of others that may also be interested in participating. The snowball "grows" in this way.

As I stated earlier, my principal objective was to attract as diverse a cross-section of adoptive families as possible throughout the United States. I was also interested in obtaining respondents who had experienced successful as well as troubled adoptions (from their viewpoints). To achieve these objectives, I used a number of creative strategies.[1] Unlike other types of samples, a snowball sample takes time to grow to an acceptable size. Most importantly, the participants in the sample do not accrue at a steady rate. The data from the questionnaire survey took four years to collect. During that time period, I mailed the questionnaire to 152 parents who either expressed interest in participating in my study or who were referred by a participant. These 152 individuals and couples became the sampling frame, or list, from which the final sample emerged. The sample itself consists of 122 completed questionnaires.[2] This sample size represents a very respectable response rate of 80 percent, or four out of every five of the prospective respondents to whom I sent a questionnaire.

Why I Choose a Snowball Sample

I thought that a snowball sample was the most reasonable option under the circumstances. Choosing a random sample that would provide the breadth and would target the respondents I hoped to reach was desirable but not possible. I aimed to target people who had adopted older children and sibling groups internationally, especially from Russia and Eastern European countries during the last decade, and whose child/children had been living with them for at least two years at the time she/they completed the questionnaire. I hoped to also attract respondents who lived in different parts of the United States. Choosing a random sample might have been possible if I could have gotten access to a complete and accurate nationwide list of all such families. However, obtaining such a list was not possible due to confidentiality/privacy issues. To my knowledge, there is no "centralized list" of Russian and Eastern European children adopted by Americans, especially older children and sibling groups available outside of the BCIS (formerly the INS). A second choice for selecting a random sample might have involved my working with a particular adoption agency or a particular parent organization. I chose not to do either for two reasons: I did not want my research to be viewed as partisan and I preferred to play the role of an independent researcher.

A Profile of the Parents Who Participated in the Questionnaire Survey

The typical respondent was the adoptive mother (84 percent). At the time they completed the questionnaire, three out of four (76 percent) respondents were married. The remaining one in four (24 percent) were either single (seven in ten) or divorced (three in ten). Age-wise, just under two thirds (65 percent) of the respondents were in their forties at the time they completed the questionnaire. Most respondents who had spouses/partners reported that their spouse/ partner also tended to be in the forties age range (66 percent) at that time. However, one in five spouses was fifty or older. The ethnic background of respondents and spouses was very diverse. Only a small percentage of respondents (11.5 percent) had any Eastern European background; even fewer spouses (7 percent) did.

As is common among most adoptive families, the large majority (70 percent) of respondents were childless before they adopted their first child internationally. Just over half (56 percent) of the respondents who already had children before they adopted internationally had only one child in their family. Almost one in four respondents, however, were already parents of two children. The remaining one in five parents had at least three children.

The number of children adopted into a single family varied from one to six. Adopting one child was typical (48 percent) for these respondents. But adopting two children was almost as likely (41 percent). A small number of respondents (11 percent) adopted at least three children. Two of the families in this study each adopted two sibling groups.

A Description of Their Internationally-Adopted Children

The parents who participated in the questionnaire study adopted a total of 208 children. Just over half of their children were adopted from Russia (55 percent).The next largest number of adoptees was born in Romania (17 percent). Adoptees from Bulgaria (8.7 percent) and other Eastern European countries (8.7 percent) together comprised an additional 17 percent. Only one in ten of the children adopted by these families came from non-Eastern European countries.[3]

At the time their parents participated in the questionnaire survey, most of the children had been living in their new homes for at least several years. Just over half (52 percent) of them had been living with their adoptive families between two to four years and one third (33 percent) for more than four years.

Almost all (96 percent) of the children whose parents participated in this survey were adopted between 1990 and 2000. More of them were adopted in the second part of the decade than in the first part: 61 percent (N = 125) of the children were adopted between 1996 and 2001 and 35 percent between 1990 and 1995 (N = 73). The remaining 4 percent of the children were adopted earlier than 1990 from India and Korea.[4]

The peak years for the adoptions of all children combined were 1995 for the first half of the decade and 1997 for the second half. In those two years alone, 38 percent of these respondents' adopted children came home. The peak year for these parents' first-child international adoption was 1997. For those who had adopted a second child, the peak year for these second-child adoptions was 1998, followed closely by 1997. Among respondents who adopted a single child, girls outnumbered boys by about three to two. Nearly two thirds (64 percent) of those who adopted two children chose to adopt a girl and a boy. The small number (N = 14) of respondents who adopted three or more children typically chose a combination of girls and boys (71 percent).

Just over half (53 percent) of the respondents who adopted two or more children reported that their children are either a full or a half biological sibling to another child they had adopted. Siblings tended to be adopted at the same time. However, when respondents adopted unrelated children, slightly more (52 percent) of them did separate adoptions rather than simultaneous ones (48 percent).

The children adopted from an Eastern European country ranged in age from three months (a child from Romania) to fifteen years old (a child adopted from Bulgaria). The oldest child adopted by a respondent was twenty-five years old. She was the last of six children adopted by a single mother.

Only 17 percent of the adoptees were a year old or younger when they were adopted. Another 18 percent were between thirteen and twenty-four months old. The remaining almost two thirds of the children (65 percent) were more than two years old when they were adopted. Twenty seven percent were between twenty-five months and forty-eight months old and 38 percent of them were forty-nine months or older when they were adopted.

Nine out of ten (90 percent) of the children were adopted from orphanages. The remaining one in ten was either in a foster home, a hospital, or in another setting at the time of their adoption. Many of the adoptees lived in an orphanage setting all or most of their lives before they were adopted. Since the first eighteen to twenty-four months of life are most crucial for attachment and for normal brain development, it is important to note the implications of length of time spent in deprived environments where staff-to-child ratios are high and interaction with adults and resources limited.

Just over half (51 percent) of the adoptees spent at least two years in an orphanage setting. About three in ten of the children spent between thirteen and twenty-four months in an orphanage and two in ten, twelve months or less. Only 3 percent of these adoptees lived in an orphanage for six months or less.

According to information from respondents, less than half (44 percent) of the children had spent time in their birth homes, prior to entering an orphanage. In general, parents were able to provide information on the likely reason why their adopted children entered an orphanage. The two major reasons were termination of parental rights by the courts because of neglect and/or abuse (61 percent of the children) and abandonment (17 percent of the children). In a minority of cases, parents gave up their parental rights.

Respondents were asked if any of their children had problems at the time of their adoption. Four out of five respondents said yes. About one in ten said that some of their children had problems, but others did not. Only 8 percent of the respondents reported that their child/children had no problems. How many children did this involve? According to these respondents, 81 percent of the adoptees had at least one problem. The remaining 19 percent were reported to have no problems.

What kinds of problems did the 81 percent of adoptees have? Problems were coded into five categories: physical, behavioral, emotional, psychological, and other. The most frequent type of problem respondents mentioned was physical: Overall, 60 percent of the adoptees had at least one problem that fell into this category. The next most likely problem mentioned was behavioral: One in every two of the children's identified problems was described as behavioral. An almost equal number of problems were reported to be emotional (46 percent). Next came psychological (31 percent), and, last, other problems (24 percent).

Examples of problems included in the "other" category are speech and learning problems and developmental delays.

Were children likely to have problems in a single category or in multiple categories? Respondents reported that children who had problems tended to have problems in more than one category. Although 27 percent of the adoptees were reported to have problems in only one category, parents' answers show that almost four in ten of their children (38 percent) had problems in three or more categories. An additional 16 percent had problems in two categories. A very small minority (6 percent) had problems in all five categories. When a child's problems fell into a single category, this category was most likely to be physical health (69 percent).

I asked respondents if their child or children still had any these problems at the time they completed the questionnaire. Just over half (56 percent) of the respondents said yes. An additional 13 percent said that some of the children they adopted did. Parents were more likely than not to say that the problems did not resolve by themselves. The children needed various services to address their problems. The kinds of services they needed included speech therapy (for 54 percent of the children with this problem), services for other problems (53 percent), special education (45 percent), psychological or psychiatric services (43 percent), and language services (32 percent).

When asked if they were able to arrange the needed services, the majority of respondents reported that they were. Respondents were most successful in obtaining speech and psychological services (98 percent for each), followed by other services (85 percent), special education (84 percent), and language (78 percent). Just over half (54 percent) of the respondents reported that they paid for the needed services themselves.

Strengths of My Study

A major strength of this study lies in the care and creativity I used to locate as diverse a sampling frame as possible. A second strength is my speaking personally—either by telephone or via e-mail—with each prospective participant who inquired about my study. Thus, the researcher was the closest person to the data collection. These activities were labor intensive, but crucial to my obtaining valid data from a fairly large number of respondents willing to speak honestly and at length about a very private and emotionally-laden issue like adoption. A third strength involves the decision to focus primarily on older adoptees and sibling groups while also including some parents who had adopted infants or young toddlers.

Limitations and How I Addressed Them

The most important weakness is not having access to a list from which to choose a random sample of adoptive parents who met my study criteria regarding age at adoption, number of children adopted, length of time in the adoptive home, and birth country. However, other studies of adoptive parents and adoptees are typically based on non-random samples. I tried to address this weakness by not drawing potential participants from a single source. Rather, I contacted various individuals, parent groups, and online sources where I posted information about my study.

Some might consider sample size to be a second limitation. Although small in general for a sociological investigation, the sample I obtained is of a respectable size. There is also some precedent for a sociologist to collect a sample size of 100 using a snowball approach.[5]

Sample sizes in some adoption studies vary considerably, from a low of eight respondents,[6] to forty-six respondents[7] to just over 100 respondents.[8] Very few surveys of adoptive families reported in international adoption literature have achieved larger sample sizes.[9]

The principal reason for the potentially lengthy time frame involved in collecting data through a snowball approach is the researcher's inability to predict when a sample of the desired size will be reached. This lack of predictability is especially true in regard to adoption research.

In order for me to obtain a snowball sample size of at least 100 respondents, my original target size, I had to wait longer than I originally expected. Also, even when the questionnaire sample size reached 100, I was reluctant to turn away additional parents who wanted to participate in my study until I deemed it absolutely necessary. Even then, I offered those families the opportunity to participate in Phase II of the research, the telephone interview, if they wished.

The possibility of self-selection might be considered by some to be a third limitation. What that means in this case is the greater likelihood that adoptive parents who viewed their adoption outcome positively would volunteer in greater numbers than those with troubled adoptions. I do think that people who have experienced a positive outcome are more likely, and more successful, in encouraging other families with similar outcome perceptions to participate than are those who have experienced less positive outcomes. The latter are often more isolated and may be using their energy to struggle with the day-to-day issues. Based on respondents' subjective determination of satisfaction, it did turn out that satisfied parents were most likely to participate. However, adoption surveys, especially those conducted by agencies, also seem to support this pattern. In this regard, one result of my study was not different from others. However, I tried to counteract this potential limitation be telling all prospective participants that I was interested in reaching as diverse a cross section of adoptive parents of as possible—both those who experienced positive adoption outcomes as well as those whose adoption experiences were more problematic.

Finally, anonymous questionnaires can be a mixed blessing in conducting research on sensitive, highly personal topics like adoption. On the plus side, respondents are able to answer honestly without fear of personal reprisal, since their identities are safeguarded. However, if any respondents were concerned about possible repercussions that my study might have for international adoption policy or were "in denial" about the nature and/or extent of their children's issues, then they did have an opportunity to give "socially desirable" answers. I encouraged respondents to provide honest answers to the questions I posed. And, I believe that the large majority of respondents did answer the questions honestly and openly. Despite the possibility of some respondents having a "personal agenda" for participating in this research, I do not believe that concerns about vested interests resulted in respondents providing misleading information about their experiences and views.

Overall, I am confident that the data gathered through this questionnaire provide important insights into the phenomena of international adoption of older children and sibling groups from orphanage settings in Russia and Eastern Europe.

Summary

In this postscript, I have provided details about the methodology of my phase I questionnaire survey, a description of the demographic characteristics of the parents who responded, and detailed information about their child or children. In regard to the children, just over half (55 percent) were born in Russia. A similar percentage had lived with their adoptive parent(s) between two and four years. One third of the children had been with their American families for more than four years. Parents who adopted a single child at the time they participated in my Phase I survey were much more likely to adopt a girl. The majority of parents that adopted two children chose a boy and a girl. Siblings tended to be adopted at the same time. Nine out of ten of the adoptees had lived in orphanages. Typically, the children had spent at least two years in an orphanage setting.

The large majority were in an orphanage at the time of their adoption. Fewer than two in ten of the adoptees were twelve months or younger when they joined their adoptive families.

Not surprisingly, four out of five parents reported that their child or children had problems at the time they entered their new family. Typically, the children's problems were not confined to a single area. Physical, behavioral, and emotional problems were typical. More likely than not, the children's problems did not resolve on their own. Parents reported that interventions were needed. Just over half of the respondents paid for the needed services themselves.

Notes

1. First, I attended several adoption conferences between the Spring of 1998 and the Spring of 2000. These conferences included the Open Door Society of Massachusetts (ODSMA), Adoption Rhode Island (ARI), and a specialized conference organized by the Parents Network for the Post-Institutionalized Child (PNPIC). These conferences varied in size from very large and regional (ODSMA) to smaller (ARI). Both of these conferences were attended by people in various stages of adoption (pre-and post-), representatives of adoption agencies, and professionals who work with adoptive families. The PNPIC conference consisted primarily of between seventy-five to 100 families that had already adopted internationally. At each conference, I both provided information sheets describing my study and spoke to adoptive parents. At the ODSMA conference, I also spoke to representatives of several international adoption agencies that placed older children from Russia and Eastern Europe.

    Second, in order to publicize my study to a wider audience, I sent a description of the study objectives and parameters to the Co-founders of the Parents Network for the Post-Institutionalized Child and to the Executive Director of the Open Door Society. They graciously included details about my study in their newsletters. A few adoption agencies, whose representatives I had spoken to at the ODS conference in April of 2000, also identified my study in their newsletters.

    Third, I was able to get my study identified on the families for Russian and Ukrainian Adoption (FRUA) web site and on another web site that provides information on current IA research.

    Fourth, I asked the Editor of Adoptive Families of America to identify my study on the bottom of a "Letter to the Editor" I wrote and which they published.

    Fifth, I also recruited respondents through adoptive parents who were leaders of, or involved in, support groups in their areas of the country. I provided details about my research and myself under my department Home Page so that internet browsers interested in international adoption could contact me easily.

    Finally, I also contacted the administrators of the Eastern European Adoption Coalition (EEAC) listserv several times asking for permission to post a notice about the study to their members. I did not receive any response.

2. Because her experiences were so different in different countries, one respondent completed two questionnaires. So, the sample size was 121 respondents.

3.   No information was provided on the dates that two of the children were adopted. So, the N used here was 206 children.
4.   Most of these families participated in the study because they adopted their child or children at older ages or had adopted siblings or more than one child simultaneously. This small number also reflects the aim of the study to target primarily families who had adopted from Russia and other Eastern European countries.
5.   L. Benjamin 1991. *The Black Elite: Facing the Color Line in the Twilight of the Twentieth Century*. Chicago: Nelson-Hall.
6.   See Goldberg, Ibid, 1997, 2001.
7.   See Ames and others, Ibid, 2000.
8.   See Marcovitch and others, Ibid, 1995; Rutter and others, Ibid, 1998.
9.   Exceptions are studies done by Groze and Ileana 1996, by and Price 2000 which report samples in 500-575 range. However, in both cases, these researchers worked from a preexisting list of adoptive families.

Enhancing the Success of Older-Child Adoptions from Eastern Europe: Pre- and Post-Adoption Issues and Tips "From the Trenches"

Josephine A. Ruggiero and Kathy Johnson

Toddler, older-child, and sibling-group adoptions have become more common over the last few decades in the United States. Adopting non-infants (i.e., a child age twelve months or older) is also typical for the majority of children Americans adopt from Russia and other Eastern European countries. Statistics collected by the Immigration and Naturalization Service (now known as the USCIS) on immigrant orphans adopted by U. S. citizens show that, between 1990 and 2005, Americans adopted 71,665 children from former Soviet countries.

More than 47,000 (65.9 percent) of these adoptees came from Russia alone. Nearly twenty-five percent of the Eastern European adoptees came from four other countries: the Ukraine (8.7 percent, N = 6,235), Romania (7.0 percent, N = 5,043), Kazakhstan (6.2 percent, N = 4,417), and Bulgaria (3.0 percent, N = 2,172). The remaining 6,583 (9.2 percent) of adoptees joined American families from other Eastern European countries, including Poland, Lithuania, Belarus, Latvia, Estonia, Hungary, Moldova, the Republic of Georgia, Albania, Armenia, and Azerbaijan.

According to aggregated statistics published by the INS/USCIS for 1990-2005, only a minority of these adoptees were under one year old at the time their adoption was completed. Kazakhstan, which began sending orphans out of country for adoption in 1998, showed the highest average percentage of young infant adoptees: Thirty-eight out of every 100 adoptees to the United States from this country during this time period were less than twelve months old at the time of their adoptions. For Russia, the overall average of infant adoptions was twenty-seven out of every 100 Russians. The ratio for adoptees coming to the United States as infants from the Ukraine was even lower: sixteen of out every 100. A comparable statistic describes Romanian children adopted as infants: sixteen out of every 100. Of these five countries, Bulgarian orphans were the least likely to be adopted as infants: Two out of every 100 Bulgarian children adopted by Americans fell into this age category.

Overall, between 1990-2005, the typical age category for adoptees to the United States from these five countries was from "one to four years old" with a modal age of three years old. The average percentage of children in this age category ranged from 70 percent (Bulgaria) to 44 percent (Kazakhstan).

Why does age at adoption matter? It is not so much age per se as it is the kinds of pre-adoptive experiences a child may have had: deprivation, neglect, trauma, abuse, more time spent in institutional settings, etc. According to *The Special Edition* (Spring 2000), produced by the St. Joseph Center in Scranton, PA, adoption outcomes depend heavily on information and support. This document notes that the risk of disruption in older and special needs domestic adoptions is ten to twenty times the rate of disruptions of infant adoptions.

Families that adopt children past infancy need to be well prepared (before they adopt) and well-supported (after the child/children is/are home). In this pamphlet, we raise several important issues and offer interested readers some important tips "from the trenches." We have identified these issues and collected the tips we share here through personal experiences as well as through talking with, and listening to, many parents who have adopted one or more older children internationally. Most of the families with whom we have had contact have adopted older children and sibling groups from Russia and other Eastern European countries.

Our objective in writing this appendix chapter is not to discourage older-child or international adoptions or domestic adoptions but rather to help better prepare families for what might lie ahead of them when they adopt an older child. What follows is an exhaustive list of issues to consider and a number of helpful tips "from the trenches." People who plan to adopt, and those who have already adopted one or more non-infants internationally, especially from Russia and Eastern Europe, should find this pamphlet valuable either for themselves or for a family they know.

Pre-Adoption Issues and Tips

ISSUE #1: Choice of Home Study and Placing Agency: The first, most important step in the success of an adoption is the careful choice of a home study and placing agency/facilitators.

Tip #1: Work with a reputable, experienced home study and placing agency. Although the same agency may do both your home study and locate a child(ren) for you, it is not uncommon for adoptive parents to work with a placing agency or facilitator located outside their state of residence. Home study agencies are usually licensed by the state(s) in which they are located and do business but placing agencies may not be. Find out what the state in which the placing agency does business requires. Under its current name, the placing agency/facilitator you choose should have successfully placed children from that country for several years. Home study agencies and facilitators should both have a proven history of high performance and up-to-date knowledgeable about, and/or experience in, placing children from the country (and orphanage) from which you plan to adopt. The person or persons with whom you will work most directly should be easy to find when you have concerns or questions, approachable, honest, and ethical in his/her dealings with you.

Tip #2: Check out both agencies track records' thoroughly and carefully. Contact, but do not rely only on, information provided by state licensing boards. Make a special point of talking with adoptive parents who have lived with their adopted children for at least two years. Talk with at least five or six people who (1) have adopted a child similar to the one you are considering (country, age, family circumstances, etc.) and (2) from the agency you are considering using. Ask the placing agency you plan to use for names of several adoptive parents who have adopted a child with problems. Ask the adoptive parents how the problems were presented to them by the agency before the adoption and how accurate that picture of the problems has turned out to be. Tell them you do not want issues to be sugar coated or denied.

Tip #3: Check both agencies' philosophies and practices for biases against "non-traditional" prospective adopters. For example, single women and men may face more in-depth scrutiny than married couples and which the former might perceive as discriminatory.

Tip #4: Think twice about working with a placing agency or facilitator that is located very far from your home. If the agency is reasonably close geographically, plan to talk to the Director and/or social worker in charge of adoptions in person. Personal contact can give you a good "feel" for what working with the agency will probably be like. If post adoption problems arise, are they able and willing to help? Do they have resources to offer, or to refer, in the area where you live? It is too easy for staff at a distant agency to forget about you once the adoption is complete. Be cautious about accepting a child/children being placed by an agency or facilitator via the Internet.

ISSUE #2: Pre-Adoption Preparation. The next most important decision a pre-adoptive parent can make is to find out up front how much and the nature of the pre-adoption preparation they will get if they sign on with a particular home study agency. Look for group sessions featuring, as speakers, adoptive parents who have adopted the kind of children you're interested in more than two years ago. The reading material assigned should also be up-to-date research. If possible, ask to see the reading packet before signing with an agency.

Tip #1:   Filling out paper work (forms) is NOT equivalent to pre-adoption preparation.

Tip #2:   Do NOT be lured to an agency by claims of a short, painless pre-adoption process. Your best bet is to choose a home study agency that has prepared prospective adopters thoroughly in sending-country risk factors and issues in adopting a child/children that has (have) spent, early (formative) years in abusive and/or deprived social environments, including neglectful, abusive birth homes or institutional settings.

Tip #3: A good home study agency does more than focus only on "quali-fying" clients as potential adopters. A good agency should also require pre-adoptive parents to spend 10 or more hours familiarizing themselves with key issues and risk factors and what post-adoption services will be available either through the home study agency or in the local "therapeu-tic" community. Pre-adopters should read relevant literature and discuss with it the preparing social worker. The home study agency should put pre-adopters in touch with other adoptive parents and, at least, direct them to an online support group as part of their home study preparation. In addition, they should follow up with the family for at least one year after the child enters his/her new family.

Tip #4: Take the initiative: prepare yourself well regarding the potential risk factors (i.e., Pre-adoption experiences of abuse/or neglect, country-related risks, age at adoption, etc.) If possible before you adopt, make time to become friendly with a family that has adopted children about the age you are considering. Spend time with them and their children. Unfortunately, many pre-adoptive parents romanticize the outcome of life after adoptiion and do not anticipate realistically the challenges they may face.

Tip #5: Be prepared ahead of time regarding services the child/children you adopt may need. Many adoptive parents think only of a check-up by a pediatrician. However, many children adopted internationally need more services and evaluations than that, at least initially. Do not take a "wait and see" approach. If the issue is not resolving or is of great concern, seek an evaluation immediately. Become familiar with the services available in your area before the child enters your family. Look especially into services offered to disabled/special needs children, either through the county or the school system. Almost all children adopted after infancy, especially from an orphanage setting, are considered special needs when they join their new families. They should qualify, at least initially, for services from the county or state. Look into evaluations, intervention programs, day care, and mental health professionals who are qualified and experienced in the issues your child might have.

Tip #6: Check out the conditions and therapies your health insurance provider will cover. Find out how many visits for each condition you can expect your insurer to cover. Be sure to find out whether pre-existing conditions are excluded from coverage. Discuss with the insurance company what conditions in an adopted child would be considered pre-existing, especially as the label applies to behavioral disorders.

Tip #7: Learn at least a few phrases of your child's native language and be open to supporting your child's desire to connect with his/her birth culture and traditions at some point in his/her life. Practice speaking the phrases you have learned often. Look for cultural activities that you and you child can explore together.

ISSUE #3: Complete and Honest Disclosure of ALL KNOWN information about the child and his/her pre-adoption history.

Tip #1: Informed consent on the part of the pre-adoptive parent(s) and older children   (even those as young as three years old) for whom adoption outside his/her birth country is the plan is essential to the potential success of any adoption. Reputable agencies understand that they have a fiduciary responsibility to pre-adoptive parents with whom they work to obtain and pass on every scrap of information known about a potential adoptee before they expect pre-adoptive parent(s) to accept the referral. However, many agencies claim that there is little or no information available. Others rely on sending-country "intermediaries" that may edit or omit the information they send to the placing agency for which they work. Some agencies only pass on official "written" information and do not interview the child's current caretakers. However, the caretakers are the people who know your child best. Ask for their input, especially about your child's likes, dislikes, routine, friends in the orphanage, etc.

Tip #2: While pre-adoptive information about a child or sibling group may be sketchy or unknown, information since s/he entered the sending-country's institutional and court systems should be available. Pre-adoptive parents should expect to get information on (1) whether the child was abandoned, released for adoption by birth parents, or removed from the birth parents custody, (2) the child's birth and/or milestones while in care, (3) his/her physical and mental health, (4) typical behaviors, (5) interactions with staff and other children in the institution(s), (6) length of time in all institutional settings (number of pre-adoption moves and broken attachments are especially important), etc. No information about the child and his/her pre-adoption history should be summarized as "notes," or omitted.

Tip #3: Be persistent in your request for information. Don't settle for verbal assurances that the child is "healthy" and/or will be a "blessing" in your life. Ask for the background information before the placing agency sends you the photo. Don't be hooked by the photo alone. Ask for the name of a family who has adopted from the same orphanage and whose child might know the child you are considering. Have that family ask their child what your potential child is like, would they want him/her for a friend, etc.

Tip #4: Request all records and other information both in the native language and in English. Once you have the documents, make arrangements for a thorough review and independent translation of the documents into English. Something important may have been omitted. Obtain and translate all information before you accept the referral and, most definitely, before you finalize the adoption in the sending country.

Tip #5: Consider hiring a western-trained pediatrician to visit and examine the child/children before you make a decision to accept the referral. A group of pre-adoptive parents may wish to share the cost of the physician's expenses. Also consider asking a family or groups of families traveling to adopt from the same orphanage before you do to observe and interact with the child you have been offered while they are there. Ask them to videotape the child, if possible. This is a tape you can share with an experienced international adoption physician. Agree in advance to pay for extra expenses they incur on your behalf.

Tip #6: Don't be pressured into taking on a child with more serious issues than you can manage or adopting more children than you honestly think you want to parent. Family, friends, facilitators, or placing social workers may not the best people from whom to ask for, or receive, advice in this important decision.

Tip #7: Consider hosting a child through a summer hosting program. The local branches of the national groups are usually composed of volunteers, many experienced adoptive parents themselves. The child will be placed in your home for a number of weeks during the summer and will attend camp during the day. As a family you will attend group sponsored events on the weekends and should have 24-hour translation and other support services available to you. Hosting a child gives both you and the child a chance to live together as a family and see if the match is a good "fit." Most families that host a child report knowing within three weeks whether or not the child is a good fit for their family. A group like this should also have a support system and resource list available that you can access not only during the hosting program, but after the adoption as well.

ISSUE #4: Joining a Support Group

Tip #1: Get involved before you adopt: Before you get your child, join a support group of adoptive parents who adopted a child/children from the country/region where you are planning to adopt. You can learn a lot and will connect with a community of people who will support you after you adopt. People who join a group ahead of time are usually happy that they did. People who do not often say they wish they had.

Tip #2: Look for support both near and far: if your home study agency or placing agency do not know of any, ask some of the people they give as references. Consider joining an internet support group. Sometimes internet support groups have listservs for parents whose children have specific issues, pre-adoptive experiences, or are older. If you are planning to adopt from Russia or another Eastern European country, check out the EEAC on-line subscription page at http://eeadopt.org/home/services/mlists/subscribe/index.html.

ISSUE #5: The Cost of Adopting Internationally

Tip #1: Cheaper may come with hidden costs: Although cost is definitely an issue, do not allow cost alone drive your decision to use a particular agency or facilitator. Agency costs may increase without notice while you are waiting to complete your adoption. Also, there may be hidden or less obvious costs that make the total expense more comparable to that of other agencies. For example, travel and lodging costs may vary considerably from country to country and for a given country even within a relatively short period of time.

Tip #2: Look into adoption funding/incentives: Start with your employer. Also, look into foundations that support adoption, state and/or federal tax incentives. Help to defray the costs of adoption is out there.

Tip #3: Consider adopting a child already in the United States: Sometimes, along with domestically-born children, internationally-adopted children are placed in the U. S. child welfare system. In adoptions (or re-adoptions) through the child welfare system, prospective adopters meet with, and get to know, the child and/his/her case worker before the adoption is finalized.

Post-Adoption Issues and Tips

ISSUE #1: Impact of Adoption on Family Functioning

Tip #1: Be prepared for bumps in the road: Adding a child or children to your family is a major life change. Expect the change to be stressful as well as potentially rewarding. Accept the likelihood that, at least at the beginning, parenting an older child may be more stressful than rewarding.

Tip #2: Take care of your closest relationships: If married or in a long-term relationship, make sure that you and your spouse or partner are equally involved in, and committed to, the decision to adopt an older child or children. Couples need a strong relationship to withstand the challenges of parenting an older child or children. Single parents need a strong support system of friends and relatives.

Tip #3: Prepare, make time for, and support the children already in your home: prepare children already in your family for the kinds of changes likely to occur when another child or other children is (are) added to the family. Support the child/children already in your home and find post-adoption services to help them deal with issues raised by a challenging sibling.

Tip #4: Is changing birth order a good idea? Consider the ramifications of a decision to change to the birth order of the child/children already in the home by adding a child who is older than him/her/them. Doing this may not seem like a big deal to you, but it may have important negative consequences to the child/children already in the family who can feel that their position has been usurped.

ISSUE #2: The Challenges and Stresses of Parenting a Post-Institutionalized Child/Children

Tip #1: Parenting (or re-parenting) the tough ones: Be aware that traditional parenting methods may not work with older, post-institutionalized children—especially those who have control or trust issues. Read Nancy Thomas' book, *When Love is Not Enough* (www.amazon.com) and check out the resources available to parents and educators through the Love and Logic Institute (https://www.loveandlogic.com).

Tip #2: Reign in the fanfare: for the first month or so, minimize contact between your recently-adopted child and people outside the immediate family. Restrict stimuli from the outside (e.g., gifts, fawning over the child, etc.). Do as much of the initial care taking as possible. Work on attachment right away.

Tip #3: When does "adjustment" become more than that? It is important NOT to take a "wait and see" attitude when problems continue or escalate. Read Cathy Helding and Foster Cline M.D.: *Can This Child Be Saved? Solutions for Adoptive and Foster Families* (1999) and *Adopted and Foster Child Assessment* (CHAFCA) (1999), to help you understand what your child's issues may be.

Tip #4: Practice proactive parenting: be prepared to advocate for your child/children in the schools and elsewhere. Some school districts may provide services without much pressure from a family. Most will not. Know your child's rights and your own. Consulting *Wright's Law* should be a big help (http://www.wrightslaw.com/). Also be proactive in getting accurate diagnoses of your child's issues. Do NOT assume that it will be easy or that you should wait for the "professionals" to make referrals. Also be on the alert for misdiagnoses, because certain conditions may share or have overlapping characteristics. For example, Post Traumatic Stress Disorder (PTSD) may be misidentified as Attention Deficit Hyperactivity Disorder or even as Asperger's Syndrome. Misdiagnoses can be a very big problem when children are being tested by the school district as their evaluators may not know how to identify conditions affecting post-institutionalized children. In such a case, children may end up being treated for conditions they do not have and not treated for the condition(s) they do have.

Tip #5: Be kind to yourself: make (find) time for yourself daily, or at least weekly. Do something that you enjoy and which is a stress reducer. Meditate, exercise, do yoga, make a "spa" morning for yourself (even at home). Follow through on your plans.

Tip #6: Respite may keep you going: arrange a break from your child/children as often as weekly. Respite may be available at no cost to you. Check the services available in your state.

Tip #7: Say something when advice is not helpful: expect friends, family, even neighbors and acquaintances, to offer unwanted advice or disagree with your parenting approach. Have they "walked in your shoes?" If not, remember that you, and other families that have a child/children like yours, are the real experts.

ISSUE #3: Decisions About Guardianship in the Event of Adoptive Parent(s)' Death(s) or Incapacitating Illness.

Decisions about who will care for your child or children in the case that they are still minors when the unexpected happens: incapacitating illness or death. The issue of guardianship is important to both couples and single parents. Planning for your child's future care is particularly important as older parents adopt young children.

Tip #1: Do not be hasty: make the decision about guardianship after your child has been home for a while and both you and the prospective guardians are familiar with his/her needs.

Tip #2: Confused about the best choice of guardian(s)? Do not assume that a family member is always the best choice. Sometimes, family and/or friends do not work out as guardians. Below are three examples of people having trouble making, or failing to make, arrangements for their children should something happen to them.

Carolyn, a single woman in her middle fifties, adopted three siblings from Russia. Carolyn didn't have any relatives who were willing, or able, to take the children if anything happened to her. However, when she first got home with the children, a couple, friends of hers, indicated that they would care for the children if something happened to her. Fairly soon after the adoption, however, it became obvious that all three children had serious learning issues as well as some physical problems and attachment issues. Their various needs got so time consuming that Carolyn had to cut her work hours drastically, which plunged the family into poverty. She had always assumed that the couple would step in. However, when she became ill with lung cancer, Carolyn called the couple. She discovered then that neither that couple nor anyone else she knew felt they could parent all three of the children. When Carolyn died without a will, the state in which she lived at that time took custody of her three children. The children went into two different foster homes because the state claimed that it couldn't find one home for all three. A social worker for the state is now trying to find a permanent placement for the children. However, he's having a difficult time as he does not have a lot of experience with children that have the kind of issues these children face. Carolyn's children are not only mourning the death of the only loving parent they'd ever known, but also they are not able to grieve their mother's passing together.

When Sally, a single woman, adopted a toddler from Romania she and her brother both assumed he and his wife would take care of her son should something happen to her. Unbeknownst to Sally at the time she adopted her son, he suffered from both autism and attachment issues. Once her brother and his wife got to know the child and realized the extent of his problems, they decided they could not parent him along with their own children. However, they did not mention their decision to Sally until after her first cancer surgery. After checking with all her other relatives and friends, and having them tell her they did not feel they could parent her son either, Sally is now looking into group home options, possibly with her brother as an advocate for the child.

After Mary and John adopted an older child in Russia, family members on both sides were thrilled. All of them wanted to be designated guardian should something happen to the Mary and John. The couple is very family-oriented, believing that a child should stay in the family if something happens to the parents. So, they immediately picked possible guardians from among their siblings. They also began working with their daughter on attachment and trust issues. After a year of struggle, the couple realized that their family members did not understand what their daughter had experienced before her adoption and what her parents were trying to do to help her. At that time, Mary and John realized that they had to look elsewhere for guardians should something happen to them. As they approach their second older-child adoption, and have to show a will for the home study, they are seriously considering naming other adoptive families as guardians instead of family members.

Tip #3: What does a guardian do? Parents' expectations for their child's guardian(s) should be discussed with the guardian(s) and ambiguities or areas of disagreement ironed out to the satisfaction of all parties.

Tip #4: Put it in writing: the names and expectations for guardians should be included in a legal document such as a will. Keep more than one copy of this document. Be sure that a copy will be readily available.

ISSUE #4: When Stress Becomes Too Much: Considering the Options

Tip #1: Consider the options and look carefully before you leap. What are you looking for in an out-of-home placement: A short-term vs. a long-term arrangement? Are you planning for the child to re-enter your family after time spent in the placement? What do you know about the options available to your child, how they can be arranged, their cost, and who will pay for the out-of-home care? There may be more options available than you know.
Consider, for example, the following options:

Option #1: Group home placement (temporary: 6-12 months).

Option #2: Foster care: Regular vs. therapeutic foster care (temporary but the latter type is usually longer term and more difficult to obtain) Ideally, therapeutic foster parents have more training and understanding of your child's behavioral and other issues than do people trained as foster parents through the child welfare system.

Option #3: An institutional placement (larger than a group home, more staff, probably a longer-term arrangement).

Option #4: Are there more acceptable (to you) options? Such options may include boarding school, military school, or the transfer of guardianship (and the child's move to a family member or friend who may live out of state). Seek legal advice to see if the option you are considering is both feasible and legal in state in which you live.

Option #5: Terminating the adoption and giving up your parental rights (permanent). Choosing this option is likely to end any future contact with the child.

Option #6: Facilitated re-adoption: if you want to be involved in finding another home for the child privately instead of placing him or her
in state custody, you can find out more about the re-adoption option by
contacting adoption networking groups, private adoption agencies, or
lawyers familiar with private re-adoption placements.

Tip #2: Ask savvy questions. Try to find out as much as you can about
each option you are considering. Tour the residential placements you
are considering. Meet the staff, find out about their experience and
credentials. Find out if the staff that will interact most with your child
understands the kinds of issues your child has and has worked successfully with children who have those issues before. Remember: clueless,
inexperienced staff, or those who have their own "agendas," will not be
able to do much to help your child function better at home.

Ask how much and what type of involvement you will have with your
child while s/he is in placement. Participation of families in "therapy"
with a staff member is usually a given. Parents may also be required to
participate in other forms of monitored activity with their child. If a child
is expected to return home, weekend visits are also expected. If, however,
parents say that they are not sure whether the child will come home, the
social worker handling the case will probably require all family visits
to be "supervised" by an authorized staff person in an approved setting.
Overnights and unsupervised visits do not take place in such cases.

Tip #3: Determine whether your goals for your child and their goals are
a good fit. Be sure that you know what those goals are. Once you do,
determine whether or not those are your goals as well. If not, can you
work with placement staff to adjust the goals?

Most important is being clear about your expectations and the way
"success" is defined. For example, from a family perspective, "success"
should mean that the child is able to re-enter the family showing greater
self control and significantly improved behavior and functioning in the
family, including more cooperative forms of interaction with family
members, than when s/he left home. However, "success" to the placement staff typically means that the child has met their goals (based on
a star or check system) well enough to "graduate." Typically, from the
placement's perspective, success means that the child is doing what the
staff expects of him/her in a highly-structured, less intimate environment
than a family. In group homes, rewards are used regularly, and often lav-
ishly (from a parent's perspective), to reinforce conformity.

Tip #4: Take off the rose-colored glasses. Group homes in the United States are generally not set up around the family model where house "parents" live with the children as a family and others come in as needed. In group homes, a few staff may be around for years, but many staff come and go. Also, group home staff has different levels of training, experience, commitment, and, very likely, burn out.

How much should you expect from the "typical" residential placement in regard to improving your child's functioning upon return to the family? A realistic caveat is to be reasonable in your expectations. It is unlikely that a child's post-placement behavior will improve dramatically or remain improved over the long-term. A lot depends on the child's ability and commitment to do better in a less structured, more intimate environment and on the family's ability and patience in providing support for the child's small, as well as big, accomplishments as a family member.

Unfortunately, for middle-class families, the negative consequences of their child living in a residential placement may outweigh the positive ones. Parents need to consider these as well in making their decision about choosing an option. Will the values parents are trying to teach the child be reinforced in that setting, or undermined? In addition, a child may (1) not transfer the skills and coping mechanisms s/he learned in a group home setting to the family setting; (2) unrealistically expect the family to be as structured as the group home and his/her parents to act as staff did (i.e., always be available, play with them if no one else is around, routinely take them on weekend "field trips" to fun settings, eat out a lot, etc.); (3) gain weight and/or use food as more of a control issue to cause arguments; (4) expect parents to provide playmates for them (i.e., children who were used to having "built-in" playmates may become angry and depressed in their absence and have trouble developing new relationships with peers; (5) fear or delay coming home (e.g., the latter by escalating behavior problems on visits with family).

Parents also need to be aware that they may need to give up their parental rights, at least temporarily, if the state gets involved in providing residential or foster placement for their child. They will also probably need to hire a lawyer and make regular appearances in court if required by the laws of their state of residence and the child welfare agency.

Conclusion

Based on our experiences and interactions with families that have adopted older children internationally, primarily from Russia and Eastern Europe, the factors that affect the success or failure of older-child adoptions are not a mystery. However, neither are these factors clearly identified and typically discussed in detail outside of professional social work and psychology journals. The objective of this booklet is to raise important issues and offer tips to the people who most need them: adoptive parents in all stages of the process.

It is clear that people who adopt a child past infancy need to be well-informed and well- prepared in advance. They also need to have access to a variety of services and support for as long as it takes after the adoption. The home study agency plays a crucial role in the success or failure of older-child adoptions as does the placing agency, if different from the former. The staff of both agencies has a fiduciary responsibility to the adoptive family and the child/children they place. They must put the best interests of the newly-created or changed family unit above all other interests, financial included.

Endnote

Some of tips are based on comments made by respondents in questionnaire and/or telephone interview surveys conducted by the first author.

About Kathy Johnson:

Kathy Johnson is a former member of Kidsave International and the organizer of an adoptive parents' support group in southern California. She is a single parent of two children, adopted separately, both as infants—one from Russia and one from the Republic of Georgia.

Bibliography

ABC *Nightline*. 1997. (July 22). "Unlocking the Mysteries of the Brain: Emotionally Scared Adopted From Eastern Europe."

Ames, MD., E., S. J. Morison, L. Fisher, and K. Chisolm 2000. "Some Recommendations from a Study of Romanian Orphans Adopted to British Columbia" in *International Adoption: Challenges and Opportunities*, T. Tepper, L. Hannon, and D. Sandstrom, Editors, pp. 33-39.

Barth, R. P. and M. Berry. 1988. *Adoption and Disruption: Risks, Rates, and Responses*. New York: Aldine DeGruyter.

Bartholet, E. 1999. *Nobody's Children: Abuse and Neglect, the Foster Care Drift, and the Adoption Alternative*. Boston: Beacon Press.

Bartholet. E. 1993. *Family Bonds: Adoption and the Politics of Parenting*. Boston: Houghton Mifflin Company.

Bartholet. E. 1994. "What's Wrong With Adoption Law," *Trial* (February), pp. 19-23.

Belkin, L. 1988a. "Adoptive Parents Ask States for Help with Abused Young." *The New York Times* (Monday, August 22).

Belkin, L. 1988b. "Adoptive Parents Lose Court Case." *The New York Times* (Sunday, November 13).

Benet, M. K. 1976. *The Politics of Adoption*. New York: The Free Press.

Benjamin, L. 1991. *The Black Elite: Facing the Color Line in the Twilight of the Twentieth Century*. Chicago: Nelson-Hall.

Benfield, JR, R. 1996. Private correspondence (August 6), p. 6.

Berry, M. 1990. "Preparing and Supporting Special Needs Adoptive Families: A Review of the Literature." *Child and Adolescent Social Work*. Vol. 7, No. 5 (October), pp. 403-418.

Boer, F. H. J. M. Versluis-den Bieman and F. C. Verhulst. 1994. "International Adoption of Children With Siblings," *American Journal of Orthopsychiatry*. Vol. 6-4, No. 2 (April), pp. 252-262.

Bogert, C. et al. 1994. "Bringing Baby Back." *Newsweek*. (November 21), pp. 78-79.

Bowlby, J. 1951. *Maternal Care and Mental Health*. Geneva: World Health Organization.

Cermak, S. and V. Groza. 1998. "Sensory Processing Problems in Post-Institutionalized Children: Implications for Social Work." *Child and Adolescent Social Work Journal*, Vol. 15, No. 1 (February), pp. 5-37. Children's Bureau Factsheets/Publications. http://www.acf.dhhs.gov/programs/cb/publications/afcars/rpt0100/ar0100a,.htm.

Claus, D. and S. Baxter. 1997. "Post-Adoption Survey of Russian and Eastern European Children: Completed by Rainbow House International." http://www.rhi.org/Anews/SurveyResults1997.html.

Cloninger, C. R., M. Bohman, and S. Sigvardsson. 1981. "Inheritance of Alcohol Abuse." *Archives of General Psychiatry*. Vol. 38, pp. 861-868.

Cobb, N. 1996. "Infants through the Internet; Some would-be Parents Scan Cyberspace for a Match." *The Boston Globe* (April 28).

Cohen, D. 1978 79. "Adoption." In *Readings in Marriage and the Family*. Guilford, CT: Dushkin Publishing, pp. 116-119. Metro/Region, p. 1.

Cole, E. 1985. "Permanency Planning—A Better Definition." *Permanency Report* (Summer), p. 4.

Cordes, R. 1993. "Parents Kept in the Dark Find Ray of Hope in Wrongful Adoption Suits." *Trial*. Vol. 29, (November), pp. 12-14.

Cradle of Hope Adoption Study Center. 1998. "Adoptions from Eastern European Orphanages Overwhelmingly Successful." (March). http://www.cradlehope.org/surv/html

Crary, David 2007. (January 6). Foreign Adoptions in U. S. Drop in 2006. http://news.yahoo.com/s/ap/2007106/ap_on_re_us/foreign_adoptions&printer=1 and condensed version of same, entitled "Adoptions of Foreign Children by Americans Decline Sharply," 2007 (January 7), *The Providence Journal*, Nation, p. A6.

Deane, B. 1997. "International Adoptions: Can Love Beat the Odds?" *Woman's Day*. (April 22), pp. 95-98.

De Woody, M. 1993. "Adoption Disclosure of Medical and Social History: A Review of the Law." *Child Welfare*. Vol. LXXII, No. 3 (May June), pp. 195-218.

Egbert, S. C. and E. C. LaMont. 2004. "Factors Contributing to Parents' Preparation for Special-Needs Adoption." *Child and Adolescent Social Work Journal*, Vol. 21, No. 6 (December), pp. 593-609.

Elbow, M. and M. Knight. 1987. "Adoption Disruptions: Losses, Transitions, and Tasks." *Social Casework*. Vol. 68, pp. 546-552.

Essley, M. and L. Perilstein. 1998. "Good News on European Adoptions." Unpublished Manuscript, Cradle of Hope Adoption Center, Silver Spring, MD.

Fishman, K. D. 1992. "Problem Adoptions," *The Atlantic Monthly* (September), pp. 37-39, 42, 45-46, 49-50, 52, 55-56, 59-61, 64, 66, 68-69.

Fragin, S. 2000. "Did She Try to Sell Her Child?" *Redbook* (May), www.redbookmag.com.

Freiss, S. 2005. "Overseas Adoptions Have a Somber Side." Special to *USA Today* (September 13).

Geraghty, M. 1995. "The Myths and Realities of Orphanages." *The Chronicle of Higher Education* (January 6), p. A5.

Goldberg, R. 1997. "Adopting Romanian Children: Making Choices, Taking Risks." *Marriage and Family Review*. Vol. 25 (1/2), pp. 79-98.

Goldberg, R. 2001. "The Social Construction of Adoptive Families: A Follow-up Study of Adopting Romanian Children." *International Review of Sociology*. Vol. 11, No. 1, pp. 89-101.

Goldfarb, W. 1943. "Effects of Early Institutional Care on Adolescent Personality." *J.Exptl. Educ.* Vol. 12, pp. 106-129.

Goldfarb, W. 1944. "Effects of Early Institutional Care on Adolescent Personality: Rorschach Data." *Am. J. of Orthopsychiatry*. Vol. 14, pp. 441-447.

Goldfarb, W. 1945. "Psychological Privation in Infancy and Subsequent Adjustment." *Am. J. of Orthopsychiatry*. Vol. 15, pp. 247-255.

Groza, V. and D. Ileana. 1996. "A Follow-up Study of Adopted Children From Romania." *Child and Adolescent Social Work Journal*, Vol. 13, No. 6, pp. 541-565.

Groza, V. and S. D. Ryan. 2002. "Pre-Adoption Stress and Its Association With Child Behavior in Domestic Special Needs and International Adoptions." *Psychoneuroendocrinology*, Vol. 27, No. 2, pp. 181-197.

Hart, J. 1997. "For Adoptive Families, Love Is Not Always Enough." *The Boston Globe* (May 14), Metro/Region, p. A1.

Hastings, D. 2001. "Life and Community: Russia's Exported Children." *The Moscow Times* (February 9), online copy.

Herrmann, K. J. and B. Kasper. 1992. "International Adoption: The Exploitation of Women and Children." *AFFILIA*, Vol. 7, No.1 (Spring), pp. 45-58.

Hoffer, E. 1942. *True Believer*. Scranton: Harper Collins

Hollingsworth, L. and V. M. Ruffin. 2002. "Why Are So Many U.S. Families Adopting Internationally? A Social Exchange Perspective." *Journal of Human Behavior in the Social Environment*. Vol. 6, No 1, pp. 81-97.

Horn, M. 1997. "A Dead Child, a Troubling Defense." *U.S. News and World Report* (July 14), pp. 24-26, 28.

Hutchings, B. and S. A. Mednick. 1975. "Registered Criminality in the Adoptive and Biological Parents of Registered Male Criminal Adoptees." In *Genetic Research in Psychiatry*. R. R. Feve, D.Rosenthal, and H. Brill, Eds. Baltimore: Johns Hopkins University Press.

Immigration and Naturalization Service, Statistics Branch, Selected Un-Numbered and Numbered Tables and Varying Titles, listed here from earliest to most recent: Table 6D. Immigrants Admitted Under the Act of September 11, 1957 by Class of Admission and Country or Region of Birth: September 11, 1957-June 30, 1963; Immigrant Orphans Admitted to the United States by Country or Region of Birth: Years Ended June 30, 1964, June 30, 1965, June 30, 1966, June 30, 1967, June 30, 1968, and June 30, 1969; Immigrant Orphans Admitted to the United States, By Country or Region of Birth, Years Ended June 30, 1970, June 30, 1971, June 30, 1972, June 30, 1973, June 30, 1974, and June 30, 1975; Table 12. Immigrant Orphans Admitted to the United States by Country or Region of Birth, Year Ended June 30, 1965, July through September 1976, and September 30, 1977-1980; IMM2.5. Immigrant Orphans Admitted to the United States by Country or Region of Birth, Fiscal Years 1981-85; IMM 2.5. Immigrant Orphans Admitted to the United States by Country or Region of Birth, Fiscal Years 1981-1985; Table(s) 14. Immigrants Admitted as Orphans by Sex, Age, and Region from Selected Countries of Birth, Fiscal Years 1986-1991; Table 15. Immigrant-Orphans Adopted by U.S. Citizens by Sex, Age, Region and Selected Country of Birth, Fiscal Years 1992-2001;

Table 12. Immigrant-Orphans Adopted by U.S. Citizens by Gender, Age, and Region and Country of Birth, Fiscal Year 2002; and Table 10. Immigrant Orphans Adopted by U.S. Citizens by Gender, Age, and Region and Country of Birth, Fiscal Year 2003.

Jewett, C. L. 1978. *Adopting the Older Child*. Boston: The Harvard Common Press.

Johnson, A.K., R. L. Edwards and H. Puwak. 1993. "Foster Care and Adoption Policy in Romania: Suggestions for International Intervention." *Child Welfare*. Vol. 72, No. 5 (September-October), pp. 489-506.

Johnson, M. D. D. 1997. "Adopting an Institutionalized Child: What Are the Risks?" *The Post*, Issue #9 (January February), pp. 1-3.

Judge, S. L. 1999. "Eastern European Adoption: Current Status and Implications for Intervention." *Topics in Early Childhood Special Education*. Vol. 13, Issue 4 (Winter), pp. 244-252.

Kagan, R. M. and W. J. Reid. 1986. "Critical Factors in the Adoption of Emotionally Disturbed Youths." *Child Welfare*. Vol. 65, pp. 63-73.

Keck, G. C., R. M. Kopecky and L. G. Mansfield. 2002. *Parenting the Hurt Child: Helping Adoptive Families Heal and Grow*. Colorado Springs, Colo: Pinion Press.

Kety, S. S., D. Rosenthal, P. H. Wender, and F. Schulsinger. 1976. "Studies Based on a Total Sample of Adopted Individuals and Their Relatives." *Schiz. Bulletin*. Vol. 2, pp. 413-428.

King, P. and K. Hamilton. 1997. "Bringing Kids All the Way Home." *Newsweek*. (June 16), pp. 60-65.

Kingsley, E. P. "Welcome to Holland."

Lash, C. 2000a. "Corruption, Lack of Regulations Have Resulted in Troubled Orphans: More U.S. Adoptions of Russians Fail." *Post Gazette*. (August 13), online.

Lash, C. 2000b. "The Boy They Couldn't Raise." *Post Gazette*. (August 13), online.

Lash C. 2000c. "Overwhelmed Families Dissolve Adoptions: More American Parents Find they Can't Cope With 'Troubled Children.'" *The Post Gazette* (August 14), online.

Leung, P. and S. Erich. 2002. "Family Functioning of Adoptive Children With Special Needs: Implications of Familial Supports and Child Characteristics." *Children and Youth Services Review*. Vol. 24, No. 11, pp. 799-816.

Lewis, J. 1992. "Wrongful Adoption: Agencies Mislead Prospective Parents." *Trial*. Vol. 28, pp. 75-78.

Mainemer, H., L. C. Gilman, and E. W. Ames. 1998. "Parenting Stress in Families Adopting Children From Romanian Orphanages." *The Journal of Family Issues*. Vol. 19, No. 2 (March), pp. 164-180.

Marcovitch, S., L. Cesaroni, W. Roberts, and C. Swanson. 1995. "Romanian Adoption: Parents' Dreams, Nightmares, and Realities." *Child Welfare*. Vol. 74 (Sept./Oct.), pp. 993-1017.

Massey, S. M. "Russia's Maternal and Infant Health Crisis: Socioeconomic Implications and the Path Forward." Highlights of Policy Brief. http://psp.iews.org.highlights.cfm?view=detail&id=33.

McKelvey, C. A. and J. Stevens. 1994. *Adoption Crisis: The Truth Behind Adoption and Foster Care*. Golden, CO: Fulcrum Publishing.

McQuiston, J. T. 1996. "Doctor Helps Couple Avoid Adoption Trouble." *The New York Times* (July 13), Section 1, p. 25.

Miall, C. E. 1987. "The Stigma of Adoptive Parent Status: Perceptions of Community Attitudes Toward Adoption and the Experience of Informal Social Sanctioning." *Family Relations*. Vol. 36 (January), pp. 34-39.

Miller, M.D., L. C., M. T. Kiernan, M. I. Mathers, and M. Klein Gitelman. 1995. "Developmental and Nutritional Status of Internationally Adopted Children." *Archives of Pediatric and Adolescent Medicine*. Vol. 149, No. 1 (January), pp. 40-44.

Mills, C. W. 1959. *The Sociological Imagination*. New York: Grove Press.

Mirabella, M. 1996. "Brazil's Older Orphans Seeking Homes in the Web." *CNN Worldview*, Transcript #260 5 (September 19).

Modell, J. S. 2002. *A Sealed and Secret Kinship: The Culture of Policies and Practices in American Adoption*. New York: Berghahn Books.

Morison, S. J., E. W. Ames, and K. Chisholm. 1995. "The Development of Children Adopted From Romanian Orphanages." *Merrill-Palmer Quarterly*. Vol. 41, pp. 441-430.

MOSNEWS.com. 2005. "13,000 Russian Children Are HIV-Positive."(April 14). http://www.mosnews.com/news/2005/04/14/hivchildren.shtml.

Nelson, K. A. 1985. *On the Frontier of Adoption: A Study of Special Needs Adoptive Parents*. New York: Child Welfare League of America.

ODS News. 1996. "Income Tax Credit and Ban on Race Discrimination in Adoption Now U. S. Law." (October), p. 1.

Partridge, S., H. Hornby, and T. McDonald. 1986. *Legacies of Loss, Visions of Gain: An Inside Look at Adoption Disruption*. Portland: University of Southern Maine.

Peterson, E. 2003. "Adoptive Mother's Bond at 3 Million." *Daily Herald*. (December 23).

Price, P. 2000. "FRUA's Health & Development Survey." *The Family Focus*. Vol. VI-3.

Prendergast, K. 2001. "Couple Accused of Cruelty to Adopted Teenager." *MediaNews Group, Inc.* (July 23).

Reid, W. J., R. M. Kagan, A. Kaminsky, and K. Helmer. 1987. "Adoptions of Older Institutionalized Youth." *Social Casework*. Vol. 68, pp. 140-149.

Report of a Conference on Post-Adoption Services, Sponsored by Casey Family Services. 1995. Workshop XI: J. M. Pavao, Presenter (December 7-8).

Romano, Michael. 1996. "Mother Arrested in Death of Child." *Rocky Mountain News*. (February 13).

Rosenthal, J. A. and V. Groze. 1990. "Special Needs Adoption: Study of Intact Families." *Social Service Review*. (September), pp. 475-505.

Rosenthal, J. A., D. Schmidt, and J. Conner. 1988. "Predictors of Special Needs Adoption Disruption: An Exploratory Study." *Children and Youth Services*. Vol. 10, pp. 101-117.

"Russia on the Ropes." 2002. *Parade Magazine* (December 15).

Rutter, M. L. and others on the English and Romanian Adoptees Study Team. 1998. "Developmental Catch-Up, and Deficit, Following Adoption After Severe Early Global Privation." *Journal of Child Psychology-Psychiatry.* Vol. 39, No. 4. pp. 465-476.

Rutter, M. L., J. M. Kreppner, and Thomas G. O'Connor. 2001. "Specificity and Heterogeneity in Children's Responses to Profound Institutional Privation." *British Journal of Psychiatry.* Vol. 179. pp. 97-103.

Sack, W. H. and D. D. Dale. 1982. "Abuse and Deprivation in Failing Adoptions." *Child Abuse and Neglect.* Vol. 6, pp. 443-451.

Saul, S. 1997a. "Broken Dreams/In Some Foreign Adoptions, Hope Fades To Hard Reality." *News Day.* (January 2), p. A05.

Saul, S. 1997b. "Agony Not Joy/Greatly Torn, Some Give Up Adoptees They Can't Handle." *News Day.* (January 3), p. A06.

Saul, S. 1997c. "Couples Wait With Empty Cradles As Adoptions Stall, Agencies Taken to Court." *News Day.* (January 5), A08.

Schmidt, D. M, J. A. Rosenthal, and B. Bombeck. 1988. "Parents' Views of Adoption Disruption." *Children and Youth Services Review.* Vol. 10, pp. 119-130.

Seelye, K. Q. "Couple Accused of Beating Daughters Tell of Adoption Ordeal." *The New York Times.* (Sunday, November 2), Section 1, p. 37.

Serbin, L. A. "Research on International Adoption: Implications for Developmental Theory And Social Policy." *International Journal of Behavioral Development.* Vol. 20, No.1, pp. 83-92.

Shapiro, M. 2001. Faith, Love, Hope. *Rosie Magazine,* 128, 7 (May) p. 150-60.

Spitz, R. A. 1946. "Hospitalism." in Anna Freud et al. Eds. *The Psychoanalytic Study of the Child.* Vol. 2. New York; International Universities Press, pp. 52-74.

Tepper, T. 1995. Conversation with the Co-Founder of The Parents Network for the Post-Institutionalized Child (December).

Tremitiere, B. 1979. "Adoption of Children With Special Needs—the Client Centered Approach." *Child Welfare.* Vol. 58, pp. 681-685.

USA Today. 2003. "Mother Charged in Death of Adopted Son." (December 23), p. 3A.

Verhulst, M. D., F. C., M. Althaus, and H. J. M. Versluis Den Bieman. 1990a. "Problem Behavior in International Adoptees: I. An Epidemiological Study." *The Journal of the American Academy of Child and Adolescent Psychiatry.* Vol. 29, No. 1 (January), pp. 94-103.

Verhulst, M.D., F. C., M. Althaus, and H. J. M. Versluis Den Bieman. 1990b. "Problem Behavior in International Adoptees: II. Age at Placement." *The Journal of the American Academy of Child and Adolescent Psychiatry.* Vol. 29. No. 1 (January), pp. 104-111.

Verhulst, M.D., F. C., M. Althaus, and H. J. M. Versluis Den Bieman. 1900c. "Problem Behavior in International Adoptees: III. Diagnosis of Child Psychiatric Disorders." *The Journal of the American Academy of Child and Adolescent Psychiatry.* Vol. 29, No. 3 (May), pp. 420-428.

Verhulst, M.D., F. C., M. Althaus, and H. J. M. Versluis Den Bieman. 1992. "Damaging Backgrounds: Later Adjustment of International Adoptees." *Journal of the American Academy of Child and Adolescent Psychiatry.* Vol. 31, No. 3 (May), 518-524.

Wolkind, S. and M. Rutter. 1985. "Separation, Loss and Family Relationships." In *Child and Adolescent Psychiatry: Modern Approaches.* M. Rutter and L. Heršov, Eds. Oxford: Blackwell Scientific Publications, pp. 34-57

Working, R. and A. Madhani. 2003. "Parents Often Not Ready for Needy Foreign Kids." *The Chicago Tribune* (December 28), online copy.

Working, R. 2004 . "Adoptee Deaths Rare, Experts Say; 12 Russian Cases Troubling, Puzzling." *The Chicago Tribune* (May 21), online copy (5/24/04).

Working, R. and A. Rodriguez. 2004. "Rescue of Boy Ends in Tragedy." *The Chicago Tribune* (May 21), online copy (5/24/04).

Zeppa, S. 1998. "'Let Me In, Immigration Man': An Overview of Intercountry Adoption and the Role of the Immigration and Nationality Act." *Hastings International and Comparative Law Review.* Vol. 22, No. 1 (Fall), pp. 161-185.

Name Index

Ames, 28, 156-57

Barth, 133, 152
Bartholet, 147, 149, 172
Belkin, 152, 171
Benet, 171-72
Benfield, 136
Benjamin, 189
Berry, 133, 152-53
Boer, 34
Bogert, 30
Bowlby, 29, 31, 42

Cermak, 28
Claus, 28
Cloninger, 33
Cobb, 21
Cohen, 172
Cole, 150
Cordes, 135, 152
Cradle of Hope Adoption Study Center,
    52
Crary, 180

Deane, 128
De Woody, 135, 152

Egbert, 62
Elbow, 134
Essley, 28

Fishman, 129
Fragin, 130
Freiss, 130

Geraghty, 31
Goldberg, 28
Goldfarb, 29
Groza (formerly Groze), 33-34, 41, 134

Hart, 134
Hastings, 40

Helding, 202
Herrmann, 28
Hollingsworth, 25
Horn, 128
Hutchings, 33

Jewett, 133
Johnson, MD, 28, 166
Judge, 28

Kagan, 133-34
Keck, 145
Kety, 33
King, 128
Kingsley, 65

Lash, 129
Leung, 34
Lewis, 135, 125

Mainemer, 28, 131
Marcovitch, 28, 189
Massey, 31
McKelvey, 20, 24, 152-53, 171, 173
McQuiston, 32
Miall, 173
Miller, 28, 30
Mills, 125-26
Mirabella, 21
Modell, 171
Morison, 28

Nelson, 152

Partridge, 133
Peterson, 130
Prendergast, 130
Price, 28, 53, 189

Reid, 133-34
Romano, 129
Rosenthal, 33, 133-34

217

Rutter, 28, 31, 189

Sack, 133
Saint Joseph Center, 194
Saul, 135
Schmidt, 133-34
Seelye, 130
Serbin, 28
Shapiro, 146
Spitz, 29

Tepper, 28, 130
Thomas, 201

Tremitiere, 134

USA Today, 130

Verhulst, 32-34, 42, 50

Wolkind, 31

Working, 130

Wright and Wright, 202

Zeppa, 28

Subject Index

Adopted children
  Older adoptees, 14, 97, 145-46,
    158, 172, 188
  Sibling adoptees, 4, 34, 132
  Pre-adoption history of risk, xi,
    33-35, 78, 81, 91, 93, 95, 128,
    135,145, 198
  Health problems (including phys-
    ical, emotional, psychological,
    behavioral, and combinations
    of problems)
      Anxiety Disorder/issues, 33,
        113
      Attention Deficit Disorder
        (ADD), 86, 91-92
      Attention Deficit/Hyper-
        activity Disorder
        (ADHD), 81, 86, 101,
        108, 110, 113-14
      Depression, 32-33
      Mood Disorder/Bi Polar
        Disorder, 111, 113
      Oppositional-Defiant
        Disorder (ODD), 90,
        109, 111
      Pervasive Developmental
        Disorder (PDD), 89
      Physical (correctable), 22,
        37, 86
      Post-Traumatic Stress
        Disorder (PTSD), 92, 95,
        100-01, 108, 111, 143,
        202
      Reactive Attachment
        Disorder/issues (RAD),
        91-95, 101, 103-04,
        111-12
      Speech Delay, 109
Adoption
  Adoption in the United States,
    1-6, 8-17

Growth in Eastern European
  adoptions, 3-12
Adoption agencies
  Obligations, 157
  Responsibilities, 128, 149, 151,
    157
Adoption costs, 37-39, 102, 106, 115,
  130, 137, 143, 152, 157, 162, 176,
  200
Adoption law, 136, 172
Adoption policies
  Domestic, 31-32, 117-21, 128,
    141-43, 178, 183
  International, 25, 28, 36, 97, 110,
    112, 128, 132, 141-43, 154,
    183, 190
Adoption practices
  Domestic, 3, 25, 35, 117, 119,
    127-28, 136, 141-43, 147, 163,
    165, 179, 182, 195
  International, 3, 28, 36, 65,
    118-19, 128, 141-43, 147, 149,
    163, 166, 179, 182, 195
Adoption research
  Domestic, 28-40, 133-34, 136-38,
    167, 196
  International, 28-40, 47-62,
    131-34, 136-38, 156, 183-89,
    196
  Older child, 21, 27, 37-38, 50, 67,
    73, 76-77, 80-82, 92-94, 99-
    100, 103, 105-08, 115, 127,
    130, 133-34, 136-38, 144-52,
    154, 158-59, 166-67,
    174-75, 179, 181, 184-85,
    190, 193-94, 198, 201, 204,
    208
Adopters' positions on government poli-
  cies, 117-22
Attitudes toward adoption, adopters,
  adoptees, 19, 171-73, 183

Clients' rights
Adoptees, 149-50
Adoptive parents, 150-51, 174

Differences/similarities in issues relative
to adoption
Domestic adoptees, 28-35, 38-40
Eastern European adoptees,
28-35, 38-40
Dissatisfaction with the decision to adopt
internationally, 53, 97, 121-22

Future of international adoption,
179-82

Hague Convention, 117, 181
Home study, 36, 47-48, 56-57, 75-76,
79-82, 87-90, 92, 94-95, 101-02, 104-
06, 108, 110, 112-13, 115, 142-43,
145, 149, 151-52, 155-57, 195-96,
200, 204, 208

Impacts of existing adoption policies and
practices, 125-38
Issues relevant to older-child domestic
and international adoption
Differences, 27-40
Similarities, 27-40

Media coverage of adoption, 22, 40,
128, 130
Models of Adoption practices
Revised, 142-44
Traditional, 141-42
Motivations to adopt, 86

Post-adoption support, services, 55-56,
94, 133-34, 138, 146, 157
Pre-adoption preparation, 50, 52, 55-57,
74-81, 84, 86-92, 94-95, 97-98, 100-
05, 107-08, 110, 112-13, 115, 142,
145, 155-56, 161, 196
Private troubles, 125, 127, 138
Process of international adoption, 47,
183
Public issues, 125, 127, 138, 141

Real-life case narratives
Mixed, 85-98
Positive, 73-84
Problems, 99-116

Reasons for adopting internationally
Pull factors, 21-22
Push factors, 20-21

Satisfaction with the decision to adopt
internationally, 40, 47, 52-54, 68, 85,
87, 104, 110, 121-22
Scenarios
Arriving in Paris, 66
Landing outside of Paris, 66
Where are we?, 66-67
Sending countries
Bulgaria, 3, 5, 7-8, 11, 14-17, 75,
80, 82, 102-03, 185-86, 193-94
Kazakhstan, 3, 5, 7, 13, 181,
193-94
Other Eastern European countries,
3, 6, 9, 11, 16, 22, 25, 68, 132,
153, 174, 180, 183, 185, 193-
94, 200, 208
Romania, 3, 5-8, 11-13, 17, 25,
28, 30, 76, 87, 89, 96-97,
100-01, 105-10, 114, 131, 156,
181, 185-86, 193-94, 204
Russia, 3-6, 10-11, 17, 22, 24-25,
28, 30-31, 40, 50, 68-69,
73-75, 81, 85, 87-88, 91-95,
103, 111-14, 129-30, 132, 134,
153, 166, 174, 180-81, 183-85,
190, 193-94, 200, 203-04, 208
Ukraine, 3, 5-7, 11-12, 22, 28, 79,
181, 193-94
Social Movements on behalf of
Adoptees, 174
Adoptive parents, 174-75
Birth parents, 174
Strategies for change in
Adoption policies, 141-42, 154,
190
Adoption practices, 141-47
Study Methodology
Decisions, 190-91
Limitations, 190-91

Ticking time bomb, 176
Tips for enhancing adoption success
Pre-adoption issues and tips, 195-200
Post-adoption issues and tips, 201-08

For Product Safety Concerns and Information please contact
our EU representative GPSR@taylorandfrancis.com Taylor & Francis
Verlag GmbH, Kaufingerstraße 24, 80331 München, Germany

T - #0245 - 270225 - C240 - 229/152/11 - PB - 9781138509344 - Gloss Lamination